How to
Write What
You Want
and
Sell What
You Write

By
Skip Press

CAREER PRESS
3 Tice Road
P.O. Box 687
Franklin Lakes, NJ 07417
1-800-CAREER-1
201-848-0310 (outside U.S.)
FAX: 201-848-1727

HOW TO WRITE WHAT YOU WANT AND SELL WHAT YOU WRITE

ISBN 1-56414-152-7, $10.99

Cover design by A Good Thing, Inc.

Printed in the U.S.A. by Book-mart Press

To order this title by mail, please include price as noted above, $2.50 handling per order, and $1.00 for each book ordered. Send to: Career Press, Inc., 3 Tice Road, P.O. Box 687, Franklin Lakes, NJ 07417.

Or call toll-free 1-800-CAREER-1 (Canada: 201-848-0310) to order using VISA or MasterCard, or for further information on books from Career Press.

Library of Congress Cataloging-in-Publication Data

Press, Skip, 1950-
    How to write what you want and sell what you write / by Skip
Press.
        p.   cm.
    Includes index.
    ISBN 1-56414-152-7 : $10.99
    1. Authorship--Marketing. I. Title.
PN161.P74 1995
808'.02--dc20   95-5415
                                                                         CIP

Acknowledgments

I would like to thank the following people, without whom this book would not have been possible:

Linda Venis, who brought me into the UCLA Extension Writers Program and helped me come up with the right title.

Ray Montalvo and all the other fine people at UCLA.

Rose Goss and Karl Widmater, with whom I worked on two magazines.

Agent Larry Sternig, who shared so much of his gentle wisdom. Agents David Andrew and Sasha Goodman, fine folks to have on your side.

Trevor Meldal-Johnsen and John Dalmas, who showed me the way when it counted the most.

Jerry Jenkins, Steve Weakley and Mike McGreevey, for sharing so much so quickly.

Michael Savage and Bob Axelrod, for doing so much to make my plays a success.

Ed Hunt, for filmmaking know-how.

Mike Conley, fellow evolving writer.

All my students who made major changes after learning they could—most notably, Julie Comins and Laura Seraso.

Every gracious interview subject I've ever had, particularly Richard Donner and Tennessee Williams.

My magnificent wife, Debbie, and our amazing kids, Haley and Holly.

Mrs. Stinson, my first-grade teacher in Palmer, Texas, who did so much to set my mind afire with the possibilities of creation.

My grandmother, Mary Elizabeth Jacobs, who bought me my Golden Encyclopedia and owned a personal library I so much admired.

And last but not least, all the people who mail me the checks.

Contents

Introduction

Books about writing. Bah! There are tons of 'em! Somebody get me a shovel! You can't teach anybody to write! Writers are born, not made. Too many writers are born, matter of fact—or should we say, people who want to be writers. Just ask any editor with red ink in her veins!

Now that we've gotten that out of the way, let's get to the real meat of the matter. Forget every assumption or generality about writing you've ever heard or read. You can teach someone to write. You can learn to write. In fact, you can keep getting better at writing for as long as you're able to think and act coherently.

Students have told me that I saved their writing lives, that they couldn't understand why all their other writing teachers had made it all seem so complex.

I understand why those other teachers stumbled, and so should you. They were more interested in process than communication. Good writing is simple in concept, though it can be elaborate in execution. What are you doing when you are writing? You're communicating. You learned to talk, didn't you? I trust you learned your ABCs. How about grammar? Did you learn it well? If you didn't, you may need to brush up. Get a copy of *The Elements of Grammar* by Margaret Shertzer. Study it, then get *The Elements of Style* by William Strunk Jr. and E.B. White. I won't fix the work you missed in English class, but if you have your basics in order, I'll take you the rest of the way. At the very least, I'll point you in the right direction and give you a road map to where you want to go.

I have a workmanlike view of the world of writing. What do I mean by workmanlike? When I was just starting out as a professional writer—a career I dreamed of, even counted on, from a very young age—I wasn't picky about what I was paid to write. That's why I put my name to articles about air conditioners, quickest taxi arrivals and the best pizza in Los Angeles. I loved the perquisites that went along with writing those articles, and I learned about the drawbacks. (After becoming sick as a dog on the eighth day of eating nothing but pizza, I didn't go near another pizza parlor for six months.)

No one taught me how to write articles; they simply told me how long they wanted them, and I winged it. I learned each new form of writing "flying by the seat of my pants." I've been holding that basic flight pattern for the last 15 years. If you do some research, you'll discover that the majority of highly successful writers have a workman-like view of writing. They have simply written whatever it took, perfecting their craft as they went along.

Here's another tip. One of the best things I learned early on was this: No matter how good your writing is, if it isn't presented in the proper length, format and "look," you're immediately branded an amateur.

When I began writing screenplays, there was only one book available that explained the proper format. (Wow, has that changed!) The correct format for an audiovisual script was explained to me verbally. The best length for various kinds of short stories—the length acceptable to editors—was explained on a postcard from my agent.

When I needed to know about stage play formats, the way speeches should look on a page or tricks about article writing, I gleaned inside tips from experts. I lived in Los Angeles then, so there were plenty of successful writers at hand. I've found, however, that many other hopeful writers don't naturally seek out experts even when they live in major metropolitan centers.

Since I often secured writing jobs in areas of writing I knew nothing about, I had to display total professionalism if I wanted to keep the job. So I learned to: 1) get it right the first time and 2) ask a pro if I didn't know. Don't know any pros? Well, you do now. In essence, with this book in your hands, you know me.

I'll also tell you where to find other experts. So pat yourself on the back—you just moved ahead in the game. In teaching writing over the years, both formally and informally, I discovered that although most of my students had a very strong urge to get published or even to become professional writers, they didn't know how to sort out their own desires, capabilities and strengths. They rarely knew proper formats, or thought to find out about them. I determined that, by explaining in brief detail different writing markets, then providing the proper format for each, I gave my students an advantage. They could then do a minimum of two things: 1) hone in on the form of writing offering them the best immediate chance of success and 2) give their work a professional "look" right from the start.

Beyond that, I told them that one becomes a better writer by: 1) writing; 2) writing; and 3) more writing. Thank you, Mark Twain.

I realized I had a pretty good system when I got the Instructor Evaluation Forms back from my first class at UCLA Extension Writers Program. Most of my students rated me a "9," the highest possible rating. A couple of troublemakers gave me a "7" or a "6." One of my best students thanked me profusely for not presenting another "touchy, feely, thank-you-for-sharing-that-with-us" type of class. She was extremely grateful for my honest, practical, useful advice. Like 25 percent of my students from that first class, she got published within a year of taking my course. Twenty percent of the students became full-time writers in a year. I've maintained that 20 to 25 percent first-year success rate with every course I've given.

This book will tell you what sort of submission is expected for a newspaper "op ed" (opinion editorial) piece, an audio-visual script, a year-end report, a screenplay or even a nonfiction book proposal. There are other places to get this information, of course. You could buy the entire Writer's Digest Book Club list, including a book about nothing but writing query letters. In contrast, my book is one-stop shopping. In *How to Write What You Want & Sell What You Write*, I've attempted to cover virtually the entire field of writing in practical, workable, proven terms.

Although I've sold darn near every type of writing that exists, my own advice is mixed with that of established professionals in specialized topics. I try to cover all the bases. In this book, I don't spend too much time on any one subject, but I do give you the basics. After reading and applying the principles and formats given here, every single want-to-be writer out there (and those interested in switching fields of writing) should know what basic first steps to take. You'll discover exactly how to get started and rapidly achieve quick, no-nonsense results.

People buy "everything-you-need-to-know" books about medicines, cars, gardening, home electronic repair and taking care of babies. Why not one about writing? Turn the page, and let your adventures begin!

Chapter 1

❖❖❖❖❖❖❖❖❖❖❖❖❖❖❖❖

The big picture

I never set out to become the writer I am. I'm a generalist, a full-time writer kind of a guy, making a good living. It amazes my friends and confounds my enemies, but I am rarely between deals. My burden is usually finding the time to deliver all the writing I've sold, but that's okay. I've had worse problems in my lifetime. I'm usually happy typing away, meeting a deadline, and I've made money writing just about everything. I love being interviewed by reporters, appearing on talk shows and being a guest speaker. I'm the busiest writer I know, and I have a mouth to match. You may have correctly guessed that I plan to stay that way. Retirement? What a silly word! Retire from doing something I absolutely love? Pish, posh, balderdash. I'd have to be daft.

Guess what? I can tell you how to have this much fun, too.

From an early age, I always thought I would become the great American novelist, not an all-purpose wordsmith. In wanting to write my first novel, however, I became confused about where to start. I knew that a journey of a thousand miles began with the first step, but I didn't know where to step first. I didn't even know what shoes to wear. How long should my book be? What should it look like on the page? Should it be single-spaced, or double? Coming from small-town Texas, I had no one to advise me, and no idea where to go to find advice.

After the confusion came the distraction. Maybe you've shared some of my wrong turns. Inspired by seeing The Beatles on Ed Sullivan's TV show, I became a musician and songwriter for a number of years. I had some success as a performer, but I didn't sell a single song. Living in Hollywood, I tried screenwriting, with moderate initial success. To support myself through these endeavors, I did office work to pay the rent. Finally, I got back to my original purpose of writing books, and my creative life began to flourish.

Do those detours sound familiar? Did you go to law school to secure financial security and, now that you've got the BMW and the nice house, did you suddenly realize that you'd rather be like John Grisham, ex-lawyer/author of *The Firm* and other bestsellers?

Are you a secretary who thinks you can write better training manuals than the ones you try to use?

Are you like me—someone who did not finish college, who did hard-labor jobs along the way, all the while convinced that one day you'd write and sell books and films?

As a teacher, have you noticed that the books your kids study are no better than ones you could write?

Don't sweat it. You may be right about your literary capabilities. You may be the next Tom Clancy, peddling insurance while you try to sell your first novel. Where you stand with your writing aspirations at this point doesn't matter. I can help you improve your circumstances. As I mentioned earlier, if you can't use English well, you're lacking some education. You need to handle that; it's not my jurisdiction. If you have the rudimentary skills of writing under control, however, I can offer you at least three things:

1. Help in improving your overall writing.
2. Proper, expected formats to use.
3. Places to get in touch with people who will buy what you write, whatever kind of writing that might be.

The latter may ultimately be the most important. I've had foreign (English as a second language) students who were stunned that I was interested in their concepts, not the way they turned an English phrase. After all, Cervantes wasn't worried about the Queen's English when he wrote *Don Quixote*. Ideas, ideas, ideas are what matter. Great ideas are independent of language; language is merely a tool we use to communicate ideas to others. Inspiration literally means the breath of life, and life breathes in any language—great ideas can come from anywhere. I simply try to help great ideas germinate, reach full bloom and make it to market. Since I've made a living doing many different kinds of writing on a regular basis, I assume others can learn to do so. As I write this, I may or may not be well on my way to becoming the great American novelist, but I'll at least be able to pay for my kids' college educations. I'm living the life I envisioned from childhood.

I don't mind sharing what I know with anyone, because I've seen it demonstrated over and over again that good works have a way of coming back to you. I never feel threatened by possible competition. Any time I help someone get their career started, or help boost someone's career, I get some kind of unexpected return dividend. Always, always, always.

And you know what? I rarely run across a person who, when they learn I'm a successful writer, doesn't express a deep desire to write. That's a big reason I wrote this book. In talking about writing, doing writing and teaching writing for a decade and a half, I've discovered that most people have an urge to at least write something. Usually, their main problem is not knowing where to start. That's where I was in the beginning, and that's what this book is designed to handle for you.

There is only one thing I ask of you, if you find this book helpful. Help someone else. Share the knowledge. Don't get territorial and fall into the trap of thinking there's a scarcity of places to sell your work. With the way media has exploded in the past decade, the big complaint I hear from the people writing checks (you know, those who actually pay for writing) is how hard it is to find good writers. That will not change in our Age of Information, so don't get greedy.

Consider this: If we had an entire society where everyone was able to write professionally, imagine what an amazing, literate culture we'd have. Wouldn't you like to contribute to the formation of such a society? So you see, I can't lose by helping you.

Okay, my speech is over. Let's get down to specifics. So far in my career, I've written and sold the following: advertising copy; "advertorial" articles (a business pays for an ad and gets an article written about them); biographies (or "bios") and other public relations materials, like press kits; children's stories; corporate speeches; ghostwritten books; how-to videos; jokes; magazine articles; marketing materials; nonfiction books; novels; poetry; radio scripts; screenplays; short stories; slide shows; stage plays; technical manuals; technical studies; and television. I probably left something out, but you get the point.

I've been a member of more professional writing societies than I care to count. I've been a board member. I'm listed in Who's Who books. That's all nice, but none of it matters except to point out that I've seen a bit of the world, from the bottom to the top. I can show you around the territory. Remember, I've always operated by getting the job first, then worrying about how to write it, going straight to the experts when need be. Though I don't claim to personally be an expert at any one form of writing, I know enough to make a living at my craft. I'll share everything I know with you. When I don't know, I'll provide an expert (or several) to tell you what to do.

In this book, I've done a lot of basic research for you. I will show you the generally accepted form for just about any kind of writing you can imagine. When I offer experts' opinions, they'll be great ones—Tennessee Williams on playwriting, for example, or at the other end of the spectrum, a successful TV producer. If you choose, you'll learn how to write and sell comic books, greeting cards, jokes to your favorite comedian or comedienne (believe me, none of them writes all their own material), and every form of script you can imagine. If you want, you may even gain some insight into speechwriting. Frankly, I feel you'll end up amazed at what you can potentially write and sell.

Beyond that, my friend, it's you and the blank page, or that blinking cursor on your computer screen.

Your primary focus

I always try to start as large as possible and whittle down as needed. If you think small, your brain will atrophy. Aspire to be the most successful writer who ever lived, in whatever area of writing you choose. You might end up like Stephen King, who started off wanting to be a great writer of Western novels, *à la* Louis L'Amour or Zane Grey, and ended up being a guy who could write a grocery list and have it made into a Hollywood movie. King did not originally intend to be a great horror master, but he did intend to be a very successful writer. Your success will have to do first with how big you dream, then how hard you work to get there. Anything you can dream, you can achieve. The secret in getting there will be in mapping out a path through the jungle and up to the top of the mountain. Your primary image of your potential success is very important, so let's look at it.

Creating your image

A popular business phrase is "worst case scenario"—that is, the very worst that could happen if you took a certain path. Similarly, "creative visualization" has come into popularity in the last couple of decades. Olympic athletes and others mentally picture a desired result, such as coming in first in the 5,000-meter race or going out with Miss October, with the idea that their projection will be realized. This isn't a new concept. To Hopi Indians, the idea of creative visualization isn't terribly exciting, because their ancestors have been doing it for about 10 centuries. Hopis call the practice "sitting in pictures," and they use it for practical purposes, like getting it to rain.

Don't laugh. Hopis are the only Native Americans who have never been displaced from their original land. The most peaceful of all tribes, they try to work within the balance of nature. When they "sit in pictures" to improve conditions, it works.

Here's why I'm telling you this: When I found out about the Hopis' "sitting in pictures" practice, described in *Blue Highways* by William Least Heat Moon, a little light went off in my mind. I realized that creative visualization, supposedly developed by psychologists and New Age thinkers, had actually been around for a very long time. I saw that, as a writer, I'd been "sitting in pictures" and writing about them for a long, long time.

I'm not much of a fan of psychology, pop or otherwise. Superficial "new" ideas don't mean much to me, because they're usually not new. I've learned that most "modern" ideas are derived from very old, even ancient, sources. The more I learned about mental pictures, the more it became obvious to me that many people have practiced creative visualization since the world began. This includes writers and other learned people who pass things on by oral and written means. All artists do it: actors, dancers, musicians, painters, sculptors, you name it. When someone evokes an emotional response in you, they often evoke a mental picture, good or bad, or at least the communication of a concept (which may be in idea, if not pictorial, form). This is important for any writer to understand.

So now we have a starting point for writing. We know mental pictures exist, as the expression of concepts. Words are a writer's main tool, but toward what end? Good writers use words creatively to effectively communicate concepts and paint mental pictures. These pictures then evoke emotional responses and bring about an understanding. Hopefully, the emotional responses aroused and the concepts communicated are positive ones, with a result of increased understanding of life. Even horror writers can do that, believe it or not.

If all that sounds easy enough, it is. You do the same thing, to some degree, every time you talk to someone. Successful writers simply turn communication into an art form. The best writers communicate so well that they transcend simple communication and move into the realm of aesthetics. Page by rapidly turning page, they "get you going" and keep you going, and you're happy to go along.

Truly great writers create works that have a lasting, beneficial effect on generations of readers, often helping to bring about a change of understanding and/or social custom in their own society. Take William Shakespeare, for example, who is more responsible than anyone else for making English the most popular language on Earth. He did not write from an ivory tower, to be understood a hundred years after his passing.

These are the basics of all writing. You should continually work to master the mechanics of how these things are accomplished. You will get there by learning simple principles, then staying ever vigilant about improving your skills. Coasting isn't in my vocabulary, and it shouldn't be in yours if you're serious about writing professionally.

Choosing the proper frame

Now let's get to your personal writing aspirations. I would hazard a guess that fear of the unknown is perhaps the greatest fear you will ever encounter.

When people get the idea that the unknown is unknowable, they can become immobilized by fear. Or they become angry, which is equally unproductive. Either way, they don't get any closer to realizing their dreams. Fear is usually the first hurdle I have to get over with any writing student. Once they get over the fear of having their writing rejected, and stop being depressed from taking rejection personally, they get angry, because often the people doing the rejecting don't offer a better direction. When someone does take pains to explain the rejection, it's usually because they see promise in the writing and would like to see it improved so it becomes salable.

I'd personally like to strangle the smug little sage who said "A journey of a thousand miles begins with the first step," because he left something out. Before anyone goes anywhere, it's good to know where they're going and how to get there. In beginning to write, how are you supposed to figure out your destination if you don't know the correct mode of travel to begin with? That's why I always tell students specifically what I didn't like about their writing. A lot of angry frustration is avoided this way.

Once you discover where you want to go as a writer, you can backtrack from there and map out your plan of action. It's a process of simple deduction. If you've been a dabbler with writing, if it's always been on your "one-of-those-days" shelf, if you've got any spare time at all and haven't at least started writing something you really want to write, you're probably in one of three categories:

1. A delusional dilettante who will never adopt a professional attitude and seriously attack writing and selling.
2. Someone who doesn't know where to start, and therefore is hung up in fear of the unknown.
3. Someone who is angry because of the rejection received where no one bothered to mention specifically what he or she "did wrong." (Remember, they may not be "right.")

Strange as it may seem, I didn't write my first novel until a professional writer told me that the generally accepted length for mainstream novels was 100,000 words. (If you count 250 words to a page, double-spaced 8½" x 11" paper, that's 400 pages of manuscript. These days, publishers are generally looking for shorter books or 75,000 words or so.) When I heard 100,000 words, I finally had a frame within which to work. Since I knew the ending I wanted for my story and where I wanted it to begin, when I did my outline it was easy to calculate the average length of the parts of my book. I simply broke down the story into what I thought were logical chapters, then divided the number of chapters into 400 pages. After I'd written a chapter or two, I could roughly calculate how many hours and days it would take me to complete my book. The process became reassuring and predictable. It was suddenly something known, which I understood and didn't have to fear! Does that give you some relief?

Wouldn't you benefit by having a frame to work within? Think about it. How many times in your life have you worked within a framework? Johnny, you'll go to school for 12 years, then you'll get a high school diploma. Four more years, Tina, and you'll graduate from college. Three years, Larry, and you'll get through law school. Twenty years with the firm, Margaret, and you'll get your gold watch.

What if someone had told you, at any point along those journeys, "you'll just go till you get it right"? Would that have been a little discouraging? Darn right. That's why you need to have a writing goal and some parameters within which to work.

I feel comfortable working within boundaries. Other writers I've known operate more loosely. Some simply get an idea, sit down and start writing, letting the story flow. More often than not, they are soon flooded with confusion. The piece never gets done, or perfected. I must tell you that I don't know a single writer like that who is very successful. Quite the opposite: I know one hopeful novelist who writes "on a flow" and hasn't sold a thing, after nine books.

"What the public will buy" is another—perhaps the most important—writing parameter. It's discussed thoroughly in this book. It took me a long time to realize writing was a job. A hard job, I might add, with hard-to-please customers. I've dug ditches for a living, been a union carpenter and labored in a foundry, yet I don't know any harder work than writing. It takes constant discipline and mental alertness, so it helps when I lay down guidelines for myself from the beginning. In interviews with highly successful writers, I've never known a "big name" writer who didn't maintain strict discipline with his or her writing schedule and have some fairly concrete outline when beginning a new work, even if the story changed as they wrote it. I usually have my next 10 large projects mapped out.

If you haven't already noticed, *genre* books—like romance novels and detective thrillers—tend to be roughly the same length each time. "Big" books such as the latest epic from James Michener or Tom Clancy are usually just that, big and fat. There are practical reasons that different forms of writing come in certain lengths and are presented in the same format each time. It always comes down to what is commercially acceptable to a publisher, with the parameters having been developed over a long time of doing business. Big writers write big books because they can. The readers will stay with them and will pay more money for the books.

Similarly, Hollywood has very strict guidelines for both film and television. Movie scripts are single-spaced, usually varying in length from 90 to 120 pages. Why? Because on screen, film time averages roughly one minute per page. When a script is 120 pages long, the film will be two hours. When a film is two hours or shorter, movie exhibitors can maximize their number of daily screenings. This means they can sell more popcorn and goodies, which is where they make their largest profits. Television situation comedy (sitcom) scripts, on the other hand, are roughly 48 pages long, double-spaced. That works out to 24 minutes of on-screen time, leaving plenty of time for commercials. (We'll get further into the structure of scripts, and how you, too, can chase the Hollywood dream, in a later chapter. The above examples merely illustrate how having guidelines is not only important but expected.)

Yes, girls and boys, it all comes down to the buck and the buying public, but isn't that the way of the world? Would you rather write one book that wouldn't be recognized as brilliant for three generations, or would you like to enjoy the fruits of your labor in this life?

Remember these important points:

- Form a big picture of the success you will achieve as a writer, as though you're already living the best dream you can imagine, as if it currently existed. *Write it down!*
- Conceptualize what you want to achieve with each completed writing project, just as you would visualize a story before writing it. Each piece is a step on the way to your bigger dream.
- Find out (roughly, at least) how long your current project should be.
- Make sure you use the acceptable, established format of the professionals in the field. If you don't know the proper format, find out. Don't guess.
- Once you've established your parameters, write on a regular (hopefully daily) basis.

Does that help you take your first step? A thousand miles or a thousand pages, it should. If you're not more comfortable about embarking on your journey by now, read this chapter over again and make sure you fully understand everything I've written. Sketch the steps out on paper if need be, or work it out with toy soldiers the way a general mapping out a battle would. American scientist Alfred Korzybski stressed the importance of understanding each word in a piece of text, with each one like a link in a chain, hooked to the next. If the chain is broken by lack of correctly understanding one word, the meaning of the entire text may be lost. So make sure you understand each successive concept I give you. Then I'm certain you'll see the big picture clearly.

Getting to the exhibition

If it's any good at all, there is someone, somewhere, who will publish your work. I'm not talking about vanity presses—those companies who charge you for the delight of seeing your work in print. With enough perspiration and a little bit of inspiration, every hardworking, decent writer can get published somewhere. You might be so far ahead of the market with your concepts that you'll have to self-publish first, sell lots of copies yourself and then come to the notice of a large national company. That's happened with now-famous authors. One example is poet Rod McKuen, who sold 35,000 books of his poetry before hooking up with Random House. For now, though, let's discuss traditional publishing.

The first thing I ever had published was a short poem. The publisher was in prison, and my poem graced the pages of the inmate newsletter, which he edited. I wasn't in prison, just in correspondence with this particular inmate via a "help-a-prisoner" public service situation. He published not one but two of my poems, and I was thrilled.

My next multiple publication (and the first time I was paid) was with a publisher of a local giveaway newspaper called *The Piccadilly*. Referred by a friend, I wrote my first piece on a trial basis. If the publisher didn't like it, I wouldn't get paid. My first assignment was to find the best price on air conditioners in Los Angeles. The publisher paid me $25 and sent me on another assignment. This time, I had to determine the quickest response time and best congeniality of local taxi services. I angered most of the cab companies in Los Angeles when I suddenly "changed my mind" as each cab arrived, but I got another *Piccadilly* check. The third article came with perquisites ("perks"). I had to find the best pizza in the City of the Angels. This meant, as I explained carefully to the proprietor of each establishment I visited, I had to have a large version of their best pizza. I fed some friends a couple of times for free, ate nothing but pizza for a week (at a time when my finances were very tight) and got my third article published.

Bang! In three weeks, I had three "clips" (so-called because you clip out the published article, photocopy it and use it as a sample of your work). I also had three checks. I gloated over my success while I lay in bed, recovering from my dietary disaster.

I thought big long-term, but I started small short-term. I was willing to build my career slowly. Every city has a publication where you can get started and acquire those all-important clips. Why do you need clips? One reason is because you don't have a resume that shows the accomplishments of 15 years as a professional writer and leaves out the starvation. Since you have to convince editors you can write, showing them a clip with your name on it helps. Even today, if I wanted to break in with a new magazine, I would send an editor a sample of my work, if asked.

So that's your first assignment: Get some clips.

What? You don't want to write nonfiction? You're a serious writer who will eventually make people forget the name Ernest Hemingway? Okay. So sell a story. Do I hear gulping sounds? In case you haven't already figured this out, it's much harder to sell fiction than nonfiction. That rule applies from short local sales all the way up to books on *The New York Times* bestseller list.

At some point, people begin to take you seriously. It's like you've suddenly earned your membership, survived the hazing and magically gained entry into some sort of literary fraternity or club. Believe me, that happens a lot quicker when you have published enough words. To some extent, it doesn't matter *where* you've published. People just seem to be impressed by volume and persistence. If you publish a book, you're taken a lot more seriously, even if you published it yourself (no one needs to know).

A student in my first formal class, Julie Comins, moved to Aspen, Colorado, after finishing up with me at UCLA. Los Angeles was the place to be for the pursuit of stardom, but Julie was sick of the entertainment rat race, where the rats wear disguises. She was also a poet, with aspirations of publishing a book of poems, maybe even a novel.

Since she knew quite a bit about the celebrity "behind-the-scenes" aspect of the ski resort of Aspen, I encouraged her to write a Jackie Collins type of novel featuring Julie's own unique humor and point of view.

I was thrilled one day when Julie sent me a thick package containing some of her published work. Before my class, she'd never had a thing printed. I saw that she had taken to heart my suggestion that getting some writing published—whatever kind—is better than nothing. Julie had taken an administrative job at Aspen's *Daily News*. One of her duties was typing classifieds, and she barely knew how to type. Then, one day, the editor learned of Julie's theatrical background. It wasn't long before the "In the Front Row with Julie Comins" column began appearing in the paper. Not long after that, Julie received a scholarship to the Aspen Writers Conference and spent 10 days studying nonfiction writing with Pulitzer Prize-winning journalist Madeleine Blais. Julie is now a professional and will no doubt write me next from the chalet she's purchased with the money from her first novel.

Similarly, my student Duke Bates wrote dark narrative stories, like a slightly more serious Stephen King. Duke, however, lacked confidence that he would ever be published. Duke had tried many times and failed. When I learned about his day job—computer conversions for businesses—I suggested he find a magazine where he could sell an article about what he did. This idea stunned him, because he'd never considered journalism, but he almost immediately wrote and sold "Seven Easy Steps for a Computer Conversion" to a national magazine. Duke's confidence level went through the roof. The other students were amazed—one of their peers had written and sold an article to a national magazine before the term was over!

I'll go along if you only want to write fiction. I make the majority of my income from writing fiction. Consider this, however: For 500-word articles in *Disney Adventures* magazine, I used to get $500, or a dollar a word. No writer gets that kind of money for short stories except from big national magazines like *The New Yorker* or *Esquire*, and those editors usually want to "know who you are" before they'll give your work serious consideration. By knowing who you are, I mean your story has to arrive via a literary agent they trust, or you should have already published a novel or two.

I had a literary agent who specialized in short stories. The great Larry Sternig, who's now retired, helped break my work into magazines with national circulation. I got lucky; my science-fiction author friend John Dalm had recommended me to Larry. Try finding an agent like Larry these days. One agent I know at one of the big three literary agencies (Creative Artists Agency, International Creative Management and William Morris), handles the short stories of all his agency's authors, while also representing novels for his individual clients. Does this tell you anything about the market for short stories these days?

Still, if you're focused on fiction, you can try a local newspaper (or any periodical) for your short story. It might surprise you, because such publications usually don't get a lot of submissions like that. Be prepared to be asked if it's humorous, though. "Hometown" publications for general circulation tend to lean in that direction. "Alternative" papers tend to favor dark, twisted fiction, usually of a psychological bent.

When you're beginning, getting published is about all that matters. I'll probably say that again, before this book is done. Just don't sell anyone all the publishing rights. (More on that in another chapter.)

The matter of style

I learned how a writer's style develops in my first year of full-time writing. I didn't get to be a full-time writer by selling enough writing to support myself. Rather, I won a lot of money on a TV game show and went on a temporary vacation from the workaday world. In my year off, I wrote the novel I'd always wanted to write, learned the proper screenplay format and completed two screenplays, sold my first script—a radio play for a science-fiction radio show called *Alien Worlds*—and wrote a couple of movie "treatments" (expanded synopses of movie stories). My style "emerged" with all this writing. I first got a glimpse of it after completion of the novel. Or, after my first 100,000 words.

I once calculated that it took roughly four screenplays to equal, word count-wise, a novel. Interestingly enough, the fourth screenplay I completed, co-written with Mike Convey, was the first one I ever made much money on. Matter of fact, we made money on that script three different times. Although we eventually sold it outright for a nice price, it still hasn't made it to the screen! I'll explain in the screenplay chapter.

I've never counted up all the articles I've ever written, but with each article conservatively about 1,000 words, I can tell you with no hesitation that by the time I'd written my 100th article, my journalistic style was very well established. Once again, 100,000 words. That's another reason I advise people to write and publish wherever they can, long before they start worrying about money. Whatever field of writing you choose, you simply have to do a lot of writing before you acquire the professional quality that is always in demand. From my observation, 100,000 words seems to be the turning point. Try that as your first big goal and see if it works. At 100,000 words, you might arrive at the place where you join the "club" I previously mentioned, but don't be surprised if it takes a bit longer to gain membership.

I told you about my friend who wrote all those novels without selling one. Remember what else I said about that writer? Potential marketability wasn't the greatest concern. The style is firmly established, and I happen to enjoy the books tremendously. Unfortunately, the style is not one that currently fits in with broad public taste. Notice I said "currently." The history of literature is rife with books that became bestsellers after the authors were gone. *Moby Dick,* for example, was a big disappointment during Herman Melville's lifetime.

Artistic success before you die

I wrote from the time I was a small child, though not very much for many years. I let myself get discouraged by teachers who should have known better. Then in 1974 I got a job in Los Angeles writing business letters. That lasted almost four years. I won't even try to figure how many business letter words I wrote. One week I put out 1,350 letters to customers. Out of a contact I made during that time, I sold my first script. Shortly thereafter, I met the publisher of *The Piccadilly,* where I got my first clips.

When I started writing seriously, I couldn't find anyone to teach me the rules of writing. No one handed me a road map, and I didn't want to go back to college. I went on a long tour of the School of Hard Knocks and Rare Checks. The books available when I was starting out didn't quite do the trick. They only gave me pieces of the big picture.

I want to save you from traveling the hard roads. Mark Twain wrote about "roughing it." I'll show you how to smooth it. In closing this chapter, let me offer you a step-by-step process that might help you become a full-time, professional writer quickly, or at least help you make your first big sale.

Skip's process—not to be skipped

Survey local publications, particularly community newspapers. Read them and see what they buy. Contact the editor. Comment on a specific fine piece you enjoyed in the last issue. If necessary, offer to write something for free. This is your "foot in the door," and I've rarely seen the process fail. Get some clips and start a portfolio.

Try to determine what you most want to write. Narrow down the field. If you like romance novels, find out which ones are on the bestseller list. Read at least three different top authors. Buy a book or two on writing in your genre. If possible in your geographic area, take a course on your chosen specialty from a working writer. Or take a correspondence course from a working writer.

Figure out what you will have to write to get 100,000 words done. Make a step-by-step "battle plan" on what you'll have to do to have the time to write 100,000 words.

Join a writing group. If none is available locally, start one. In this day of online computer services and the forums they offer, it's easy to find kindred souls. The resources available to groups are geometrical in proportion to those available to an individual. (There's a chapter later in this book on writers' organizations and where to find them.)

Unless you have a very big problem with low self-esteem, stay away from "touchy feely" classes and groups. You'll be amazed how much your confidence will rise through accomplishment alone. "Thank you for sharing that with us" doesn't go very far in getting you published. Completing a major project does.

Buy a current *Writer's Market*, published by Writer's Digest Books, available in any large bookstore. It's the most excellent source of potential markets going. The book is divided into categories, so if you know what you'd like to sell, you can go straight to that category.

Read it, don't scan it, and make notes. Then contact the appropriate editors.

Write something every single day, even if only a page. Screenwriter/director John Milius (the films *Apocalypse Now*, *Red Dawn* and others) reportedly writes two pages per day. In two months, that's a 120-page script. Other writers, like Michael Crichton (*Rising Sun*, *Jurassic Park*), become virtual hermits while completing a project, but chances are you don't have that luxury. So go at it bit by regular bit.

In social situations, don't call yourself a writer unless you pretty much make a living at it. The exception is when you are with a group of your peers, as in a writing group or class. I consider all my students to be writers, and say so. At parties, when I tell people I'm a writer, they inevitably ask, "Have you sold anything?" When you have sold professionally, and can recite a list of your accomplishments, the people who make that kind of snide comment are taken down a couple of notches, which is its own sweet satisfaction. Don't set yourself up for sneers.

Sell, sell, sell! Set a few hours aside each week (or as much time as you can), in locating and contacting markets. Even if you make a big sale, keep promoting. There are few things more disheartening than being "on a roll" with sale after sale, then forgetting to tell people about yourself, and ending up with nothing to do when commitments are fulfilled. Writers who get a lot of paid writing assignments are usually as good at selling as they are at writing.

Be true to your personal goals. If you decide you really want to write the great American novel, and only the great American novel, go for it. There is something admirable in that type of focused, persistent integrity and it will come across in your work. I've learned to build the pyramid from the ground up rather than starting with the capstone, but there are people who get rich quick and make a big name for themselves with their first major creation. You may be one of them.

This chapter has been a summation, a general direction provider. It didn't cover all the bases, but I hope the rest of the book will. I would like you to be so well-rounded in knowledge of the writing world after reading this book that you can launch or improve your career immediately. Even if you read only one chapter, or a few that personally appeal to you, I want you to be able to confidently approach writing and selling. I will never claim to be the world's foremost authority on the written word. I'll never try to be, but I do have a policy of trying to make the path easier for those who come after me. That's why I've given away a lot more advice than I've been paid for. I believe in working for the common good, which Plato espoused. I also believe in the Buddhist principle of cause and effect, more commonly known as "what goes around comes around."

I truly wish that you come around to greatness.

Chapter 2

❖❖❖❖❖❖❖❖❖❖❖❖❖❖❖

Who cares who queries?

Other than the quality of your text, the most potent tool in selling your writing is the query letter. This is a letter sent to an editor accompanying and/or describing your manuscript. A query letter simply asks the question: "Will you buy my writing?" Everything in a query letter should also *answer* that question.

Even if you send the world's greatest unpublished manuscript, you still need to include a letter to say something about who you are, what you have to sell, where you can be found and why you contacted that person in the first place. Who, what, where and why—anything else is fluff, which makes good editors impatient and prone to slam-dunking your manuscript in the round file under the desk.

You can, no doubt, visit your local bookstore or library right now and find an entire book on writing a great query letter. This month's issue of at least one writing magazine will probably feature an article about composing the world's best query letter. None of this will change the fact that you'll still be inquiring whether the editor you contact has any need for what you've written and, if so, how much they'll pay you for it (providing they pay).

Note that I said the editor you contact. I didn't say the magazine or publisher. The first secret to writing a query letter that will sell is to address it to a real person, not just a title. Who might that be? Do some homework. If you read about a magazine in *Writer's Market*, go to the local newsstand and buy a copy of the magazine to study. If you can't find it at the newsstand or in your local library, write away for one. Once you get a copy, find the portion of the magazine known as the "masthead." The masthead is the column of text on a page near the front that lists where the office of the magazine is located, who publishes it, who works on it, how often it comes out, its circulation, etc. (Usually, you find the masthead of a newspaper on the editorial page.) If you see many names in the editorial department, chances are you shouldn't waste your time writing the publisher or editor-in-chief. They'll probably just give your letter and manuscript to a junior editor. A large magazine will have an articles editor, a fiction editor, etc. Smaller magazines may have only one person wearing all the "hats." You'll know if they're small because they'll pay only in copies (and a few copies at that), if you meet their standards and they make an offer to put you in print.

Call me ambitious, but I used to go through lists of publishers looking to buy and only sent my work to paying publications. Please note: This was after I'd sold something. Before I was a paid (read: "professional") writer, all I wanted were copies of my printed work, and I was thrilled to get them. After I was published, I sent my work to places that paid the most, first. If they rejected me, I'd move to the next one down the line in financially rewarding rank. I eschewed literary journals, which I've never thought mattered much to anyone except the people publishing them.

You may see this as mercenary logic, but I never met a writer who paid the mortgage writing for prestigious literary journals. I believe writers should not only be paid, but paid very well, because writing is the hardest work I've ever known. I advise you to get paid as soon as possible. You'll feel a lot better about yourself as a writer.

If you got your letter

I always advise my students to try to find a common ground with anyone they communicate with. That includes other writing students, readers certainly, and editors particularly. By "common ground," I mean you should try to find something you both know or can agree on. You build from that foundation for communication. You've experienced some form of this a thousand times. "My fellow Americans," began President Lyndon Baines Johnson. "Friends, Romans, countrymen," said Marc Antony. "Four score and seven years ago, our fathers set forth..." President Abraham Lincoln intoned solemnly, setting the scene for his famous speech at Gettysburg. Tell your audience something to show them you're on the same track, before you tell them something new and harder to comprehend.

I'd like you to switch seats now. Travel in your mind to a swank office, high in the lofty stratosphere of Manhattan publishing. You are a successful editor, and your office is filled with cutting edge technological wonders. Decorated like something out of *Architectural Digest*, your work space is a source of great pride. You have half a floor of room, two secretaries, and hot and cold running drinks. Your lunch is catered and you get a daily manicure. You knock off work at 4:00, and that's on a long day. It's a short walk to your private elevator. Down below, your chauffeured limousine awaits, ready to sweep you off to yet another night of highly expensive dining and dancing. The maitre d' brightens on seeing your face, and immediately escorts you to the best table in the house.

Sure. Reject that mental scenario, because it's a ridiculous pipe dream. Most editors I know are pleasant enough, but they are also harried. They never seem to have enough time, I don't think their office would win a neatest-place-to-work prize, and I'm certain none of them jet to Bermuda every weekend for a nice little vacation. Most editors are hardworking people. Most of them have stacks of things to read and few have secretaries.

In other words, you don't need to give editors an excuse to use your manuscript to test the new shredding machine because you start off your query letter telling them how your work is the best thing since sliced pumpernickel.

Think about it. If that editor—the real one I've just described—was your significant other, your wife, husband, girlfriend or boyfriend, what approach would you take to brighten their day? What if they were simply a good friend, or a new acquaintance you liked? Would you make sure to keep your workday communication with them short, bright and to the point? Hopefully you would. Would you throw in a bit of humor, to try to help them have a better day? If you wanted to build that relationship, you would. So why not see an editor as a real person, someone you might actually like to get to know one day? Believe me, if you sell them something, you will get to know them, maybe better than you initially imagined. You might end up on each other's holiday card lists, or something even more friendly.

When you query, be friendly and cordial, but get to the point. Don't waste time. As your writing success grows, you'll be surprised at just how small a world it can be, in publishing and in our world at large. You'll also see the true importance of first impressions. Getting to the point in brief but friendly fashion will help your chances of making that great first impression.

A few years back, I added a cartoon to my personal stationery. It's in the upper right-hand corner, a clever caricature by John Caldwell of Mark Twain sitting at a desk looking perplexed. Several dialogue balloons hover over Twain's head: "Strawberry Finn? Blueberry Finn? Cranberry Finn? Boysenberry Finn?" he wonders. You might try something similar with your own personal stationery. Making 'em laugh helps.

And by the way—*get your own personal stationery.* In these days of inexpensive desktop publishing and word processing programs, there's really no excuse not to have it. It shows an editor or publisher that you take your writing seriously and have invested some money in playing the game.

Some samples to sample

So what do you write in a query letter? Some examples of my own letters follow. As I review them with you, I'll toss in comments (in italics) to illustrate points. These points are *not* something you include in the text of your letter. In your letter, you should try to use as little in the way of bolding, all caps, justification and other such fancy text elements as possible. My query letters may not be the most perfect you'll ever see, but they'll get you started.

The first sample letter, on page 33, didn't work. Why? Like all my query letters (unless I have a justifiable excuse), this letter was one page. I always keep them short and to the point, so that's not the problem. As I said earlier, you shouldn't send a letter to the top dog in a big publication. In the example given, I forgot my own rules. I probably didn't help myself by saying what was wrong with the article I had read, but that wasn't why I got no response. When I did not hear from Mr. Achee, I followed up with a phone call. This is a perfectly acceptable practice, but I waited the time prescribed by the magazine (replies in six weeks or whatever). My phone call was at first fruitless, which intrigued me. I figured that my mention of writing for a competitor of *Disney Adventures* (their biggest competitor at the time) would get some attention, but it didn't.

I subsequently learned that *Disney Adventures* had a historically high personnel turnover rate. Achee was gone as publisher by the time I called. I persisted and finally got through to Andy Ragan, a nice guy who was then associate editor. I explained everything to Andy. He was intrigued, and we hit it off. That started a relationship which resulted in sales of stories I originated as well as assignments from Andy. My query letter didn't work, but my persistence did.

Persist, persist, persist! Writers without persistence are losers.

Now, refer to the letter on page 34. I know what you're thinking: "Look at that first paragraph. If I could toot my horn like that, I could get an editor's attention, too. What a braggart!"

Well, I could have left out that first paragraph entirely. Why does an editor of a magazine care if I've sold a screenplay, unless it's a magazine about the film business? What *was* right about the letter—and what got me the job—was the second paragraph. It showed Tina that I'd done my homework. I at least knew what her listing in *Novel & Short Story Writer's Market* said. Actually, I'd written one of the two computer articles I mentioned for her magazine, *ComputorEdge*, but that was for another editor. Tina didn't know me from blue beans when I first contacted her. Her magazine was the largest of its kind in the U.S. at the time, so she had her hands too full to keep up with everyone who had ever written for *ComputorEdge*. Therefore, I approached her as if both she and the magazine were brand new to me.

Why didn't I send her my old *ComputorEdge* clip? I didn't want to run the risk of alienating her. With a new editor, writers are often up against a "new broom sweeps clean" mentality. Some editors want to show they can do a better job than anyone from the old regime. Thus, they use writers they know or writers who contact them anew.

Back to the letter. All of the paragraphs after the second one get right to the point. They walk you through the content of the article, step by step. Any editor could see what my article was about and decide on the spot whether or not it was worthy of assignment. If a decision from an editorial board was necessary, all the editor would have to do is copy my letter and distribute it.

In the last paragraph, I put in a pitch for humor. Humor almost always works for editors. Notice that I mentioned my resume and a sample article last. That way, the editor knew about the other pieces of paper I had enclosed. (Don't assume they'll figure it out without your direction.)

Possibly you're thinking, "This is all well and good, easy for you to say, Skip." I had a long background when I wrote those letters, I was already successful, and had a resume to send along. What about a writer just starting out?

On pages 35 and 36 are samples of the type of letter I wrote in the beginning of my career. Obviously, the first one of the two is tongue-in-cheek. But if your proposed article was laid out as in the letter, you'd probably sell it, if it fit the magazine.

Should you always follow a letter with a phone call? If you're proposing a major article, it usually doesn't hurt. However, if you're sending in anything else—a book manuscript or a screenplay, for example—it could hurt your chances. In those instances, it will be tougher to discover who to send your work to, but you can find out. The personnel who review your material may be subject to weekly musical chairs, even more so in Hollywood. If you're trying to sell something larger than an article or short story, you'll probably be better off with an agent. We'll get into that later. If you don't have an agent, can't find an agent, don't know where to start in finding an agent, don't want to follow my advice about agents, or think you can beat all the odds and sell your manuscript because it truly is the greatest thing since sliced pumpernickel and you simply have to let the right person know, then I have another query letter for you that you might find useful (see page 37).

First, though, do some homework. If you can't find an editor to send your manuscript to, call the publisher and ask who handles unsolicited manuscripts. When I say "unsolicited," I mean they didn't ask to see your work. You just picked them to send it to and took your chances. (You'll probably be told "We don't accept those," but it's worth a call.) If you're trying to sell a screenplay, call the studio and/or production company you want to sell to and ask who their Director of Development is. This is the designated reader (not buyer) of scripts. (You'll probably be told "We only deal with agents or lawyers." In other words, they won't accept a submission of your work directly from you, for legal protection purposes. Again, all you can waste is some patience and a phone call.)

Note that in the example of the query letter on page 37 I mention a one-page synopsis. You should have a short synopsis, preferably one page or less, with any large work you send in, unsolicited or not.

Script readers go through dozens of scripts in a week, writing synopses or summaries on each of those scripts they either recommend others to read or those they turn down. The report is usually known as "coverage" and will be filed for future reference, should another production company at that studio receive your script. It works pretty much the same with book publishers, only they aren't as organized because the financial stakes aren't usually as high. It might cost in the hundreds of thousands to publish a book, yet even a low-budget film might cost well over a million dollars. So save them some time (and see if you really do have your work focused) and write a synopsis to accompany your work. Even if you send in a completed manuscript, you still need a good letter to introduce it to the reader.

Don't take rejections personally

I once wrote a play about a despondent writer who thinks of committing suicide, then changes his mind, only to lose his life in an accident a few moments later. He is brought back to life by his guardian angel, who is an apprentice angel and plenty mad about her bungling writer. One wall of the writer's apartment, when the play was staged, was plastered with real rejection letters.

My own very real rejection letters.

If you sincerely want to make it as a writer, grow some thick rhinoceros skin. If you let the inevitable rejections affect you personally, you'll drive yourself crazy and feel like the worst person in the world. Even if you write perfect query letters and fantastic manuscripts, you'll still get rejections. Since I want to do everything I can to help you get a few less stinging darts tossed at your feelings, here's one more tip to help you write a better query letter.

As you may have noticed in my first letter on page 33 when I referred to *Boys' Life*, many magazines have a long "lead time." This means they plan the theme of each magazine and schedule their articles well in advance. What this means to you is that you can usually write an editor of a magazine and ask for a publishing schedule. They might call it something else, but they'll know what you mean.

Think about it. If you were an editor planning a Christmas issue, wouldn't you want to buy your articles starting in March or so? If you planned on doing an issue that you wanted read by every armed services veteran in America, wouldn't it make sense to have it come out on Memorial Day or Veterans Day?

As a writer, you should consider things like this. If you have a piece about a unique Thanksgiving your family had, don't write the editor in October! You can find out what's on their mind by asking for their publishing schedule. They might not always stick to it, but it's at least what they're planning.

Don't downplay your hunches

No matter what your homework tells you, if you have a sneaking suspicion that you can sell your piece to an editor despite everything you've read about the company, act on it. You'll only waste postage if you're wrong.

I once read about *Grit* in a market listing and was intrigued. *Grit*, a tabloid-sized newspaper, was geared to families when I was a kid, bringing news and homey advice to rural areas. Kids went door to door selling subscriptions to *Grit*, which featured comics that I didn't see in my local newspaper, like "The Phantom." *Grit* held fond memories for me, and the idea of making a sale to them was a boyhood fantasy. Problem was, the only fiction need they listed was full-length novels for serialization. At the time, I didn't have a novel that I thought would be right for *Grit* readers. Still, I had this funny feeling that if the magazine serialized books they might buy short stories.

So I sent the managing editor my resume and mentioned the short stories I had for sale. My hunch paid off. Mike Rafferty, the managing editor, read my letter and called me. He wanted to do exactly what I had proposed—publish some short stories. I sold Mike several stories that I had already published locally (meaning his national readers had probably never seen them). So I not only sold on a hunch, I made money on something I'd already sold in the past!

Never, ever, discount your own instinct about what you might sell to whom, no matter what my own or conventional wisdom tells you.

I hope you get something out of my advice about query letters. A big sale, hopefully. When you get your first great response from a query letter, write and let me know. You'll get another great response!

A query letter that didn't work

February 4, 1991

Randy Achee, Publisher
Disney Adventures, W.D. Publications, Inc.
500 South Buena Vista Street
Tower Building, 29th Floor
Burbank, CA 91521

Dear Mr. Achee:

I'm presently writing for *Boys' Life* magazine and have some other freelance accounts. *Boys' Life* has a four-month lead time and as a result it's difficult juggling what will be of interest when the issue comes out. It occurred to me, after looking over your magazine, that I might do "double duty" with my interviews. What's right for you might not be right for *Boys' Life*, etc.

In your February 11th issue, you had a lengthy article on stunts, yet didn't cover Kim Kahana, who has the most famous stunt man school going. Also, the writers got one thing wrong—there was trick photography when Harold Lloyd did *Safety Last*. The clock Harold is hanging from was actually on a platform several feet above the roof of a building. If Harold had fallen, it would have only been a few feet. This isn't widely known but better research would have revealed the truth (and copies of "how he did it" shots might have been nice). I try not to miss details like that, particularly when young "Bet I can do that" readers are at stake.

I'm enclosing my resume for you to look over. I would enjoy writing about Hollywood for your magazine.

Best,

Skip Press

A query letter that did work

September 27, 1991

Ms. Tina Berke, Editor
ComputorEdge
The Byte Buyer, Inc.
Box 83086
San Diego, CA 92138

Dear Mr. Berke:

I'm currently writing for three national magazines—*Boys' Life, Disney Adventures* and *Grit*. One upcoming assignment is an interview with and article on Steven Spielberg. The current cover story (September) of *Boys' Life* is mine (in case you know a Boy Scout who subscribes). I sold a screenplay recently and am working on another one that has been "optioned" by some producers.

I recently wrote a computer business article (my second) and I'd like to do more. Your listing in *Novel & Short Story Writer's Market* says you buy material helpful to first-time computer buyers. I may have something for you.

An article I'm developing is called "Man Over Motherboard," a chronicle of my experiences in buying our first computer and setting it up, which included three trips back to the shop. I've found my experiences are the norm. Here's how it's gone:

I got ambitious. I wanted a fax/modem, so I bought the card and installed it personally. That's one of the reasons I was back to the shop three times. Now, I can fax an article, no problem. Modem? If I get lucky. I also bought and installed a hand-held scanner, which enables me to scan photos and incorporate them into my articles. Of course, I haven't used it once and don't know how.

I have Windows, a screen-saver named After Dark and a virus-checking program that hasn't helped me one bit. I also have 21 separate manuals, none of which I've read all the way through. I'm not alone in this, as you probably know.

A "friend" with "10 years' experience, knowing everything about PCs" came over and "just put some simple things which will really help you" on my computer. This caused two of the trips back to the shop. He was amazed that I was reading my DOS manual. In his 10 years, you see, he never read it.

I can give your readers a few laughs and some helpful tips. I'm perfectly willing to write my piece as fact, or fiction. My resume and a sample article are enclosed.

Best,

Skip Press

A sample query letter if you haven't previously published

January 2, 1995

Ms. Baleful Glance, Editor
Local Magazine
123 Main Street
Your Town, USA 12345

Dear Ms. Glance:

I've been following your magazine for several months now...(*Do your homework, read the magazine and don't lie.*)...and I've noticed that you seem to have a fondness for articles about hog-calling techniques and other aspects of country living. (*Wow, she'll say, a writer who's actually done some homework.*)

That's why I thought you'd be interested in my enclosed article, "Peccary Persuasion Along the Orinoco." I was marooned in the Amazon Jungle after a failed love affair some time back, and I found solace among a lost tribe, the Heybuddies, who are the best callers of wild pigs in the known world. (*You've got her, because she's probably never heard of the Heybuddies, and neither has anyone else.*)

For example, as a passage into manhood, a Heybuddy male of the age of 12 is led into the jungle by an elder, then abandoned. The young man must then squeal like a pig at the top of his lungs until he either: 1) is eaten by a python or some other animal or 2) attracts a wild peccary suitable for eating. He is, I should mention, given a week's instruction in peccary persuasion before being led off into the jungle.

My article describes the entire rite in a manner I feel would fascinate your readers. I've noticed that your letters to the editor tend to be most vocal when commenting on youthful topics. (*You give her a taste of your piece and close with a sales pitch on how you think her readers would like it—if you've actually read the letters section of her publication and use that in your pitch, she'll be amazed.*)

I have provided a self-addressed, stamped envelope for you as requested. (*A self-addressed, stamped envelope is commonly referred to as an "SASE."*) I look forward to hearing from you at your earliest convenience.

Sincerely,

Brilliant Writer (Your Name)

(*Remember, if this letter goes on your own stationery, all the better. If it doesn't, don't be surprised when the postperson passes your house without stopping six weeks later.*)

A sample query letter if you have previously published

February 1, 1995

Mr. See Nitall, Managing Editor
Bigtime Magazine
777 Park
New York, NY 12345

(Remember, don't waste time writing the top editor, because he or she will likely pass it on to a lower-echelon editor first. Besides, lower-level editors like to be singled out and noticed.)

Dear Mr. Nitall:

After studying the *Writer's Market* listing and the last three issues of your magazine... (*or* I've been reading *Bigtime Magazine* for years and recently)...I concluded that you'd be interested in my article, "Peccary Persuasion Along the Orinoco."

As anyone who has been following the news in recent months knows, pigs are the most popular items of interest to the American public today—if not to readers around the world. (*Show him how your piece reaches the broadest audience possible.*) I came to write this piece after being marooned in the Amazon Jungle by a jealous lover. Reluctant to immediately return to civilization (my erstwhile lover runs the Rhode Island mob), I found solace among a lost tribe—the Heybuddies—who are the best callers of wild pigs in the known world. (*You've got him, because he's probably never heard of this.*)

For example, as a passage into manhood, a Heybuddy male of the age of 12 is led into the jungle by an elder, then abandoned. The young man must then squeal like a pig at the top of his lungs until he either: 1) is eaten by a python or some other animal or 2) attracts a wild peccary suitable for eating. He is, I should mention, given a week's instruction in peccary persuasion before being led off into the jungle. (*You give him a taste of your piece, but cut it short, because editors of bigger magazines don't have as much time.*)

I enclose a self-addressed, stamped envelope, along with my resume. (*If you have a resume that the editor would care about, which is to say, one that fills at least half a page, single-spaced, with your literary accomplishments.*) (*Or*) I enclose a self-addressed, stamped envelope, along with an article I recently published in *Hog Caller News*, as a writing sample. (*Obviously, the editor will want to see how you write before making an assignment. Wouldn't you, if you were writing the checks?*) I look forward to hearing from you at your earliest convenience.

Sincerely,
Your Name

Query letter for an unsolicited manuscript

February 1, 1995

Ms. U. Don't Know Me
Director of Development
Bigtime Studios
1 Bigtime Place
Hollywood, CA 90028

Dear Ms. Don't Know Me:

My enclosed screenplay, *Don't Call Me Red*, is about the first Martian to be elected to the United States Congress after we colonize Mars, the Red Planet. (*This sentence is called the high concept in Hollywood terms. If you can't say what the screenplay (or book) is about in a sentence or two, you usually don't have your piece focused, which is to say, not well written.*)

I know that in the past, your company has made successful films I've enjoyed like *First Woman in the Moon* and *Saucers from Hell*. I believe my film could be another great success for you, and I picked your company as the first to see it. I enclose a one-page synopsis of my script, along with a self-addressed, stamped envelope. I look forward to hearing from you at your first available opportunity.

(*If you have a resume the reader would care about, send it. If your resume doesn't much relate to the subject of your script, it won't matter.*)

Sincerely,

Your Name

Chapter 3

❖❖❖❖❖❖❖❖❖❖❖❖❖❖❖❖

Artful articles and superb short fiction

The basics

By now you've probably figured out that I have a fondness for journalism. I was a journalist when I began on my road to success, but it's not the only route to riches for writers. Most of the successful writers I've known or read about, however, put in a lot of hard work at some form of paid writing that allowed them to learn as they went and at the same time made high demands on them to deliver the goods. Journalism readily offers this opportunity.

I am a fan of journalism because you have to get to the point right up front. You have to grab the reader's attention and keep it. Remember this if you are convinced you only want to write fiction. It's hard to author a novel. It's very hard to write a great one. You have to learn a lot of tricks, some of which I'll explain later. Not many writers write hugely popular works as their first work. They build up to it. You learn to write "page-turner" text the more you write. If you can learn to write and sell articles on a regular basis, or if you get a job writing for a periodical like a newspaper or monthly magazine, it's inevitable that your writing skills will be honed and improved. So if you're looking for a place to start, I'd advise you to write some articles, or even get a job working for a periodical. Articles are easier to write and sell than short stories, and the market for them is much bigger.

Did you know that articles have been made into major Hollywood films? It's happened time and time again. Producer Peter Guber developed *Midnight Express* from an article he read in the newspaper.

Screenwriter Floyd Mutrux read about modern-day cowboys in Houston, Texas, in *Esquire* magazine. He secured the rights and developed *Urban Cowboy* from it. (He later sold his interest and someone else got screenplay credit.) You can make a big name for yourself by writing articles.

The first thing you need to know about article writing is what it looks like on the page. Once you're past that hurdle, you'll have the editor convinced that you are at least clued in on how your words should look on the page. Please note that you'll probably find someone who will tell you they want a different format than the one I give you. That's fine. This format given here is one I've used and seen used for two decades. I'll explain all the parts later. Meanwhile, here it is:

Your Name   About 1,000 words
Your Street Address
Your City, State & Zip
Your Phone Number

                            TITLE
                         by (Your Name)

     The text of your article or story begins at least four lines down from your name, and continues double-spaced to...

                          THE END

Now let's break down that format. Your name, address and phone number go at the top left because that's what someone reads first on a page. Some editors also like to see the following on subsequent pages:

Your Last Name   Page Number

Some editors like this format on subsequent pages:

Article or Story Title/Your Last Name   Page Number

(If you have a long title, you'd abbreviate it in this type of header.)

Other editors prefer numbered pages only. I advise you to use the title/last name and number header. Why? Because if your work gets broken apart, it will be easy to put back together with the necessary information on each page.

If you have an agent, the agent may instruct you to leave your name and address off, or type their name and address on the page under yours. They might simply paste their label over your name and address. However that happens, the editor or editor's assistant will return the manuscript to the name and address in the upper left-hand corner. If they want to buy your manuscript, they'll write a letter informing you of same at that address. They might even call you. So get your particulars in order.

Why "about 1,000 words"? Editors have space constraints in their publications. Small articles are generally 1,000 words long—or four double-spaced, typewritten pages of 250 words each. The word count per page is based on an average of 25 lines per page, 10 words per line. This means you'll have roughly one-inch margins on all sides of the page. If you have a word processing program that counts words for you, you're ahead of the game. If you don't, the above is a rough guideline.

Any time you're researching a listing about what a magazine will buy, you'll probably see a notation about article size. Normal articles are generally 2,500 words or so. A 10,000-word article or short story is very large by modern periodical standards. Beginning writers mostly sell short articles, sometimes as short as 500 to 750 words. That's why you tell the editor how long your written piece is in the upper right-hand corner. It's the second thing they look at.

Next is the title, centered. I advise you to put the title in caps. Some editors might prefer a different look, but don't sweat it. Titles are important. Good ones give you the essence of what the piece is about. So put it in the center and make it noticeable.

Below that is the "by" line: who wrote it, right below the title. Even though you've listed your name in the upper left corner, you still need the by-line. Why? Maybe you're using a pen name. You could list Joe Smith if that's your real name in the upper left, then put Jack Benimble on the by-line if that's your chosen pen name. The editor will see the distinction.

Note that the double-spacing begins with the title and continues throughout the article. The exception to this would be if you inserted a block quotation in your text, or a poem or lyric. For example:

"Once when I was a young lass, I read the following poem which made me

weep and long for my lost love:

Now you're gone
I'm all alone
And my, am I so sad

I completely forgot about this cherished verse of my youth until my 25th

high school reunion. It was there I saw Johnny, the captain of the football team

and president of the Poetry Society..."

At the end of your writing, put "THE END" in capital letters, centered. Don't get fancy; you'll run the risk of irritating the editor. That same editor who never gets manicures or rides in limousines, remember?

As I mentioned earlier, having parameters helps me pace my writing. I hope that by having the above format to use, you'll be better able to plot out your articles. A short story uses the same format. And it's my contention that a great article and a great short story are constructed with roughly the same elements.

In the Information Age

By the way, as I was writing this book I came across a bright young fellow in Alabama named Watt Key who developed some interesting software to take care of your formatting woes and a lot more. Green Turtle submission software gives you a database, address storage, a submission recorder and tracker, a label maker, reports, onscreen help and a full-featured word processor with mail merge capabilities. You might simply try using this program to take the pain out of formatting and submitting for your articles and stories. Write to Watt Key, Green Turtle Software, P.O. Box 1044, Point Clear, Alabama 36564, or call (334) 928-0874, for details about the program.

Start with the essentials

Any piece of writing begins with a premise—the concept, the central idea, the thing you want to get across to the reader. The premise should answer the question, "Why is this tale so special?"

Give that some thought. If you read a book and are thrilled by it, chances are you'll tell a friend. You'll do the same with a movie you like, or someone on TV who catches your eye. You'll talk about a magazine article you enjoyed. Along that line, did you know that editors generally consider that three to five times as many people read their magazine as buy it? If the magazine circulation is 100,000, they figure 300,000 or more people read it.

No matter how many people find the writing in question to be special, it begins with the person who buys it for broad public distribution in the first place. So you have a double duty. You have to convince an editor that your work is special so it will be bought. That's the query letter. Then you have to convince your reader it is special, and the editor is Reader #1.

This all starts with a premise. In Hollywood terms, the premise is called the "high concept." Here's an example: "A learned man is able to turn a poor girl into a cultured lady." That's the premise of George Bernard Shaw's *Pygmalion*, which inspired the musical *My Fair Lady*. Dolly Parton starred in a film which tried to reverse genders and use the same premise. *Rhinestone* didn't work, because Sylvester Stallone couldn't sing nearly as well as Eliza Doolittle and didn't have half her charm.

Stallone worked just fine with a similar premise, however. "Journeyman ne'er-do-well boxer gets a surprising shot at the heavyweight championship and triumphs." That premise is the essence of Stallone's *Rocky* and all its sequels.

Let's look at some other premises. "Your fat can make you thin." That's the central concept of an amazing diet regimen by a doctor friend of mine, Calvin Ezrin. In fact, it's the title of his book of the same name. A learned endocrinologist, Dr. Ezrin discovered that insulin imbalance brought on by excessive carbohydrate intake was the source of dietary failures. He coauthored an earlier book, which had all the same information, called *The Endocrine Control Diet* but it didn't sell the way he thought it would. Why? Because most people couldn't tell you without thinking about it that the word endocrine refers to our glandular system. The title didn't reveal the premise or give the reader a rough idea what the diet was all about. *Your Fat Can Make You Thin,* on the other hand, reveals the premise. The book merely elaborates on that primary idea, showing you how you can cut your carbohydrate intake way back, concentrate on a protein and vegetables diet, and with proper exercise and medical supervision get to and maintain one's ideal weight. (As a further but cursory explanation, lacking enough calories from food, the body is forced to turn fat into substances called ketones to provide the extra calories. Thus, your fat literally makes you thin.)

Now let's move on to what really matters in your story—and in any story, matter of fact.

What makes your tale special?

You should always be able to answer this question about your work. What are you doing when you write? I say you are taking the reader to some place new. It might be a place where they haven't been, or some place where they've been but have never seen with your unique perspective. In Dr. Ezrin's case, he was revisiting that old diet road that so many people had been down before. Having lost 50 pounds or so on his program in a few months and gotten educated on how to keep the pounds off forever, I was happy to go on that road, because it is my belief that his unique understanding of the mechanics of the human body saved my life.

Everyone likes to think they are special. When considering life as a writer, people enjoy thinking they fit that old proverb that each person has at least one good book in them. People also like to be able to offer something worthwhile to the world. When they take the time to read an article, they want it to be something they can use to make their lives better, even if it only entertains them for a while and gives them some relief from the stresses of life. Keep that in mind when you're forming a premise for a piece of writing. Why is your idea special? What does it tell the reader that he or she hasn't heard before? If it travels a path already visited, what's your unique angle?

Another thing to remember is that you, as a writer, are often able to put into words something that other people can only conceptualize. They don't have the vocabulary to fully and specifically express their emotions, their vision, their philosophy. That's why politicians have speechwriters to tell their constituents what they are all about.

With a premise, you usually offer one of the following:

• A new reality.
• A fresh look at modern reality.
• An examination or reexamination of an old reality.

Or a combination of any of these. Remember what I said about finding common ground? If you plan to introduce a new reality to the reader, you need to get on common ground first. You can do that by comparing the new reality you're about to explain with a reality you're pretty sure your reader will understand. Similarly, a look at an old reality usually needs to be grounded in modern examples. If you are reexamining a modern reality, you will still need to compare. For example:

> "We've all heard that you starve a fever and feed a cold, haven't we? A doctor in Houston has proven that this old wives' tale isn't always true."

(Please note this is just an example, and that I don't know any medical specialists from Texas.)

Got the idea about premises? You should take pains to get your premise in order. If someone asks you, "What's this about?" you should be able to answer quickly and coherently with no hesitation. It's the old 25-words-or-less approach. Many screenwriting teachers will tell you that, if you can't describe your entire story in a sentence or two, you don't have it fully focused. I agree with that and feel it applies to any type of writing.

A friend of mine, Howard Steninger, dabbled in poetry. He was never very serious about it, but he did come up with one poem that I loved. It is a haiku poem (a Japanese form) of five syllables:

```
Watching
   falling
      snow
```

See why I like it? You can see the snow, the wind and the rhythm of the falling flakes. It's a perfectly realized premise and execution that conveys Howard's experience magnificently.

The premise is often expressed fully in the title, but not always. The title might merely allude to the premise. It might convey a double meaning or make you wonder what the story is about. A good example of the latter is a book, *The Adventures of Huckleberry Finn.* Adventures? Great, you know what that is. But what's a "Huckleberry"? The word has a nice roll on the tongue, and you want to learn all about a person with such an odd name. And that's what you do when you read the book.

For now, though, just work on your premise. See if your title expresses what it is. Try to make your premise as special as possible. If you treat every piece you write as something that might be enjoyed for centuries, you will uniformly turn in work that has a special quality. Then, like cream, you will rise to the top as though by a force of nature.

Planning by parts

As a writer, you'll hear beginning, middle and end over and over and over. These have been the agreed-upon parts of an article, story or creative work since before the ancient Greeks. They are such a given it would seem we wouldn't need to discuss them, but I inevitably find that my students aren't quite sure what these parts really mean.

Actor/comedian/composer/musician/talk show host Steve Allen once said that you should begin a story where it truly begins. By that, he meant that writers will often ramble around, provide back story (explanation of prior events) and use other devices to begin a story, boring the reader with details. So where does your story really start? What action (note that word) takes place that sets in motion a major event? That's the beginning of your story. For a very basic example of this, take the Book of Genesis in the Bible. Adam and Eve were created in God's image. They were living in Paradise, the Garden of

Eden. They were innocent, free of care. Then Eve heard a whisper, said hello to the snake and decided to chomp an apple of wisdom. God got mad, the angel arrived with the flaming sword and they had to start working for a living. Where did that story really start?

"Hey, Eve! Tired of being ignorant? Take a look at this!" Hiss, hiss, wag of tail. The apple glistened in the midday sun. That's where it began. That's where the premise kicks off. There is the action that set everything else in motion.

The beginning of a story provides the following items: a) point of view; b) the main character(s); c) the setting; d) something happening. In other words, you establish the elements of the entire story. Once you've done that, you're finished with the beginning.

Have you ever thought about the opening scene of a movie? Often, you see a broad panorama, with a character going somewhere. Something is happening, and you're in on it. That broad opening view is called an establishing shot. If the movie begins in New York then shifts to Chicago, there will be a new establishing shot in the Windy City. You'll probably see the title "Chicago" briefly displayed on the screen, and/or a year such as "1950." Ron Howard spoofed this process in his film *Splash* when he shifted the opening action from the Atlantic Ocean off New England to the Big Apple. "New York," said the title, "This Morning."

Once you know where you are and who is doing what, you can move on to the middle. The middle of a piece of writing usually deals with one theme: transformation. The main character is changing, and/or struggling to bring about change. Often, the hero or heroine is on a literal journey or quest. In any good story, the main character is embarked on an inner transformation as well. Look at the transformation undergone by Sylvester Stallone's "Rocky." In the middle of that story, he went for it. He put in the hard work, ran the miles, pulled himself up by the bootstraps and listened to his trainer, Mickey. As we headed into the end portion of the story, we knew all about Rocky except for an unanswered question: Could he do it? Could he win? We wanted to know. We were dying to know. That question was repeated in four more *Rocky* movies, and we always wanted to know. In essence, the first *Rocky* was the beginning to all the rest.

If you're writing an article, you introduce your subject in the beginning. In the middle, you will describe what you found, how it is special and how it may affect the world around us, if at all. Even if you're writing a recipe, you'll have a beginning, middle and end. The middle will be the using of the ingredients to prepare the food. Before we retire for dinner, though, let's discuss endings. The end is very important. Usually, I get the idea for something, and I work it. I get the premise in order. Often at the same time I get the main idea, I see the logical progression of the story to its end. So I often start off with a beginning *and* an end in mind. It's much like I discussed earlier in forming the big picture. Like the Greek legend of the goddess Athena springing fully born from the brow of Zeus, I'll have a general idea of the full story as soon as the concept comes alive in my mind. You might find that you have a similar experience. You'll know how you want it to end, you'll figure out how it begins and get it outlined. Then you start writing and the fun begins. The middle, where the transformation takes place, will more easily write itself when you have the ending in mind.

This doesn't always work when you're researching an article. You might not know how it will end. Once the research is done, however, you will. You'll know what you want your article to convey to the reader. You can write toward that point. Just as you need to have your premise in good order, you might find it beneficial to work out the end, too.

What does the ending do? It tells you whether the transformation was achieved or not. Did Han Solo change his irresponsible ways we first witnessed in *Star Wars*? Obviously he did, because he's right there with the rebel forces in *The Empire Strikes Back* (the second film), fighting alongside Luke Skywalker and Princess Leia. In *Return of the Jedi,* the end of the trilogy, he's transformed completely. When it is revealed that Luke is actually Leia's brother and therefore not a romantic challenger for Leia's hand, Han Solo gets the girl. Even more to the point, he has changed (transformed) to such a degree that Princess Leia is now perfectly willing to become Han's mate.

Perhaps the beginning, middle and end could be summed up more simply in the following manner:

1. What change is imminent or what should change?
2. What changes are put in motion?
3. Did the desired changes take place?

I often observed that the only constant in most people's lives is change. All writing I've ever felt to be memorable is about change, and usually great changes. "It was the best of times, it was the worst of times…" Charles Dickens said in the beginning of *A Tale of Two Cities*. In other words, it was a time of changing conditions. In that story, enormous change.

I would hope that your efforts as a writer help bring about positive changes. I would hope your work also helps smooth over the changes of time and circumstance for your readers. Lastly, I would hope that you never stop changing with your writing. By that, I mean I hope you always get better as a writer. Before your great changes begin, though, make sure to get your basics in order. Then you'll be prepared for anything.

Chapter 4

❖❖❖❖❖❖❖❖❖❖❖❖❖❖❖

Genres, generally

By now you might see a pattern in my presentation. I've been laying out, step by step, the path I took to success. I want to steer you away from the wrong turns, detours, dead ends and traffic tickets I got along the way. Which gets us to the next rest stop: genres. What's a genre? It's a type of writing, a category, a tag a publisher can hang on a title, to explain to bookstore owners what is being sold. After all, those bookstore owners need to section off their stores, don't they?

You might have a favorite genre. Let's say you like "whodunits," or romance novels. Maybe you have an inclination to write children's books. If you can pick a genre to write in, you'll give yourself another useful parameter within which to work. In describing your book to an editor or publisher, you'll be able to more easily tell them what kind of book it is. They'll have a higher estimation of you, because once again you will have shown them you've done your homework and have a professional approach. If you look in *Writer's Market*, you'll see that publishers are divided up by genre as well.

At this point you might be in a bit of shock. Perhaps you're someone who merely wanted to write an article or short story when you picked up this book, and here I am talking about writing big old books. Get over it. You *should* write a book. Think big or your brain will atrophy. When someone comes to me after having written a book, I immediately have a great deal of respect for them, whether the book is any good or not. At least they had the gumption to finish a major project. That's admirable.

Beside, knowing genres will help you in calculating what sort of short story or anything else you want to write.

Are you convinced your work transcends genres? Maybe it does, but not likely. I've had beginning writers tell me they didn't want to get pigeonholed. "What's your story about?" I'll ask. "Well, you'll just have to read it," they say.

Oh, no I won't! Since they can't tell me what it's about, they probably don't have a focused story. They've rambled, so I'm not interested, because my rambling days are over. If they said, "It's a whodunit in which the hero discovers he's actually a heroine," that might pique my interest. They might not have something I'd personally be interested in, but at least I'd know they knew their story and the genre in which it fit.

In Hollywood, you have to put a handle on your story. "It's a buddy movie," you explain, or "It's a road picture," or "It's a buddy movie on the road with a sci-fi backdrop." (An example of a buddy movie on the road would be the old Bing Crosby and Bob Hope pictures, such as *Road to Morocco*.)

More on movie categories later. Right now, we're at a rest stop. Grab your favorite beverage, kick off your shoes and take it easy. Study the following list carefully, but don't take it as gospel. Times change and genres do, too. Here are the various publishing categories I've found, with commentary on where to find more information.

Young people's books

These range from ages 2 to 20 or so. By "20 or so" I mean they are meant for people who are not yet of legal age, which in most states is the age of 21. I've had plenty of adults read my Young Adult novels and enjoy them, including a justice of the Supreme Court, but we're talking categories here, not taste.

Picture books. Aimed at ages 2 to 6. The *Hello Kitty* books are an example. If you also illustrate these books, you'll make more money. In fact, a writer/illustrator in this genre is preferred by publishers. Otherwise, most of the time a publisher has its own illustrators, so in most cases you don't need to find your own artist. There are exceptions. If you happen to know a superb illustrator, go ahead and let him or her illustrate your book, but don't be surprised if a publisher uses someone else. These books are generally 300 words or less.

Young readers. These are aimed at ages 6 to 8. They have pictures with more text. The same rules regarding illustrations apply here. These books are generally 500 words and up in length.

Middle grades. These are aimed at ages 8 to 12. James Barrie's *Peter Pan* falls into this category, as does *The Wind in the Willows*. These are your classic "children's" books and stories that make billions in Disney animated feature versions. Length varies.

Young adult. As I mentioned previously, these are aimed at ages 10 and up. *Flowers in the Attic* by V.C. Andrews or books by Judy Blume are well-known examples. The difference with this genre and classics like *The Hardy Boys* and the *Nancy Drew* series is that the main characters are approaching adulthood and dealing with "adult" problems (though rarely experiencing sex). My "You Solve It" Mysteries with Alexander Cloud and Jilly Adams for Z*Fave, a division of Zebra Books, are examples of this genre. They run 20,000 to 50,000 words and up.

Lower reading skills. These books are also called "hi-lo" (high interest, low reading skill) and "reluctant readers." They are intended for teenagers, high schoolers (or adults) who have only third- to fifth-grade reading skills. They are mostly marketed to schools and libraries. In fiction, this genre is usually packaged with 10 or so novels in a genre such as "fantasy" or "adventure" and each set is accompanied by a teacher's guide. In these books, the characters are teenagers in challenging situations who learn something as a result of the story. This is a good "break in" category for a writer. They are easier to write and sell than other novels. They average 6,000 words and up. The main drawback to writing in this genre is that most manuscripts purchased are "buy-outs," meaning you don't get any royalties, just a one-time fee as a writer for hire. You also surrender the copyright, but you can often negotiate and retain theatrical rights to such stories.

Comic books and graphic novels. Graphic novels are basically expanded comic books, although they are sometimes published in hardcover. They are very popular with kids of all ages (translated: adults, too). The graphic novel sub-genre became important with *The Dark Knight Returns*, on which the first *Batman* movie with Michael Keaton was based. The comic world has been particularly interesting to Hollywood in recent years. For example, the "Judge Dredd" movie character portrayed by Sylvester Stallone originated in a comic book.

Young adult textbooks. These books are generally created and distributed by companies specializing in textbooks and nonfiction for junior high and high schools. They are often sold in "packages" as mentioned in the "hi-lo's." My *The Importance of Mark Twain* for Lucent Books is an example. It was part of a set about important world figures. These books are generally 20,000 words and up. For a sample catalog from this kind of publisher, you might contact: Lucent Books, P.O. Box 289011, San Diego, CA 92128-9011; (619) 485-7424.

Young adult nonfiction. The eight-volume *Star Families* I did for Silver Burdett Press is a nonfiction example in this genre. They are of similar length to textbooks, usually shorter. They cover a specific area of interest and can be expanded to include more subjects if the initial books are popular. My *Star Families* were about children of famous people who went on to their own fame, such as Natalie and Nat "King" Cole.

Take note: Every genre that exists for adults by and large has a similar place in young people's literature, usually minus violence and sex. There are exceptions to the no-violence-and-sex rule, particularly in comic books. It will vary by publisher.

Suggested reading: *Writing Juvenile Stories and Novels* by Phyllis A. Whitney, 1976, The Writer, Inc.

Recommended organization: Society of Children's Book Writers and Illustrators. (See listing in Chapter 7.)

Speculative fiction

This genre is most often broken down into the subcategories of science fiction, fantasy and horror. I lump them together because they share a common theme—their stories are far outside the bounds of "normal" life and bear heavily on "what if" premises. In legendary test pilot Chuck Yeager's words, they "push the envelope" of human existence. The length of these books are generally the same as adult fiction. You'll find length guidelines in books on where to find publishers, such as *Writer's Market*. In recent years, 75,000 words (a 300-page, double-spaced typed manuscript) is a general rule, although paperback novels may be shorter in length.

Fantasy. This is a story that has no "rational" explanation. Magic may be used in the story, or circumstances that cannot be easily explained according to known laws of the physical universe. Classic examples of this genre are *The Charwoman's Shadow* by Lord Dunsany and *The Dragonriders of Pern* (my personal favorite) and sequels about the fantasy world of Pern by Anne McCaffrey. The subcategories:

- **Sword & sorcery.** The name explains it. This has long been a popular fantasy genre. The ancient poem "Beowulf" is an example. *Conan the Barbarian* is the modern archetype for this type of story. Curiously, the Conan books (which preceded the comic books of the same name) were written not by a world explorer, but a man in West Texas who lived with his mother.

- **Action fantasy.** This genre is amply illustrated by movies like *The Neverending Story* and *Labyrinth.*

- **Role-playing games.** These are actual games. They started with the introduction to the marketplace of "Dungeons & Dragons." They are often very intricate and all of them are written. I emphasize that they are written, because students often seem surprised when I tell them this. They seem to think the games were just stamped out by a computer or something. This is a relatively new outlet for fiction writers, and has enjoyed great popularity, particularly among teenagers and college students. As the world of interactive CD-ROM computer games expands with titles like the mega-successful "Myst," there will be more and more demand for this category.

Science fiction. This is based on current fact expanded into "what if," keeping in mind our current knowledge of the workings of the physical universe. In other words, the emphasis is on science. Classics of the genre include *The Foundation Trilogy* by Isaac Asimov and *Stranger in a Strange Land* by Robert Heinlein. Science fiction not only predicts the future but inspires it. H.G. Wells basically started the genre, along with his contemporary Jules Verne. Many of the scientific developments of our modern age were first envisioned in science fiction, for example, satellites were written about by Arthur C. Clarke long before they were orbited. In recent years, fantasy and science fiction have been lumped together as "speculative fiction." That way, the term "SF" can be used for both. Science fiction as a category is still generally used, however. When I say SF I mean science fiction. SF has many sub-genres within its own category. Some examples:

- **Detective story mixed with SF.** A good example of this is *Do Androids Dream of Electric Sheep?* by Philip K. Dick, which was made into the movie *Blade Runner.*

- **Cyberpunk.** This refers to outlaw computer geniuses of the future—what current "hackers" (people who break into computer systems over phone lines, often using stolen telephone credit card numbers) may become. Think of the film *War Games* with Matthew Broderick combined with the film *Blade Runner* and you'll have an idea of this sub-genre. Better yet, read *Neuromancer* by author William Gibson. Gibson's *Johnny Mnemonic*, a film starring Keanu Reeves, is yet another example, as is the Fox Television show *VR5.*

- **Action SF**. A quick review of highly successful big budget Hollywood features of the last decade or so reveals a huge appetite among the public for this type of writing. Recent examples are *Total Recall* with Arnold Schwarzenegger (from *We Can Remember It for You Wholesale* by Philip K. Dick).

Suggested reading: "Beyond The Idea: Projecting the Future in Science Fiction" by Roger Zelazny, and "Science Fiction Today" by Isaac Asimov (both from the "Specialized Fiction" chapter of *The Writer's Handbook*, 1989, The Writer, Inc.).

Recommended organization: Science Fiction Writers of America. (See listing in Chapter 7.)

Horror. Huge careers are built on this genre, probably much more than SF or fantasy. In modern times, Edgar Allen Poe started it. I say "in modern times," because scary stories told around the fire have been with us for a long, long time. Authors Bram Stoker (*Dracula*) and Mary Shelley (*Frankenstein*) greatly expanded this genre. Stephen King is the king of current horror authors, with Anne Rice (*Interview with the Vampire* and other titles) the queen. Clive Barker, with his *Hellraiser* and other gloomy tales, has also become a darling of horror fans. By the way, a great many horror movies are made because:

- They're usually cheap to make.
- People, as a rule, love to be scared.
- It's often seen as the quickest way for an aspiring director to make a big splash in his/her career.

Here's another curious note: The vampire theme in Hollywood films is far and away the most popular theme of all time, from the early *Nosferatu* to the recent *Dracula* directed by Francis Ford Coppola.

Suggested reading: Read the classic books of the genre, much more than any "how-to's."

Recommended organization: Academy of Science Fiction, Fantasy & Horror Films, 334 W. 54th St., Los Angeles, CA 90037. Telephone: (213) 752-5811.

Interactive games. Think of "Super Mario Brothers." Very popular video game, not-so-popular movie. If, however, you can come up with a book that has any of the following, then pack your bags for Hollywood, because you've got the hottest thing on the market these days, an "interactive" property:

- A good plot involving a hero on a quest.
- A lot of action and/or violence.
- Colorful characters who also make good toys.
- Works as a book, a movie and a video game.

You can write a not-so-fabulous novel in this SF/fantasy/horror genre and still make a lot of money if the book also sells as a film and video/computer game.

Mystery, detective & true crime

This is a big, big category, perhaps because people like to exercise their analytical abilities. More often than not, when a new detective comes along on television, the public eagerly embraces the character and we see TV movies featuring the same for decades—Peter Falk as *Columbo*, for example. Similarly, the proliferation of real-life crime shows like *Cops* in recent years shows the public's seemingly endless thirst for true crime stories.

The following sub-genres are not about television, but books. Create a great detective character or characters, though, and chances are good you might see him/her/them on film or television fairly quickly. You'll also run a good chance of selling not one book, but a series. Having sold a series of detective novels and then the film/TV rights, I'm particularly fond of this genre.

High-tech or specialized knowledge thriller. This is the essence of many big-bucks novels of the last 20 years. Recent examples are Tom Clancy's *The Hunt for Red October* and other novels with his hero Jack Ryan. The tradition Clancy follows was heavily popularized by Ian Fleming's James Bond books. Another example of what I mean by specialized knowledge is the "inside the legal profession" setting of John Grisham novels like *The Firm*. Sometimes these books are written by someone who is a professional in the field, such as Robin Moore's medical-setting works. Don't fret if you don't have specialized knowledge. The specialized knowledge often comes from intensive research, which is the case with Clancy's writing. Clancy's research for *Red October* was so thorough (all done in libraries), that he was visited by intelligence officers after the book's publication. They wanted to know who gave Clancy the classified information!

Men's adventure. This category is currently in decline. Examples of these "series" books include *The Enforcer* series, the *Matt Helm* books and *The Executioner*. As sexual attitudes have changed, diseases have spread and women's issues become more prominent in our society, a James Bond "playboy" outlook on things isn't as popular in books and movies, although books that have an already-established following continue to be churned out. And though James Bond continues changing faces (new actors portraying 007), Bond movies keep getting made.

Classic detective. This ranges from "hard-boiled gumshoe" books like Raymond Chandler novels (*The Maltese Falcon, The Big Sleep*, etc.) to Agatha Christie's books (the basis for the TV series *Murder, She Wrote*) to a recent flood of Orange County, California novels (all written before the famous California county declared bankruptcy). According to a front-page article in the *L.A. Times* dated Sunday, November 8, 1992: "Over the last decade, Orange County has served as the setting for more than 60 novels ranging in genre from mystery to science fiction to romance to fantasy," including Judith Krantz's glitzy *Dazzle*. The Sherlock Holmes books by Sir Arthur Conan Doyle are still the standard for all others in this genre. If you can figure out a "new twist" to the detective novel genre and write a good book, chances are good you'll be set for life. Just keep churning out the pages and publishers will beat a hasty step to your door, bearing checks.

Police novels. "Cop" stories have been a popular theme in films and literature for a long time. In recent decades, Joseph Wambaugh, an ex-L.A. police officer, has written only about police in his books like *The Onion Field*. Perhaps the first such book of this kind, believe it or not, was *Pudd'nhead Wilson* by Mark Twain. *Wilson* incorporated the then new science of fingerprinting into this turn-of-the-century story.

Erotic thrillers. The film *Basic Instinct* is the primary modern example. This is a Hollywood favorite, which explains why *Basic Instinct* screenwriter Joe Eszterhas gets multi-million dollar paychecks. These stories sit right on the line between mystery and sex, and combine pornography with analytical detective skills. This was an increasingly popular theme for a time, but it has been satirized (the film *Fatal Instinct* by director Carl Reiner). Satirization by Hollywood sometimes means the genre is declining in favor. In the 1990s, most Hollywood studios are supposedly trying to do less violence and more family films. What Hollywood says and what it does don't always match, however.

Horse racing. Huh?! You bet. This sub-genre belongs to Dick Francis, an ex-jockey who has become hugely successful by writing about fictional crimes set around the world of horse racing. His *Driving Force* is a good example. Francis' success demonstrates that it is possible to create a genre within a genre.

True crime. As you might suspect, these are nonfiction stories. Usually, the more outrageous the crime, the better. In the 1950s, newsstands were filled with true crime magazines. More modern TV movies and "reality" TV shows such as *Hard Copy* eat this theme up. True crime books are equally popular. The first modern true crime book which really made a splash was *In Cold Blood* by Truman Capote, which explored a real-life murder of a family in the Midwest. Other examples are *The Onion Field* by Joseph Wambaugh, which described the murder of some police officers in Southern California. More recently, *Rush*, written by a female police officer who got hooked on drugs, was a bestseller. All the books mentioned became films. If you write a great true crime story, you might be on the road to a bloody fortune.

Suggested reading: Again, read the books that are successful. They are generally entertaining, and you'll learn more than you will by reading "how to" books and articles—but those can help, too.

Suggested research: This genre usually follows well-established formulas. You need an "angle" that hasn't been seen before (or done very well, perhaps) to really make yourself well-known. Jessica in *Murder, She Wrote*, for example, is a mystery writer who comes across real-life murders every single week of her life (you'd think she'd start to wonder why). If you pursue this genre, take some courses in how to be a detective. Visit police stations, or bars where cops hang out after work. The more authentic your work sounds, the more likely the reader will enjoy what you are writing.

Recommended organization: Mystery Writers of America, Inc. (See listing in Chapter 7.)

Mainstream adult

This is a broad, broad category, so if I leave something out I apologize. Like I said, public taste changes all the time. If there's a large new category in the bookstores that you notice, write and let me know.

Romance. This is basically the biggest market in the world for fiction. It's not unusual for one author to turn out dozens of books over a few years, often having other people write for them, based on the author's outline, such as the fiction factory of Barbara Cartland. This category of books is written mostly by women, or men writing under female pseudonyms. It really took off in the 1970s when the genre was broadened in theme by Kathleen Woodiwiss' *The Flame and the Flower*. Roughly, the formula for a romance novel is this: a) girl meets the man of her dreams; b) is swept off her feet; c) then, for some stupid reason, is separated from him for most of the story; d) she goes through all sorts of troubles; and e) still manages to end up with dream man at the end of the story. Sometimes the heroine doesn't get the guy, if your name is Scarlett O'Hara and the novel is Margaret Mitchell's *Gone with the Wind*. The sequel, *Scarlett* by Alexandra Ripley, wrapped that up nicely. Scarlett and Rhett went through some mighty changes, but got together at the end. Well, fiddle-dee-dee! Romance novel sub-genres:

- **Gothic.** According to *Webster's New Collegiate Dictionary*, this is defined as "of or relating to a style of fiction character-ized by the use of desolate or remote settings and macabre, mysterious, or violent incidents." As mentioned above, the original *Dracula* fit this description. So did the original *Frankenstein*. The difference with modern Gothic novels is that the main character is almost always female.

- **Historical romance.** Belva Plain's *Evergreen* is an example. The classic is, of course, *Gone with the Wind* by Margaret Mitchell.

- **Glitz.** Judith Krantz's *Scruples* is an example, while other notable authors in this category are Jackie Collins, Danielle Steele and Sidney Sheldon. Write a bestselling glitz novel and you will probably go directly to Hollywood for the miniseries and collect bushels of bucks.

- **Harlequin Romances.** As a publisher, Harlequin has defined the genre for the rest of the market.

  Their categories include: Harlequin American Romances—sexy stories with rich details of North American lifestyles and mores; Harlequin Historical Romances—set in England, France or North America between 1700 and 1900, these books emphasize the sweet and sensual; Harlequin Intrigue—passion sizzles, with the emphasis on a plot of contemporary romance and adventure, mystery or suspense; Harlequin Presents—their top seller, with strong, passionate men and women, dramatic stories, exotic locales, but (sorry, Hollywood) no sex before marriage; Harlequin Regency Romances—set in 1811-1820 England, the customs, dress and speech are covered in detail in these books, and sex is left to the imagination; Harlequin Romances—their longest-running series, featuring stories where young heroines focus on sighs instead of sizzle; Harlequin Super Romance—these are longer contemporary stories of controversial issues. The stories are sensual, with well-developed subplots; Harlequin Temptation—fast-paced and sensuous, even controversial, these books deal with topical subjects. They are adventurous, fun, glitzy stuff.

- **Woman in jeopardy.** On the Lifetime cable TV network, this is the theme of almost every film broadcast. You'll have to watch to see what I mean. When it's a "wom jep" book, usually the woman is in one place (like a house) and being attacked. An editor at Zebra who wanted me to write these said the setting seems to have a personality of its own and is almost like a character in the book.

Westerns. The classics are anything by Zane Grey (*Cimarron*, for example), and more recently anything by Louis L'Amour. With the death of Louis L'Amour, there is currently no "king" of this genre. Therefore, the opportunity for one to emerge is large.

Historical. Examples are Barbara Tuchman's *A Distant Mirror,* and *Clan of the Cave Bear* by Jean Auel. This genre is not limited to time period, but the books are generally very thick novels which imaginatively transport the reader to a world very different (yet factually accurate) from our modern one. They are tough to write if you're not good at research and detail.

The ethnic experience. This genre exploded after the smash success of Alex Haley's *Roots,* although movies about Italians—the organized crime version, anyway—have been made since the beginning of Hollywood. Irish American movies were once quite popular, at least when James Cagney was a box office star. Relatively new in American fiction, ethnic novels are becoming increasing popular. *The Color Purple* by Alice Walker is an example. Amy Tan's *The Joy Luck Club* is another good example of this genre. It's refreshing to be able to "look into" an entirely new world, particularly when you don't have ready access to that ethnic background. This idea—along with good writing, of course—might explain the genre's increasingly broad popularity.

Humor. These books are often "nonfiction" in name but fiction in truth. Columnist Dave Barry, author and the prototype for the *Dave's World* TV series, is the reigning king of this type of book. Almost always, the authors of these kind of books have syndicated columns: Barry, Erma Bombeck and Art Buchwald are examples. Radio "shock jock" Howard Stern's *Private Parts* is...well, maybe not a *good* example, but a successful one.

Humorous fiction. Kurt Vonnegut's *Hocus Pocus* is a fine example, as is the bestseller *Mostly Harmless: The Fifth Book in the Increasingly Inaccurately Named Hitchhiker's Trilogy* by Douglas Adams (author of *The Hitchhiker's Guide to the Galaxy,* which began as a radio show in England).

Nonfiction. This includes everything from biography to commentary to essays. These books are usually written by seasoned journalists. That means it helps if you have sold a number of articles, so editors think you're "ready" to write such a book. Exceptions are when people have specialized knowledge (there's that term again), such as a therapist who discovers (or thinks he has discovered) a new aspect of the human mental condition, or a salesperson or businessman who reveals his or her secrets for others to use. There's almost always a market for celebrity books. The libraries of publications resulting from the O.J. Simpson double murder case emphasize this. It usually matters most to a celebrity if they can trust you as a writer first, then whether or not you can do the job. If you want to write nonfiction books, you'll simply have to study the market, figure out where you can fit in, and draw up a step-by-step plan of achieving your goal or goals. I also advise you to pick up the latest copy of *Publishers Weekly*. You'll see more categories of nonfiction there than you ever thought existed.

Modern classic. This is the book every writer ultimately wants to write. I've discovered some common elements of many books that have become classics in this century and others, which I'll share with you now:

- Usually, a first-person narrator tells an intimate tale, often from his or her own childhood. "Coming of age" is a term you will hear used, or "rites of passage." *To Kill a Mockingbird* by Harper Lee (my personal favorite novel) had a tremendous influence on me. *Sophie's Choice* by William Styron is another example, as is *The Prince of Tides* by Pat Conroy. Steinbeck's *East of Eden*, Faulkner's *The Reivers* and Laura Ingalls Wilder's *Little House on the Prairie* are other examples. Stephen King's "Rita Hayworth and the Shawshank Redemption," adapted into the film *Shawshank Redemption* with Tim Robbins and Morgan Freeman, is another excellent example of this wonderful genre.
- Although the narrator may be young or very young when telling the tale, the story is more often than not told in retrospect, with the perspective of an adult looking back.
- The book may tell a personal story but it usually encompasses the beginnings of a larger social change, such as the

Southern attitude toward African Americans and the injustice perpetrated upon them in *To Kill a Mockingbird.*

- The writer is tremendously poetic in the way he or she tells the story. He or she is simply wonderful with words. As a reader, you are artistically transported to the time and place being described. You're taken on a wonderful ride to someplace you've never known, at least not in the manner the author describes it. It is as though you are personally living the experiences, and you are continuously emotionally moved.
- There are very few or no stereotypical characters or places. Every line of dialogue, every description of setting and mannerism, seems perfectly authentic and, most often, unique to the broader society.
- Occasionally, there is a literary device used to tell the story. The book may be epistolary—that is, told via letters, such as *A Woman of Substance* or *The Color Purple.*

If you only write one book in your life, I urge you to attempt a modern classic. You might come up with something that greatly enriches us all. I must caution you, however, that most of the writers of classics were well-practiced as authors before they penned a masterpiece.

Whether you write a classic or a romance novel, I have a simple "Suggested Reading" list which will enhance anything you write. Read the classics. Read as many classics as you can! It is essential, if you want to be a good writer, to have as broad a knowledge as possible of human history. Even though it is a daunting undertaking, I suggest you read *The Story of Civilization* by Will and Ariel Durant, which is also available (for you computer users) on CD-ROM. I recommend anything by Plato or other ancient Greek philosophers. Give Shakespeare, or Cervantes (*Don Quixote*) a read or two. You may be surprised at how good they are. Read Joseph Campbell's *Hero with a Thousand Faces* to get an idea of where we have come from as storytellers. You'll have a better grasp on where we are and where we might go.

Campbell's book has become the ruling story authority in Hollywood, thanks to screenwriting teachers like John Truby and filmmakers who swear by Campbell, like George Lucas and George Miller (the *Mad Max* films with Mel Gibson). As a side note, all of the films that Disney funds are currently examined to see if they follow the "myth" plot line Campbell explains. *The Hero's Journey: Joseph Campbell on His Life and Work* by Phil Cousineau and Stuart L. Brown (Harper & Row, 1990) is also a focused look at Campbell's conclusions on the myths and stories of Earth.

If you agree with Campbell, it might appear that humanity keeps telling the same old story over and over, with minor variations. Apparently, however, we never get tired of it. Therefore, I advise you to study thoroughly Campbell's blueprint of this recurrent hero myth, which is most thoroughly laid out in *Hero with a Thousand Faces*.

In summation, it doesn't matter if you find a genre or sub-genre in which to specialize. If your manuscript is accepted by a publisher, it will be put into a category. Maybe you don't want to specialize. Perhaps you want to write in several genres. I have, but I hope to eventually settle into writing modern classics. (I told you I think big.) If you successfully pick a genre in which you're happy writing, you might find that you'll make money quicker than you would otherwise, and also gain the time to write that classic you've always wanted to write. That is the way it happened with me. You'll get better, hopefully, every time you put words on the page, as long as you keep expanding your horizons. See if you can find a genre from which to begin.

As I cautioned earlier, everything I've given you here is simply a guide for launching your career; you need to do personal, extensive research into what the market is doing, and this market changes all the time. You need to get out there and explore.

Genre-ally, I hope I've helped you.

Chapter 5

❖❖❖❖❖❖❖❖❖❖❖❖❖❖❖❖

Nonfiction knowledge and nonsense

This book was turned down by the first publisher I sent it to, and I'm glad that happened, because the publisher who accepted it, Career Press, had no titles like *How to Write What You Want & Sell What You Write* when I sold them my book. The first publisher who seriously considered my manuscript already had a truckload of books on writing in its catalog. Since that publisher specialized in books about writing, it seemed like the logical place for my book. Then an editor there wrote to say that, although I had a very strong book in mind, it wasn't a "niche" book, the kind they'd been successful with.

See what I'm getting at? If you place your book on gardening with a publisher who has only one book on gardening—namely, yours—chances are good that publisher will put more "juice" into contacting every gardener possible to tell them about your book. (Sometimes this reverse logic doesn't make sense. In the case of art books—those big things you see on coffee tables in rooms of people's homes that they enter only on special occasions—there are only a few publishers. The books are expensive to produce and these publishers—such as Harry Abrams—have the market fairly well sewn up.)

There was another reason Career Press bought my book proposal after another publisher turned it down. The secret was format.

My agent for *How to Write*, David Andrew, looked over the proposal I'd sent out and asked me to rework it. (I signed on with David some time after my first submission and subsequent rejection.) I had always been under the impression that all you needed with a nonfiction book proposal was the first three chapters and an outline of the remainder. You wrote a good query letter, you put in a copy of your resume and/or curriculum vitae, and that was it. The rest was up to the fickle whims of puzzling publishers. I sold a number of books using that simple guideline. In retrospect, I now realize that the books I sold were not mainstream adult. The competition was not as fierce in the genres in which I formerly worked. When I moved into the big leagues, I had to learn what was expected of me as an author all over again. What I was mainly missing was an effective format.

Just as you need to submit stories, screenplays and manuscripts in an acceptable format, you need to do the same with book proposals. With most writing sales, you need to write the entire manuscript to make a sale. What I like most about writing nonfiction books is that, in contrast, you don't always need to write the entire manuscript to make the sale. You need to provide proof that you can write, which is what the chapters do. Usually, three is enough, but not always the first three. Sometimes you can get by with less than three. With the proposal for this book, for example, I sent the publisher an introduction, Chapter 1 and Chapter 18.

I'll clue you in on what else was in the proposal for *How to Write* shortly. Before I do, let me add this: If you intend to write a book about a technical subject, you'd better have someone to back it up. Note I said "someone," not "something." If you want to write a book called *Alaska on One Salmon a Day*, it could be about your personal experience. If you want to write *The Salmon Diet*, however, a book about losing weight by eating mostly salmon, you'd better have a roomful of doctors, or at least one very good one, as your recognized expert in the field. Why? Because publishers don't want to be sued by readers who feel they've been defrauded. You can write about a technical subject and have no certification in it whatsoever, as long as you find enough people who are recognized experts to back you up. This applies to article writing as well as to books. Now do you have an idea why I advised writing articles early on? If you establish yourself as a journalist and have a thick sheaf of clips to send an editor you want to sell your first book to, it can only help prove your credibility and professionalism. As with all things, there are exceptions to this rule. I'm too busy to try being an exception, so I always like to know where the experts are and what they can tell me.

What are nonfiction books? Animals, autobiographies, beauty, biographies, business, celebrity profiles, cooking, current events, diet and nutrition, entertainment, health and fitness, how-to (instructional), history, hobbies, humor, men's issues, parenting, philosophy, photography, psychology, self-help, sports, travel and women's issues are just some of the categories of nonfiction books. Is it any wonder that nonfiction books are, as an overall category, about equal with fiction in sales? In this Information Age we're supposedly in, nonfiction can only expand. Here's some even better news for beginning writers: Percentage-wise, it is generally much easier to sell a nonfiction first book than a novel.

This fact has its drawbacks. One woman I know of sells a lot of books on love. She was once married to a former friend of mine. This woman dedicated three books to her lover. The man's ex-wife told me numerous horror stories about this self-styled pop psychologist/author and her behavior. Yet the public continues to lap up her printed posturing. Why? Because, I suppose, any information on relationships—which sounds good whether it works or not—is better than nothing.

This example gives you some clue as to how much credence publishers give college degrees. I've met enough Ph.D. holders to know that many of them are good at going to school, but their degrees don't make them geniuses. Still, if you want to write about things technical, you'll need an expert on your side unless you are yourself an expert. In most cases, it is simply what is expected.

So let's get into what goes into your proposal. A nonfiction book proposal is like a film trailer (coming attraction). Just as a reader might pick up your book in a bookstore and read a few pages before making a decision on whether or not to buy, you will "hook" a publisher with your proposal or not. That means it needs to be good, fast.

Overview

The first item in your proposal is a description of the book. The introduction you read in this book is a combination of the overview and the introduction of my book proposal. Once I'd sold the book, I adjusted language in the overview intended for publishers to make it more appropriate for the mainstream public. In rereading my introduction, I decided it didn't say all I wanted to say. So I borrowed from the overview that had pleased my publisher.

The overview should fully describe what you hope to achieve with your book. Remember my advice about "why is this special?" The overview will state why it is special, hopefully in fewer pages than a normal chapter. For me, a chapter is usually around 16 to 20 typewritten pages. My introduction in this book was about six double-spaced typewritten pages long. Over the years, I've learned to say what needs to be said in as short a space as possible. I'd advise you to do the same.

Of course, your manuscript will be double-spaced. Ever wonder why? It's simply easier to read. In addition, an editor can make marks in red ink between the lines. (You'll learn about red ink when you are about to be published, believe me!) Since your introduction is the lead-in to a manuscript, it should be double-spaced as well. Number the introduction with small Roman numerals, although it's not that important. No one will reject your manuscript because they don't like your numbering. However, they might not read it if you fail to number the pages at all. (If they dropped it and the pages got out of order, then what would they do?)

The marketplace

If you spend $20 or more on a book, aren't you a bit discriminating about how that money is spent? If you don't have to watch your finances, good for you, but most people aren't in that situation. Most people comparison-shop. They look over a number of books, perhaps in a number of bookstores, before they spend their hard-earned money. Who can blame them? You should think about that when you approach a publisher. It costs a lot of money to hire a staff, get a book manuscript in shape to be printed, then shipped. Public relations campaigns must be mounted and book catalogs must be mailed. Publishers are not, as strange as it sounds to some writers, endless fonts of finance. They want "bang for the buck" just like you do. When they buy your book and take it seriously—that is, if they think it might be a big moneymaker for them—they consider the competition. You can help them decide in your favor by doing as much of their competition survey as possible. I call this section of the proposal "The Marketplace." Here's the opening paragraph of my marketplace section in the proposal for this book:

"Beginning writers have these alternatives: 1) seminars, workshops and classes at the local college; 2) correspondence schools; 3) advice from writing magazines; 4) writer's groups; 5) winging it;

6) finding a personal mentor. *How to Write What You Want & Sell What You Write* delivers all these."

I then went on to list five other books that were available in major bookstores at the time. These books were, unlike mine, niche books. They were all about only one segment of writing, such as writing articles or technical writing. I then told my potential publisher that no one book then on the market offered all the basic formats and advice on all the fields and types of writing. At the time, that was true. I said that my book would not be loaded down with theory. It would offer concise, easily understood advice, for both writing and marketing.

I did not shy from venturing into hyperbole, either. If I was shy about what I thought my book could do, how could I expect a publisher to tout it as something great?

"My book can become the bible of all writing how-to books," I proclaimed. "Delivering all the goods, it's aimed at every wanna-be writer in the English-speaking world. How many is that? The UCLA Extension Writers Program, where I teach, has a mailing list of 250,000 people! It's the largest program of its kind, but certainly not the only one."

Remember, this section of a proposal is a sales pitch. It follows your overview. You've said hello, and now your foot is in the door. You're getting the potential publisher to at least listen to all of your sales pitch, whether you'll close the sale or not. If they've read this far, you want to keep them, so you'd better be passionate in your convictions. Here's the rest of what I said in "The Marketplace" section of my proposal:

"In the most recent *Writer's Digest* listing of writer's workshops for all 50 states, there were almost 1,000 entries. With 500 video channels coming, and exploding multimedia and interactive needs, writers are needed more than ever before. The next decade could be the Golden Age of Writing. No kidding. Expansion of cable, video and computers offers something we didn't have in the beginning of the TV Age. We were used to 'broadcasting,' but for years now we've had 'narrowcasting.' That means it can be cost-effective to make a cooking show for people speaking Tagalog (the language of the Philippines and the third most common in California). Someone has to write that show. Technology has reached the point that, within five years, a person will be able to film scenes, dump them into a computer, edit their own movie, use that in creating an interactive game, upload it to a publisher via modem, and bank the profits the same way.

"When a person can do all that, will they want to access 50 books, even on CD, to find out how to write various items necessary for the complete package? What if they want to spin off greeting cards or transmit quotes from their work to be used in a speech? Or turn their screenplay into a stage play or create a camera-ready article via desktop publishing?

"Or will they want one book that covers it all, like *How to Write What You Want & Sell What You Write*?

"The answer is obvious. When this book is published, I will immediately embark on seminars around the country. It will be published, and I'll keep making writers. Hopefully, you'll help me do that."

Let's analyze my pitch. Was it passionate? It was. Were you convinced? Would you be moved to check out my claims? If you did check them out, you'd find they were true. For example, I knew that Tagalog, the language of the Philippines, was number three in the State of California because at the time I was in the middle of writing my *Awesome Almanac: California* (one of 50 on each of the various states of the U.S.). I knew about narrowcasting because I'd written and produced how-to videos in the past. The rest of my summation was simply something I had personally observed. When I acquired a computer with a CD-ROM, the idea of being able to plug in a disk and access whatever I needed to know in an encyclopedia was much more appealing than getting up, finding the right volume and looking up the information manually. It stood to reason, I felt, that people would also like to find basic information on writing and selling any form of writing in one book.

About the author

If you have one degree, or several, no doubt you studied long and hard to get those credentials. Similarly, you might have put in many years to acquire the information you want to share in a nonfiction book. If you propose to profile a celebrity, you might have years of experience writing about celebs for magazines. Should you be modest and simply provide a neat copy of your resume?

I think you know how I'll answer that. No! You need to do every-thing possible to explain to the publisher why you are qualified to write about your chosen subject. Sure, you can show them a copy of your resume, but it's not much good without explanation. I would ad-vise something else as well—a one-page narrative about yourself told in the third person. "Skip Press has received national recognition in almost all forms of media..." my "About the Author" began. I went on to relate how the first how-to video I put together sold more than 100,000 copies, how another won the Silver Medal in the New York International Film Festival, how a corporate slide show of mine be-came a video and sold 100,000 copies (and also won an award), and all the other diverse areas of writing in which I'd been successful. I men-tioned how I had sold 17 book titles in three years, as well as two screenplays. In closing, I listed all the writing societies I belonged to or had once belonged to, and spoke of my teaching at UCLA Extension Writers Program. As a final touch, I said, "His happiest accomplish-ment in the whole wide world is helping other writers get started."

It wasn't bragging, just fact. I also meant every word about my happiest accomplishment. One year, I interviewed Steven Spielberg for *Boys' Life* magazine (the magazine of the Boy Scouts of America). That same year, I sold my first four books and a screenplay. None of these feathers in my cap meant as much to me, however, as some-thing else I accomplished. I was asked to judge a short story contest of some fifth graders in Beckley, West Virginia. That's where my wife is from, and the school kids were students of her aunt, Jewell Graybeal. One of Jewell's students, Billy Hopkins, wrote a clever, hilarious story called "My Homework Ate My Dog." I not only chose it as the winner, I sold it for Bill to a national magazine called *The Children's Album,* which was written and illustrated by kids. The editor (an adult) not only published Bill's story, but hired me to write the advice page in the back of the magazine in which Bill's story appeared.

When I went back to visit my wife's family the next year, Bill's ac-complishment was written up in the local paper. A picture of us grin-ning side by side accompanied the article. Nothing in my professional writing life had ever made me feel more proud.

My entire "About the Author" pitch was one page. I didn't list every single writing society I had ever belonged to, or all my accom-plishments. I included my resume and a letter from my agent with my book proposal but did not incorporate them into the text of it. I told the publisher just enough about the author to give them a sense of security that I could deliver the goods.

If you're uneasy writing about yourself, get someone to do it for you, then edit it. I'd advise writing it yourself, however. Otherwise, you run the risk of disturbing the voice of your proposal, which should be uniform throughout.

Contents

This is as simple as it sounds. List the chapter titles on a single page. (If you can't get all the chapter titles on a single page, you're writing an encyclopedia, not a book.) You don't have chapter titles? Well, many books these days don't have them, but I always use titles. It gives me a chance to catch the attention of the reader with catchy, possibly humorous phrases that give at least a hint of what the chapters are about. Also, if I can come up with a good chapter title fairly easily, I'll know that I have my chapter focused. If you want examples, look at the chapter titles in this book. Just remember what I said about keeping 'em turning the pages. I'm all in favor of catchy chapter titles. If you have a page full of dull line-after-line titles, you run the risk of losing the reader.

Outline by chapter

Which would you rather read?

Chapter 1. This chapter is about...
Chapter 2. In this chapter, I...
Chapter 3. This is the chapter where...

Or:

Chapter 1: Life with the Oinkers. I relate my beginnings on an Arkansas pig farm, and how I acquired the nickname Porky...

Chapter 2: A Sizzling Education. When my father was appointed Ambassador to Columbia, I had never even drunk coffee, much less raised it. Here I describe my Central American school days, and...

Chapter 3: Bacon and Eggs. How I got into the diner business...

That's a further example of why I suggest you use chapter titles in your table of contents. If your book proposal is boring, you're dead. You won't sell the book. Your table of contents is followed by a description of the chapters. This chapter-by-chapter outline (which I called "Chapter Descriptions" in my proposal) will cover each chapter in one paragraph. A rough guideline is half a page, double-spaced, per chapter—that means two chapter descriptions per page. I averaged four chapter descriptions per page, but you may need more room.

The chapter outline is no time to get dry, boring and technical. Remember, the publisher or editor still hasn't seen a fully written chapter. You're still selling. You don't have to sound like a used car salesperson, but you should maintain the overall tone and style of the book you propose to write.

Writing sample

And now to the meat of the matter! This is where you show what you can do. Following your chapter outline, you provide an introduction (if you plan on having one, as most nonfiction authors do). The introduction (which you may choose to call a preface or foreword) is usually followed by Chapters 1 and 2 and sometimes 3. As I mentioned earlier, you might have a reason to include a chapter which appears later in the book in lieu of an opening chapter. Just make sure you include Chapter 1, because that's the opening to your book and it's crucial to keeping the reader turning the pages. Beyond that, which chapters you include is your call, and perhaps that of your agent or representative if you have one. In the case of this book, I included the introduction, Chapter 1 and Chapter 18 in the proposal. The first chapter, "The Big Picture," fully covers my broad view of writing. Chapter 18 is about my experiences with and advice on writers groups, so I thought it was particularly pertinent to the overall proposal. After all, part of selling my proposal was showing how I had experience with many forms of writing and writing groups.

In another book which I ghostwrote, the proposal included the first five chapters. In that case, the main supporting character of the book, a companion who walked with the author across North America, did not figure prominently in the book until Chapter 5. Since I considered this character critical to the book, I needed to have the first five chapters in the book proposal. My agent agreed, so that's how the proposal went out.

Supporting evidence

Think of this section as the "show and tell" portion of your proposal. My agent calls it "Photographs and Exhibits." In the proposal for this book, this section was titled "A Partial List of Suggested Experts." Note I said "Suggested." Since I don't claim to be an expert on all types of writing, I made sure my potential publisher knew that I would consult experts in various areas of writing, as necessary. Most of the experts I listed were friends or acquaintances. The majority of them get our family newsletter. In some cases, however, I didn't know the experts. I merely knew from long journalistic experience that I could get the experts to talk to me once I revealed that I wanted to include their opinions in my book.

People have egos, which they like to have flattered. Once, when I found out Tennessee Williams had an apartment in a security building in New York City where a friend of mine lived, I visited my friend, then went and knocked on Mr. Williams' door, unannounced. I showed the famous playwright a copy of a Los Angeles theater magazine that another friend of mine published. I told Mr. Williams I wanted to interview him for the magazine. He took it from me, looked it over a second, then agreed to the interview. He was one of the most gracious interview subjects I've ever had. He even pulled a copy of his *Memoirs* from a shelf, autographed it and gave it to me. It was a calculated, educated guess on my part that Mr. Williams would grant me an interview. After all, wasn't this the man whose character Blanche Dubois had proclaimed in his play *A Streetcar Named Desire* that she had always depended on the kindness of strangers? I mentioned this to Mr. Williams, then asked him whom he patterned Blanche after. Was it Blanche Cutrere, a girl from his youth?

"No, no!" Tennessee laughed. "It's like Flaubert said about Madame Bovary. 'C'est moi!' Blanche is me, young man."

So I knew that, when pressed to consult experts for my book, I would be able to deliver. If the ones I listed didn't work out, I could find others just as good who would. And that's precisely how it worked out. You'd be surprised how the doors fly open when you ask for someone's expert opinion for a book you're writing. If you're doing an unauthorized biography or some similar book, a different reaction is likely. But when you want their opinion about something having to do with their area of expertise, "yes" is the predominant answer.

I found a number of experts via the online service CompuServe, in various writing and entertainment business forums. What an amazing thing, doing interviews via computer with people you've never met or talked with. The Age of Information has its benefits.

In my book proposal, I listed all the experts with a brief description of their expertise. For example: Stan Lee—creator of Spider Man and other comics. You don't need to go into excruciating detail about listed experts, unless they are the primary source(s) of information for your book.

In closing this section, I explained my relationship with or access to the experts I had listed. A word of caution: Don't overdo it. If you intend to write a book about the history of real estate in New York City, don't list Donald Trump as a potential contributor to your book unless you have a very good idea that he'll participate. You run the risk of getting the publisher thinking that Trump is locked in. When you turn up later and say Trump declined, it could cause problems.

A list of experts may not be necessary for your specific book proposal. Instead, you might have a package of photographs or drawings to include. If so, you should own them, or have an agreement with their creator. Previously unpublished photos are quite desirable to a publisher, which is understandable. When most people pick up a biography, they open the book to the photo section, particularly if there are never-before-seen-pictures there. If you've had newspaper articles written about you, and/or about the subject of your book, include them in this section. Anything that might help exhibit the value of your book should be included. If you're writing a true crime book and have obtained photocopies of applicable items from the public record—marriage certificates, court filings, etc.—put them in. This part of the proposal is the "close" of your sale. Drive home how important your book will be and how much the public will like it. If possible, get your publisher thinking that people will be lining up outside the bookstores at 6 a.m. to get a copy.

People are talking

Along the lines of the previous section, support your proposal with quotes from others. This was an addition to my proposal that came from David Andrew, which, I feel, really put me over the hump with the proposal for this book. It was fine for me to make the pitch about my book. My "What People Are Saying..." section provided quotes from other people, declaring why my book was worthwhile and needed to be published. I contacted former students, recognized experts, even the head of the UCLA Writers Program for quotes. I told them why I needed quotes, and got letters from them.

For the sake of brevity, I excerpted quotes from these people on two pages of paper, single-spaced. I could have provided copies of their letters, but that meant my publisher would have had to flip through many more pages of paper. Depending on what your nonfiction book is about, you'll have to determine how many testimonials you think you'll need to support your pitch.

How can anyone give a quote on a book that isn't finished? Good question. Some of my supporters knew my work and trusted that I would turn in a superior product. In other cases, they talked specifically about work I had done with them. In one case, I wrote the quote for a screenwriter friend who was busy. I showed it to him and he signed off on it with a, "Yeah, that's about what I would have said." (After interviewing and writing about people for years, it isn't hard to write something that sounds like it came directly from their mouths.)

This is support material, remember, not the *Congressional Record*. No one lied about me or my proposed book. Here are a few examples of the quotes I used. Note that I followed each quote with an identification of the person quoted.

> *"I cannot tell you how much I adored this instructor—I've never been given so much help, confidence and practical advice in any classroom situation before. Skip is the kind of writing teacher everyone should experience. He took the fear away and helped us laugh."*
>
> —UCLA student of Skip Press

> *"When I started in the film business, I not only read books about the process, I outlined them so I could remember all that*

I read. With his book, Skip Press has successfully outlined the path to success in all fields of writing. I highly recommend it."
—Robert Bonney, screenwriter,
The Night the Lights Went out in Georgia

"Skip Press's UCLA Extension class, 'How to Write What You Want and Sell What You Write,' was an unqualified success with our very demanding, educated students."
—Linda Venis, Ph.D., Director, Department of the Arts, UCLA

In the case of the quote from Linda Venis, the mention was about my class, not my book. That way, Linda spoke only about what she knew, and preserved her integrity. Since the class I taught at UCLA Extension Writers Program was somewhat of a jumping-off point for this book, it was appropriate to have a quote from Linda. Subsequent to the time I taught that class at the program, Linda received a well-deserved promotion from Executive Director of the Writers Program to the position listed in the quote.

Do not make the mistake of including letters or quotes, however, from people whose aim is to proclaim what a worthwhile person you are. That's a turnoff to a potential publisher. If you include quotes, make sure they pertain to your qualifications to write your proposed book. Then it's okay for them to say how great you are! Humility can be a noble quality, but, in general, meek people don't sell a lot of books.

In this chapter, I purposely did not discuss the content of writing nonfiction articles. That ground has already been covered. Beside, if you aspire to be a journalist, you should try to write a book sooner or later. People in all walks of life then tend to take you much more seriously as a writer. Authors of nonfiction books are often asked by magazine and newspaper editors to write articles. They'll come to you, instead of vice versa. My friends Adrian Colesbury and Brass McLean were amazed at the doors that opened up after the publication of their first book, *Costa Rica: The Last Land the Gods Made*. Done in conjunction with a well-known photographer, the book got a great review in the *Los Angeles Times* Sunday edition travel section, was mentioned in *Auto Club* magazine and won the award for "Best Travel Narrative" in 1994 from the Publishing Marketing Association. Adrian and Brass' phone started ringing and kept ringing. Among other things, they were invited to write about a film being shot in Costa Rica. Those invitations might not have come if they hadn't written a book.

"Oddly enough," Brass told me, "we wrote the book as a last-ditch effort. Our journalism careers were at a standstill. Nobody was returning our calls. The book was a boon for us right out of the starting gate. Now, our pitches are accepted immediately, and we've gotten several unsolicited assignments from editors who have seen the book."

So write something big. Write a book. Write a big book, why don't you? If it's nonfiction, the good news is you probably won't have to write the whole book to make the sale. Now you know how to write the proposal, so you have no excuse for not getting your book sold. I hope I get to read it some day.

Chapter 6

❖❖❖❖❖❖❖❖❖❖❖❖❖❖❖❖❖

Novel means "new"

So you want to write a novel. Any editor you'll ever contact will want to know three things: 1) Do you have writing talent? 2) Do you have something they can publish profitably? 3) Will you fulfill the contract they make with you? In short, will you give them the book they want? That applies whether you send them a complete book or part of one.

In the previous chapter, you learned that it is not always necessary to write a complete book to sell it. One can often sell a nonfiction book based on a few chapters and a complete outline.

Well, the same holds true for novels, in some cases. When I got the contract for my "You Solve It" Mysteries featuring Alexander Cloud and Jilly Adams, I gave the publisher only 16 pages and short descriptions of the remaining chapters. The writing was good enough that I got a three-book deal, with my first book becoming the "lead title" (first book in a series).

I subsequently learned that in certain genres this type of sale is common. My "You Solve It" books were mass market paperbacks. The company that published them prints millions of books annually. They employ thousands of writers. Mystery publishers and romance publishers have similar operations. The writing has to meet a certain criterion of quality; they don't expect it to be great literature, just good entertainment.

If you're aiming for a big bestseller, a hardcover book with a nice dust jacket, a budget from the publisher for a promotional tour, appearances on talk shows, a big sale to Hollywood and all that, then forget the idea of writing only a few chapters and an outline. You'll simply have to write the entire book. Then, most likely, you'll need to do copious editing. The finished book better be darn near perfect.

When the editor of the century, Maxwell Perkins, received the manuscript *O Lost* from Thomas Wolfe, it was 1,114 pages long, written on onionskin paper. Massive editing was necessary to rescue the book and turn it into *Look Homeward, Angel*. Max Perkins knew talent. He worked with Taylor Caldwell, Ring Lardner, F. Scott Fitzgerald, Ernest Hemingway and many other greats. He was willing to put in the work necessary to turn Wolfe's endless (but very good) writing into a publishable manuscript. These days, editors don't have the time to do that, except for perhaps the most successful authors or notable celebrities. Nor will most editors even consider taking the time for such an effort. In most cases, the manuscript an editor receives is published—if it is published—in about the same shape as received. And the really successful authors usually don't need much editing.

Novel knowledge

Let's get some basics in order. How long should your novel be? These days, roughly 75,000 to 90,000 words (300 to 360 double-spaced, typewritten pages). When I first tried writing a novel, in 1978, 100,000 words was the norm. In 1993, a big bestseller was Robert James Waller's *The Bridges of Madison County,* which is half the size of a normal modern novel; it was also turned into a film starring Clint Eastwood and Meryl Streep. Waller's next book, *Slow Waltz at Cedar Bend,* was of similar size and also a success. Readers' attention spans have shortened considerably since the days of Max Perkins!

In Chapter 3, I told you about proper manuscript format. The format is identical for nonfiction books and novels. Your name and address, the length of the manuscript, the placing of the title and the byline stay the same. Similarly, what I told you about beginning, middle and end doesn't change. So now that you know the rough word count expected of you, let's discuss some history of storytelling. I've always felt that if you understand where you've been, it's much easier to deal with and get a grip on what the future may hold.

The story of the story: American version

Ernest Hemingway once said that the first real American novel was Mark Twain's *The Adventures of Huckleberry Finn.* I'm sure Twain was pleased by "Papa" Hemingway's comment, but the statement might have troubled Nathaniel Hawthorne. After all, Hawthorne's *The Scarlet Letter,* written in 1850, predated Huck Finn by 34 years. Hawthorne and his contemporaries, Herman Melville (*Moby Dick*) and horror master Edgar Allan Poe, helped create a unique American voice in world literature.

All three of these writers examined the psychological nature of man and the result of one's actions. Twain did, too, but he was more ebullient in his fiction. His characters were more flippant, even exaggerated. Twain brought new vigor to the American voice in literature and was the first internationally successful humor writer the nation had seen.

At the turn of the twentieth century, technology began to progress rapidly. Literature reflected and even inspired these changes. Writers in the Western world began to view mankind as one people, more so than ever before. In a day devoid of radio and television, newspapers were the main conduit of public information. Literature was the most popular form of entertainment. In the early 1900s, public writings reflected a certain mood. That is, the world at large seemed to be relatively tame. Civilization was being maintained with some ease. In the U.S., the prosperous "Gay '90s" made the oncoming century look promising. Thus it is no wonder that novelists began to speculate on possibilities. While English author Rudyard Kipling offered amazing tales of the Indian subcontinent and American novelist Edgar Rice Burroughs produced the wild Tarzan tales set in Africa, H.G. Wells, Kipling's British contemporary, helped invent a new genre called "science fiction." With books like *The Time Machine,* Wells was following on the heels of French author Jules Verne, whose *From the Earth to the Moon* in 1865 was the first popular adventure set in outer space. Wells' and Verne's writings offered potentially dark prospects for the future of mankind, but also presented possibilities for overcoming disaster.

This new science fiction inspired an explosion of American literature in the early part of the twentieth century, but there were also other changes in American writing. Beginning in the nineteenth century and continuing up through the 1950s, "pulp fiction" was a mainstay of American literature. Stories of the Wild West and other adventurous settings began in magazines and later appeared in hardcover, novel form. As an example, Edgar Rice Burroughs' *Tarzan of the Apes* first appeared in serial form in *All Story* magazine in 1912.

The science fiction segment of pulp fiction was most important. It not only inspired more writers to try their hand at this form of writing, but prompted generations of scientists to achieve in real life what had only been speculated about in fiction. Rocket ships, space suits and men on the moon were written about for decades before anyone figured out how to actually achieve such things.

During the 1920s and 1930s, two other aspects of American writing took on broad significance. One was the modern social commentary novel, as popularized by Ernest Hemingway and his pal F. Scott Fitzgerald, as well as other prominent writers of the time like Sinclair Lewis and John Steinbeck. In 1926, when Hemingway's characters in the novel *The Sun Also Rises* said things like "I feel such a bitch today" and "Oh, to hell with him!" it created a social uproar. Before Hemingway, people didn't talk like that in popular literature. Certainly not the heroes, at least. From that point on in contemporary American literature, authors have continued to challenge the level of acceptability with the outrageous. The rise of Hollywood storytelling has had a similar evolution and impact. These days, just about anything goes, even on network television.

The latest "cutting-edge" genre is "cyberpunk," a darkly futuristic science fiction, basically invented by William Gibson in his novel *Neuromancer*. Lastly, romance novels—which almost never depict explicit sex—and family entertainment are now on the rise. When standards get too loose, or the milieu of cutting-edge fiction too strange, the moral pendulum swings back toward the middle.

Your future as a novelist

So where does this short history of Western literature leave you as a novelist? It's my belief that this is the greatest time for writers in the history of mankind. There are more literate people on Earth than ever before. The computer revolution allows instantaneous translation of text, even the speaking of the translated words. Not everyone can afford the latest technology, of course, but that's only a matter of time. Paralleling the explosion of technology, information and an entertainment-hungry public is the concept of narrowcasting. In the past, a novelist who wanted to write about the life of potters in a small Japanese town might not have received much notice, except in Japan. These days, though, it is possible through computer networks to connect with potters all around the world. The task of marketing such a book to these potters might not have been economically feasible before. Large publishers prefer broadcasting, reaching the majority of people and ignoring minority elements of the society. There's simply more money in it. Association magazines (like *Pottery Monthly* or whatever) might help find potters who'd buy a novel like I mentioned, but such periodicals usually operate within geographical limitations. Now, through the Internet and other world-sweeping computer connections, it is possible to reach hundreds of thousands of people whose likes and dislikes fit within a narrow profile. This brings me to a simple conclusion—it is now possible to write whatever you want and find a way to sell it. There are probably plenty of people out there who will appreciate what you've written. You should do all you can to get on the "Information Superhighway" to take advantage of this increased "traffic."

Let's get back to the development of story subjects. If there's any unifying element to what all the writers previously mentioned were trying to do, it is to explore and understand the human condition.

Do we fully understand romantic love? Do we really know what exists on other planets? Are all the questions of religion fully answered? Obviously for most people, the answer to these questions is "no." Thus writers continue to write and readers continue to read.

I advise you to remember one constant: Novel means "new." All the writers I've mentioned—and I've mentioned some of the most classic writers of Western literature—strived to expand understanding of life as their society knew it. They concentrated on new ideas.

Maybe you'd be satisfied simply selling a novel, any novel. I'd be willing to bet, though, that when I outlined the parameters of a modern classic in my chapter on genres, that was the description that widened your eyes. Most writing students I've ever had wanted to write a classic. The writers of classics were able to accomplish the task because: 1) They mastered the basics of writing, so that technique did not get in the way of inspiration; and 2) they "pushed the envelope" of societal conventions of their time. They were all willing to risk public ridicule or commercial failure for the sake of writing something that would get people thinking. In Hemingway's case, perhaps, he was simply trying to be controversial to get attention, but I don't think so. That happens a lot more in these "media days" than in his time.

If you would be satisfied writing and selling detective novels for the rest of your life, that's fine, but I'd like to help you reach higher. Whatever you choose to write, when you attempt a novel, remember the title of this chapter. Novel means new. Even if you are writing a formulaic romance novel with a pattern that has been seen time after time, you still need a new story or a new twist to an old story.

Success in writing is a stair-step process. Even if you write one novel and it turns into a bestseller, you'll have put in some step-by-step hard work to get there. How fast you move up those steps, and how sure your step is, depends entirely on you. Just do us all a favor, and try to write something original.

How it gets done

Here's an example of how the Age of Information changed my life. One night while I was exploring the CompuServe online computer service, I got an electronic message from Jerry B. Jenkins. Jerry had read my electronic profile and thought we had very similar backgrounds. He just wanted to chat.

Well, am I glad he did! Jerry, it turned out, had written more than 100 books, of all kinds. Sports novels, young adult mysteries, adult mysteries, biographies, inspirational nonfiction, series fiction. You name it, Jerry had done it. He'd written books with or about some of the legends of the day: baseball stars Hank Aaron, Nolan Ryan and Orel Hershiser, and evangelist Billy Graham, to name a few. I'd written less than a quarter of the books Jerry had authored and was anxious to find out any secrets he might share with me.

He had a big secret all right, but it was one I already knew. Jerry simply worked hard and maintained discipline. He rose each morning at around 7 a.m. and wrote until noon. His output was roughly the same as mine: six to seven pages of fiction per hour, or 45 pages of nonfiction. Like me, he preferred writing fiction because it was more fun and did not require constant referral to notes, research materials, etc. Unlike me, he was also disciplined when it came to family time. As long as his kids were at home and awake, Jerry said, he spent time with them. That way, he felt a lot better about life and his family didn't feel cheated. That only changed (but not much) if he was nearing a deadline. Jerry turned out four to five books per year in this manner, typing about 90 words per minute (using only two fingers, I might add). When I first spoke to him on the phone, he had just signed a 27-book deal with a major publisher.

As you've probably figured out by now, I like to outline. It helps me to have my destination in mind before I embark on a writing journey. I might not have all the stops mapped out, but I know roughly where I'm going. Jerry, on the other hand, did not work from an outline. Instead, he worked from a broad mental story as well as scraps of notes made beforehand and along the way. He told me about a 460-page novel he had recently completed in only 32 days.

I asked Jerry if he had a writing philosophy, and he was quick to share it with me. It was something he tells writers at writing conferences across the country.

"The only way to write a book," Jerry said, "is with butt in chair."

If you plan to write a novel, you'll have to treat it like a business. You'll have to devote a certain amount of time to it each day, particularly in the beginning. Before you start writing your masterpiece, though, you may need to do some housecleaning. Mario Puzo, the author of *The Godfather*, once wrote a list of "Ten Rules for Writers" for a magazine. One of the rules was, if your wife was giving you trouble and distracting you from your writing, get rid of your wife.

I don't espouse "cement shoes" for your significant other, but there's some truth to Puzo's logic. Writers are born procrastinators. (Jenkins tells writers at his conferences that if they don't naturally procrastinate, they're probably not meant to write.) Too often, I play computer games, watch famous criminal cases on TV, admire the sun coming out from behind the clouds, you name it, before I seriously begin writing. Other than what I've mentioned, I don't procrastinate so much that I don't get my job done. I usually meet my daily writing goal, whether it's a chapter or two or finishing up something else. Since I make my living writing, I don't have time for long mental lapses. If I'm feeling burned out, I'll take a break for a few days, but only after a major project is done.

Even if you have only 30 minutes per day, three days a week, to devote to writing, if you maintain discipline you will get your book done. If you cannot maintain discipline, you should probably give up on writing a major project—until you can be disciplined, that is.

This applies to people in your life as well. If there is someone who continually gives you a hard time, and doesn't mean well by it, I'd suggest you either get that person to knock it off or legally arrange to have that person get out of your life. I'm quite serious about this. You've probably heard the old phrase: "If you can't stand the heat, get out of the kitchen." You'll generate a lot of mental "heat" getting a novel done. If there are people around you complaining about this and that in an unjustified manner, they'll just throw you off course. If you're upholding your familial and social responsibilities and simply trying to carve out some time each day to pursue a dream, what sane person would object?

Look at it this way. Let's say you take three months formulating the story for your novel. Maybe you make an outline, maybe you don't. (I suggest you do. Once you've written a number of books, then you can try winging it.) When your story is in order, you take an hour for yourself to write, five days a week, or the equivalent. You are faithful to that schedule. When you are at your writing station, you only write. You get up only to go to the bathroom or make a phone call, and not for long. Let's say you turn out five pages per week, or one per day. In 14 months, you will have a full size novel (75,000 words). Then you'll need to edit it. I edit each chapter as I write it, then do a once-over of the full manuscript when it's complete. With discipline and determination, I'm sure you can finish a novel using this method. One page an hour isn't much, really. You should be able to do two.

If you can't get started, answer a letter. Just write something. You'll get the gears in motion.

Seeing is composing

A famous musician I knew once revealed that he always composed with a blank wall in front of him. He would look up and see pictures, inspiring scenes that became music for him. I took that idea to heart. I keep a clean wall behind my computer. Remember the description of the Hopis "sitting in pictures" earlier? If you can see the pictures—that is, watch the scenes of your novel unfolding in front of you in imagination—then the rest is mere description. If you don't already use that method, try it and see if it works.

When I was a kid, I would draw things to entertain my younger brothers. We were too poor to own a TV. Later, as times improved for my family, I quit drawing for my siblings. When I picked up the habit years later, after my own children were born, I wondered why I'd gotten so rusty. Then I realized what I'd done as a kid. I would mentally project the picture onto the blank sheet of paper and trace around what I was "seeing." This method is the mechanics of all art.

The novel's journey

When you write a novel, you embark on a journey. The reader of your novel goes on that journey with you. Please remember that you are a tour guide. Perhaps you are doing one or several of the following things as an author:

- Taking the reader some place they cannot personally go.
- Showing the reader new aspects of a place with which they are already familiar.
- Suggesting a place the reader may never have considered or dared dream might exist.
- Reflecting upon people, places or situations many readers may know about, but few can put into the words you can with your particular expertise or artistic touch.

All the great stories I've enjoyed over the years have dramatic action. Stories bore me unless they go somewhere. They must do something. I want my main character deeply involved in something from the very beginning, and I like "cliffhanger" chapter endings. Even if the stories take place in the same locale, something happens that I want to know about. You should be similarly inclined, particularly if you aspire to write anything that anyone will pay money to acquire. Even your titles should be compelling, as far as I'm concerned.

So remember that when you write a novel, you're taking the reader on a journey. Consider this, as well: You are actually involved in two journeys at once: an inner journey and an outer journey. While events take place that form the story of your book, the main character or characters should also be transformed. People in dramatic theater call it "catharsis." Story editors at film studios call it "character arc." In other words, inner changes take place in the character as a result of having lived through the events in the story. Look at how Scarlett O'Hara changed from the beginning of *Gone with the Wind* to the end. At first, she's a spoiled belle, with the tiniest waist in the county and a mind to match. In the middle of the book, she declares to God and the sky that she is never going to go hungry again. By the end, she has done her best to ruin Rhett Butler's life, and she's lost him in the bargain. When Alexandra Ripley wrote the sequel *Scarlett*, she reformed the Georgia brat and turned her into a decent human being. It was quite a handy turn of writing to achieve such a major character transformation, but Ripley pulled it off.

Life is a series of changes. Writing is inspired by and reflects upon life. Good writing inspires a better life in others. Whether the changes of life reflected in your writing are positive or negative is your call. After all, you're God when it comes to your story (at least until you get an editor, anyway). Your characters must change, and change dramatically, if you're going to have a novel you can sell.

Red ink in your veins

Now that we've covered history, discipline and structure, let's get down to what writing is really all about—namely, editing. Get out your red pen or pencil, and roll up your sleeves. We're going to slice and dice that manuscript of yours! I have an exercise that drives my students crazy. As their first homework assignment, I have them write 1,500 words. It can be an article, a short story, whatever. They usually slave away at that, pulling their hair out, staying up nights, and some of them don't complete the assignment.

Then I drop the bombshell. "Okay," I say, "your next assignment is to cut your 1,500 words down to 1,000." After I turn off the fire hoses and get them calmed down, I explain how to edit. Basically, it comes down to two things:

1. Is it essential to the story?
2. Does it move the story forward?

Let's break that down with some examples. Here's a short paragraph for your consideration:

> Bobby knew he was in trouble. From the time he was a child, he was known as someone who had a knack for getting into bad situations. There was the time when he'd been caught stealing watermelons from Widow Whittle's garden, the Halloween he'd been mistakenly arrested as a thief, and the time at his father's birthday when he'd been accused of putting

vodka in the punch. Now here he was, with a crush on Mary Stevenson, standing on her front porch holding a corsage and feeling like a fool, and her brother Charlie just had to bring up Bobby's troubled past. Mary stood there in front of Bobby, blushing and confused. It looked like their first date was history, before it ever began.

That's not a bad paragraph. It tells you a lot about Bobby and the situation. Unfortunately, it's mostly mental. It's all in Bobby's head. We're told about action, but we don't feel a part of it. The background on Bobby is nice, and it shows the compound nature of his current situation. There's a better way to do it:

"Bobby Rivers, you're in trouble!"

Bobby gulped. Mary Stevenson, the crush of his life, stood red-faced before him, angry as a irritated hornet.

Her brother Charlie, the rat fink, stood behind her smirking.

"You'll pay for this, Charlie," Bobby managed to mutter. "I can explain everything, Mary," he added meekly.

Why was this always happening to him? Standing there on Mary's front porch, holding a corsage, Bobby felt like a fool. Their first date was history, before it ever began.

See the difference? The dialogue adds action between people. It's a scene, something happening. It brings the conflict out into the open, rather than making it mental. The story is immediately established, and moved forward. You want to know why Bobby's always getting in trouble and what will happen between him and Mary. The action happens much more quickly.

I suppose I could write a book on how to write a novel, going into a thousand subtle nuances, but the above example is roughly all you need. So where would you bring in examples of other times Bobby had been in trouble? Do it when he's going somewhere, when he's alone and thinking it over. Call it flashbacks or back story or whatever you want, just don't confuse your reader by continuously jerking back and forth over a time line to put in the background information.

There's a science fiction classic that most Hollywood types never thought would be made into a movie. It's Isaac Asimov's *I, Robot*, which is almost all mental in its narrative. It's brilliant, but movies require action. Until you become a skilled novelist, I advise you to concentrate on action. When your style is developed, when you're comfortable putting words on the page, then you can more easily be-labor back story and the like. The reader will go with you almost anywhere, simply because they feel so comfortable with you as the guide of your story. Don't you feel that way with your favorite author?

Here's another tip. Don't repeat. In editing, I do my best to use different words, even in the same sentence. Here's an example:

> If you have a wish to be a magician, it'll take more than tossing pennies down a wishing well. Years of hard work go into making magic for a living. In fact, it is one of the hardest occupations at which to succeed.

Here's how to say the same thing better:

> Want to make it in magic? Roll up your sleeves. Professional practitioners of prestidigitation commonly struggle for decades before achieving success.

In the first sentence of the first example, the syllable "wish" appeared twice. The word "magician" is in the first sentence, and "magic" in the second. "Work" and "living" are both in the second sentence, with "occupations" in the third. Similarly, "hard" appears in the second sentence, with "hardest" in the third. All these things are repetitive. You may think they don't really matter, but each time a word or meaning is repeated in the short space of a sentence or within a paragraph, it grates a bit on the reader. Just as people don't like eating the same thing for lunch each day, they also want diversity in their entertainment. I remember that every time I write a sentence.

Now study my second example. I substituted words, and I also threw in a bit of alliteration—that is, beginning words with the same sound: "Make it in magic." "Professional practitioners of prestidigitation." Because they are alliterative, those phrases have a rhyme to them. They roll off the tongue. They imply a special expertise, with the latter phrase using an uncommon word that describes making magic. They add some spice and allude to the thrill you get when watching a magician in action. If you overuse alliteration, of course, you'll be repetitive and risk turning a reader off. You'll have to judi-ciously decide.

Previously, I've told you about parameters. Try to keep your novel chapters of uniform length. By doing so, you set up a predictable rhythm, which readers (and editors) enjoy. At the end of each chapter,

I suggest a cliffhanger of action. Otherwise, if everything is neatly wrapped up, why would anyone turn the page?

Here's another parameter for you that comes from my screenwriting experience. In a movie script, it's usually a good idea to limit each scene to three pages or less, because each single-spaced page of a film script usually works out to one minute of onscreen time. After three minutes, viewers usually get a little edgy. They're ready for the story to move to someplace else, geographically, through time or both. Forty of these three-minute scenes go into a normal, 120-page film script.

I mentioned earlier that my chapters are usually 16 to 20 pages long. That's 4,000 to 5,000 words a chapter, and my chapters usually break down into approximately three different scenes. Book manuscripts are double-spaced, so a 75,000-word book would have 15 to 18 chapters. That would mean, at three scenes a chapter, I'd have 45 to 52 scenes in a book. Since it's much easier to edit down than to fill in, editing 52 scenes down to 40 is not an impossible task.

I'm not suggesting that you follow my guidelines strictly. This is simply a method that works for me. You should work out your own guidelines, based on what feels right to you. A novel is perhaps the most flexible type of writing that exists, at least with regard to form and style. In editing your manuscript, however, make sure that everything you've written is essential to the story and that each scene moves the story forward in some manner.

And don't repeat unless you have a very good reason for doing so.

Beyond that, you'll simply have to follow Jenkins' advice and write your book with your butt in a chair. In any event, you should work out a way to write a good deal each week, on a predictable schedule. Whether you're a professional typist, a hunter/pecker, or someone who dictates pages to a secretary, it doesn't matter. You just have to write, a lot. You don't even have to sit in a chair, as long as you get the writing done. I didn't have the heart to tell Jerry that Ernest Hemingway wrote all his books in longhand, standing up.

Given Jerry's success, though, he probably already knew that.

Chapter 7

❖❖❖❖❖❖❖❖❖❖❖❖❖❖❖❖❖

Groups, gatherings, goodies and garbage

Life is a group activity

All the chapters so far have discussed writing activities that are mostly solitary. Articles, stories, books and novels are the products of a single person, usually. The remaining forms of writing discussed in this book, on the other hand, concern groups of people. Naturally, writers write about people both alone and in groups, but to become a successful playwright it's a very good idea to be involved with a theater group in an ongoing manner. It's worked that way from the time of William Shakespeare and the Globe Theatre in London. That's why this chapter on groups for writers follows chapters on the basics of the most commonly pursued forms of writing.

Once I get you thinking in terms of groups that might be beneficial to your particular writing pursuits, I'll go into advice on those forms in later chapters. Here is the world of writers' groups as I have found it.

A little help from my friends

Remember the studio executive in the movie *The Player* who went to Alcoholics Anonymous only because all the Hollywood bigwigs were there? The executive himself was not an alcoholic, but all the others were. "Networking" in any profession is very important. I began networking shortly after I began to sell my writing. A friend suggested I join the Science Fiction Writers of America (SFWA). I was admitted as a member because I had sold a script to a science fiction radio show. Incidentally, I sold that script to an acquaintance—the producer of the radio show—who had called me, looking for writers. At the time I was a musician, but my acquaintance knew I "knew a lot of people." I never made a sale because of being a member of SFWA, but I gained insight into dealing with publishers, agents, etc. from reading the publications SFWA sent me as a result of my membership.

The first time I had a play produced, I joined the Dramatists Guild (DG). Similarly, the New York-based DG newsletter and their Los Angeles meetings didn't help me sell anything, but I got a lot of good advice from mailings. DG events in Los Angeles have also been enlightening. How else could I sit in a theater with 20 or 30 other people, having a discussion with legendary playwright Neil Simon? Besides, since very few people make a living writing for the theater, I didn't expect much from my DG membership.

Through another friend, I got a job as managing editor of a brand new Los Angeles business magazine. The clips from my first three articles helped me get that job. While I was working on that magazine, another friend suggested I join the Independent Writers of Southern California (IWOSC). The group offered monthly meetings, seminars, a newsletter with market tips and successful new friends who were willing to share their knowledge to help fledgling writers. I got my first regional article sale from an IWOSC market tip, then used that clip (from *Palm Springs Life*) to get a national sale to an airline in-flight magazine. A friend had edited one—not the one I made the sale to, but another airline's magazine. Since I did not do much flying in those days, I wouldn't have thought of writing for an in-flight magazine if a friend hadn't suggested it.

Do you see the pattern? When you are starting out, and to an extent even after you are established, the jobs you get through friends and acquaintances often far surpass those you get through letters and phone calls. It's really who you know that can do something for you, and vice versa. But don't think it's all just "friends." If I had not been able to write well, it wouldn't have mattered what friends suggested or helped me achieve.

Some beginning writers I know have a confused idea that they will knock out the world's greatest first novel, sell it for millions to New York and Hollywood, and live happily ever after. I always invite them to give me an example of someone who actually did that. No one ever comes forward with such a person.

Unless you want to be Emily Dickinson, stuffing your drawers full of wonderful poems that someone will discover and make millions from after your death, you must mingle. You've got to get out there and meet people to make it as a writer. Those pictures and vague impressions you've formed of writers living the life of leisure, staring out blissfully over the Mediterranean from their villa on the Riviera, are—if they're based on real people—actually souls who put years of blood, sweat and bruised fingers into getting there. If you don't believe me, get in touch with your favorite author and ask him about it.

When helping helped

One of the biggest boosts in my career came when I volunteered to head up a fund raiser. IWOSC wanted to put on a 48-hour nonstop scriptwriting marathon to acquire funds for the perennially sparse IWOSC bank account. I got the job since I had scriptwriting experience, and had produced some plays and a video. Other "IWOSCans" were mostly journalists.

Giving credit where it is due, the other committee members did most of the work during the last two weeks before the marathon, because of a 2,000-person convention I was producing at the same time. Still, my months of effort were rewarded. We got extensive newspaper and magazine write-ups, were on the Showtime cable channel, and were even on West German television. The donations we received from the event allowed the finance committee of IWOSC to resume breathing.

I gained something from the event I didn't expect—a teaching career. It was a bit roundabout, but it would not have happened if not for a connection I had made there. Everyone wanted to work during the day, when TV cameras were rolling and the newspaper reporters were present, but hardly anyone wanted to write all night. Since I had not been able to contribute much during the two weeks prior to the event, I volunteered for the "graveyard shift." I was manning the computer in the chilly open air of the Century City, California shopping mall at 3 a.m., when fellow IWOSCan Colleen Todd arrived to take my place. We talked about our careers, then Colleen suddenly asked me to speak to the class she was teaching at UCLA Extension Writers Program.

I was amazed. I'd shared writing tips and potential markets with others for years, but I had never considered teaching formally. Did I come across as more successful than I really was? After all, Colleen told me she had published books. Real writing! I had written for television and film, and sold tons of articles, but I hadn't yet published a book. Still, Colleen thought I was worthy. Since I enjoyed speaking in front of groups, I agreed.

It was some time later that I spoke to Colleen's beginning writing students. In the interim, I answered a newspaper ad and sold three young adult books to a Southern California company. They were short books, only 6,000 words, called "hi-los." That is, "high interest level, low reading level," for teens with a third-grade reading level. Still, book sales were book sales. When I spoke to Colleen's class, my success as a writer and my three books made me seem like a legend in the making to the students. Plus, they liked what I had to tell them about vigorously pursuing a career. Colleen told UCLA Extension Writers Program coordinator Linda Venis about it. I met with Linda, and before long, I was teaching a class at UCLA entitled (you guessed it) "How to Write What You Want & Sell What You Write."

Through Colleen I met Aram Saroyan, who also taught at UCLA and was Colleen's agent. When Aram found out that I was writing for *Boys' Life* and *Disney Adventures* magazines, and had sold the "hi-los," he called me about doing a young adult mystery series. I wrote up a proposal, and to my amazement soon had a three-book deal with Zebra Books. Real books, 55,000 words long. Not 100,000-word adult mainstream books, but I wasn't complaining.

Except for the newspaper ad I answered, all the work I've mentioned here came through people I met. Also during that time, I wrote almost all of my *Boys' Life's* entertainment articles. My short-story agent Larry Sternig got me that job. I met Larry through a friend.

Finding help

I tell my students that it's a common belief in metropolitan areas that, within three to five phone calls, you can reach just about anyone on the planet. I have my students make a list of everyone they know who might be able to help them directly, or who might refer them to someone who could help them make their first sale as a writer. The results inevitably astonish them. They discover they have either taken for granted who they know or learn that friends and relatives have contacts they never suspected. And since I make them complete at least one serious piece of marketable writing before our class is finished, they have a product to show someone. That means the contact will not be embarrassed by referring them, or the contact they already have won't mind reading their work.

If you live in an urban area, or even Antarctica, I firmly believe this networking principle applies. Most people are social by nature. They like meeting new people and discovering new things. A great new writer is one of the most exciting finds anyone can come across, whether for a reader, an editor, an agent, a publisher or even a heartless beast like a Hollywood film executive.

What I am telling you is that, once you have a piece of writing that you consider good, you should immediately start cultivating contacts who can help you advance your writing career. Be bold!

Legends are people, too

One of the big Hollywood tricks is "working a room." It's an art, and amazing to watch. Through a former roommate from Austin, Texas, I got into a party given by Paul McCartney and his group Wings in 1976. It worked like this:

My friend was the head "roadie" (equipment handler) on the "Wings Over America" tour. He offered to get me into the Wings concert when they came to Los Angeles, where I was living. Unfortunately, he told me the next day over the phone that he couldn't get me into the concert. There had been a cutback on free tickets for the crew, and the event was sold out.

When he called, I happened to be in the room with a public relations professional whose greatest desire had always been to meet Paul McCartney. My friend knew jazz legend Chick Corea. Thinking quickly, she suggested that Chick come to the concert. She hadn't checked with Chick first, but that's sometimes the way PR people work. My friend put me on hold, walked across the stage and asked Paul and Linda McCartney if Chick could come. The McCartneys said sure, they'd love to meet him!

My PR friend then called Chick and told him he was invited. To our relief, he thought it was a great idea. On his coattails, we went to the concert and were then invited to the party.

Since I didn't know then how to "work a room," or in this case, the entire Harold Lloyd estate in Beverly Hills, I followed and watched my PR friend as she went around the party with Chick Corea, making small talk and getting to know entertainment legends. My friend greatly boosted her career that night by stating who she was and what she did and by giving the people she met some idea of how she could help them. It was my first big lesson in just how important "working a room" could be, and how, even though I had put people on a pedestal, there was usually some way we could personally interact.

Fools on the hill

The groups I would advise you to studiously avoid are group-encounter, psycho-babble "workshops" that have a lot more to do with the hosts making money than actually advancing your writing. I remember all too well an open house for potential students at a university in which one instructor stood up and said, "I believe writing is therapy and therapy is writing," and proceeded to say that her class would "bring out the inner you." I stood up a short while later and said, "I won't try to analyze you or get you to analyze yourself. I'll simply take you from being a wanna-be to a professional writer who can sell in today's marketplace."

My class filled up, and my best student came up to me after our last meeting and thanked me profusely for not having another "thank-you-for-sharing-that-with-us, touchy-feely, inner-you" type of class.

Don't get me wrong. I actually think there is some therapeutic benefit from writing, but I lean toward the great advance in self-esteem that comes from a check in the mail. If you want to find the "inner you," I suggest you find a good minister or counselor, not a writing class. Writing is a craft and can develop into an art. You don't need to add to the confusion by getting lost in a mental or spiritual labyrinth.

The long and winding road to success

I truly hope you can shortcut your way to the top. I hope you write that first novel you always wanted to write, send it off to a publisher and make such an impact you get flown to New York on the company Lear jet and given a six-figure check.

Just don't count on it. The chances of that happening are perhaps only a little better than winning the lottery. You'll probably have to work long and hard and write a lot more than you ever imagined, before you "make it." You can help make your journey more comfortable by getting there with a group. And when you get involved with an organization, don't just sit back and listen to the monthly speakers. Get involved! Help out, make suggestions, work the room. Remember the string of events that were set in motion from one contact I made at 3 in the morning? Believe me, the more selflessly you give, the more chances you'll have to get something in return.

The last thing I'll give you in this chapter is a list of every major writers' group I felt would be of interest to beginning writers, throughout the United States. Remember, if you don't find a group located near you, you can still join one that will send you helpful mailings. Or—and I think this is ultimately better in any case—you can start your own group.

All of the organizations listed below offer worthwhile publications; most offer much more. You may be able to subscribe to the publications you want without actually joining the organization. As one example, I was able to pay the rent one month only because of a last-second, interest-free loan from the Authors Guild. Please check with the organization(s) that appeal(s) to you for full details on how you might mutually benefit from an association. Personally, I suggest you become involved in as many groups as possible, since it multiplies your chances.

American Society of Journalists & Authors
1501 Broadway, Suite 302
New York, NY 10036
(212) 997-0947; Fax: (212) 768-7414; E-mail: 75227,1650 (CompuServe)

Membership limited to professional nonfiction independent writers only. Membership qualifications are judged strictly on freelance print in general circulation periodicals. There are no associate memberships, but ASJA does open their yearly conferences and some meetings to the public. Most meetings are in New York, but an all-day yearly conference is held in Los Angeles, with an entrance fee. Dues are $165 per year, with a one-time application fee of $25 and a separate initiation fee of $75. First year dues are prorated, depending on the time of year you join.

Associated Writing Programs
George Mason University
Tallwood House, Mail Stop 1E3
Fairfax, VA 22030
(703) 993-4301; Fax: (703) 993-4302

Individual membership (open to all) is $45/year ($55 in Canada). Membership entitles you to six issues of the bimonthly *AWP Chronicle* magazine ($18 yearly subscription for nonmembers, $25 in Canada), eight issues of the *AWP Job List* per year, 33 percent discount for Award Series writing contests, and 18 percent discount to the annual conference. Student membership is $20/year with all the benefits of regular members. AWP offers a placement service for jobs having anything to do with writing—you must be a member to use the placement service. The annual fee is $40 for the placement service, entitling you to up to 25 mailings. A $10 Limited Placement Service is also available for members who do not have as much material to send out, with a $4 fee for each mailing. AWP maintains personal dossiers of writers, updated twice a year. They also offer the *AWP Official Guide to Creative Writing Programs in the U.S. and Canada*, which is edited once a year, for $23.95 ($25.95 in Canada).

The Authors Guild
330 W. 42nd Street
New York, NY 10036
(212) 563-5904; Fax: (212) 564-5363

According to their brochure, any author may join the Guild who has had a book published by an established American publisher within the last seven years; has had three works, fiction or nonfiction, published by a magazine of general circulation within the past 18 months; or is, in the opinion of the Membership Committee, entitled to membership due to his or her professional standing. There is no initiation fee. First-year dues are $90. After that, dues are based on annual writing income: $90 for less than $25,000; $150 for $25,000-49,999; $300 for $50,000-100,000; and $500 for more than $100,000. Offers many benefits, including a loan program for needy authors, their Recommended Trade Book Contract and Guide and a seasonal bulletin.

The Dramatists Guild
234 W. 44th Street
New York, NY 10036
(212) 398-9366; Fax: (212) 944-0420

All theater writers are eligible to apply in the following categories: Associate members ($75/year)—the Guild does not require previous production or publication for Associate members; Active members ($125/year)—writers who have been produced on Broadway, off-Broadway or on the main stage of a regional theater; Estate members ($125/year)—representatives of the Estates of deceased Active members; Institutional Subscriber members ($100/year)—colleges, universities, libraries, and educational theaters; Subscriber members ($50/year)—those persons engaged in a drama-related field, but not as playwrights; Professional Subscriber members ($200/year)—agents and attorneys; Student members ($35/year)—students enrolled in writing degree programs at colleges or universities.

International Association of Business Communicators
1 Hallidie Plaza, Suite 600
San Francisco, CA 94102
(415) 433-3400; Fax: (415) 362-8762

Extensive resources offered via U.S. and Canadian chapters. Yearly dues vary by region, with one-time application fee of $40. Option of paying dues monthly or quarterly, which can be deducted automatically as they come due from your credit card. If you choose this option, there is a US $10 (CDN $14) administration fee for the service.

International Women's Writing Guild
Gracie Station, Box 810
New York, NY 10028
(212) 737-7536; Fax (212) 737-9469

Membership open to all. "A network for the personal and professional empowerment of women through writing." $35 per year dues entitles one to bimonthly newsletter and "zip code parties" around the country. Ninety-eight percent of members are women. Director Hannelore Hahn observes that most nonwriters who join become writers during their membership.

International Writers Center
Old Dominion University
1411 West 49th Street
Norfolk, VA 23529-0079
(804) 683-3839; Fax: (804) 683-5901

Cosponsored by Associated Writing Programs and Old Dominion University. Free with AWP membership (see page 98). Offers more of AWP benefits with emphasis on international networking.

Mystery Writers of America
17 E. 47th Street, 6th Floor
New York, NY 10017
(212) 888-8171; Fax: (212) 888-8107

Active members are published, professional writers of fiction or nonfiction in the crime/mystery/suspense field. Only active members may vote or hold office. Associate members are professionals in allied fields: editors, publishers and writers in other fields, news reporters, critics, agents, publicists, librarians, booksellers, etc. Affiliate members are writers of crime/mystery/suspense works not yet professionally published (membership granted by petition only). Corresponding members are writers qualified for active membership who live outside the United States. Dues for all categories of U.S. membership are $65/year. Corresponding members based outside the U.S. pay $32.50/year. There is no initiation fee, but payment of a year's dues is essential for admittance to membership.

National Writers Association
1450 South Havana, Suite 424
Aurora, CO 80012
(303) 751-7844; Fax: (303) 751-8593

General membership open; dues are $50 per year. Professional membership is $60 per year, and there is an additional fee of $20 for anyone living outside the U.S. One qualifies for Professional status by three sales to national or regional magazines, a book sold to a royalty publisher, a play produced, or employment as a writer, journalist or editor. A free critique of 40 lines of poetry or a 1,500-word manuscript is a bonus for joining.

National Writers Union
873 Broadway, Suite 203
New York, NY 10003-1209
(212) 254-0279; Fax: (212) 254-0673

For regular membership, you must have published a book or three short stories, had a play produced, or have written the equivalent of any of these. Membership is $75 to $170 per year, based on your writing income. If you're not a writer, you can join the Supporter's Circle: $125/year for individuals and $200/year for nonprofit organizations and libraries. Offers very good health insurance plan, as well as resource library and publications. Health insurance and voting not open to Supporter's Circle members. Is affiliated with United Auto Workers (UAW Local 1981) and AFL-CIO.

Poetry Society of America
15 Gramercy Park
New York, NY 10003
(212) 254-9628

Membership open to anyone who writes, reads and appreciates poetry. Dues are $40/year, which entitles you to discounts at all readings and seminars, free entry to Society contests, a calendar twice a year and the newsletter twice a year. Also has a branch in Los Angeles, California.

Poets, Playwrights, Editors, Essayists & Novelists (PEN)
PEN American Center
568 Broadway
New York, NY 10012
(212) 334-1660; Fax: (212) 334-2181

Members elected by the Membership Committee. Standard qualification is the publication of two or more books of a literary character, or one book generally acclaimed to be of exceptional distinction. Also eligible for membership are editors who have demonstrated commitment to excellence in their profession (usually construed as five years' service in book editing); translators who have published at least two book-length literary translations; playwrights whose works have been produced professionally; literary essayists whose publications are extensive even if they may have not been issued as a book. Candidates for membership should be nominated by two current members of PEN, or may nominate themselves with the support of a current member. Dues are paid annually (inquire for current rates.) All PEN members receive the quarterly PEN Newsletter and qualify for medical insurance at group rates. Membership in American PEN includes reciprocal privileges in foreign PEN Centers for those traveling abroad. The PEN Cafe, an online conversation and discussion group, is available to PEN members. Friends of PEN is open also to writers who may not yet qualify for PEN membership. Affiliation with Friends of PEN ranges from the $35 yearly Supporter level to the $1,000 yearly Benefactor level.

PEN Center USA West
672 S. La Fayette Park Place, Suite #41
Los Angeles, CA 90057
(213) 365-8500; Fax: (213) 365-9616

PEN Center USA West is exclusively for those residing west of the Mississippi River. It has established five regional chapters in the western United States to provide programs for the literary community in those areas. Chapters are located in Oakland and Orange County, California; Dallas/Ft. Worth, Texas; and statewide chapters in New Mexico and Colorado. Membership is open to published or produced writers who meet the criteria of the organization and who have demonstrated work of substantial literary value. Annual membership dues are $55. The Friends of PEN arrangement is similar to that of PEN American Center; inquire for details.

Poets & Writers, Inc.
72 Spring Street
New York, NY 10012
(212) 226-3586; Fax: (212) 226-3693

A nonprofit organization of, naturally, poets and writers that advertises itself as "the central source of practical information for the literary community in the United States." Contact the organization for details. Bimonthly *Poets & Writers* magazine is the cornerstone of their publishing program: $18/year; $34/two-years; and $25/year for institutions. Has information center, workshops and Literary Network. Offers many publications, including annual *A Directory of American Poets and Fiction Writers.*

Public Relations Society of America
33 Irving Place
New York, NY 10003
(212) 995-2230

For PR professionals with two or more years of experience, there is a one-time $65 processing fee. Dues are $175 year. You may also join as an associate member. If you have less than one year's experience in public relations, it is $90 for the first year; over one year's experience but less than two is $120 per year. There is also a category for PRSA graduate members, who get started in PRSA student society chapters on college campuses (check with society for a list of campuses).

Romance Writers of America
13700 Veterans Memorial Drive, Suite 315
Houston, TX 77014
(713) 440-6885; Fax: (713) 440-7510

A national nonprofit corporation dedicated to promoting excellence in the romance writing field. General membership is open to established romance authors and writers interested in pursuing a career in romance writing. Associate membership is open to booksellers, editors, agents and other industry professionals. Annual dues are $60, with a processing fee of $10 for new members and a $10 reaffiliation fee for lapsed members. For those who do not live near one of the existing 90 chapters, they offer their "Outreach" program for members for an additional $20/year. Offers the *Romance Writer's Report,* a bimonthly magazine, and other benefits, including major medical insurance and chapter indemnity insurance. Also offers an "Information Exchange" for those who have expertise on a subject and are willing to share it. For information on the Exchange, send an SASE to Aline Thompson, 13400 Bromwich, Arleta, CA 91331, (818) 896-8246.

Science-Fiction and Fantasy Writers of America, Inc.
Peter Dennis Pautz, Executive Secretary
5 Winding Brook Drive, Suite 1B
Guilderland, NY 12084
(518) 869-5361

There is no established national office. The address changes as the officers of SFWA change. The address given above is for 1994-1995. The minimum requirement for active membership is the professional publication (acceptance and payment) of three short stories or one full-length fiction book. Collaborations with a single coauthor may be used as a half-credential. Authors' estates may join at the active dues rate as well.

Association membership is available to beginning writers who have had at least one professional publication but are not yet eligible for active status. This classification is open to those with a professional fiction publication outside North or South America or in a language other than English. Neither nonfiction nor poetry will be considered for this or active status. Allied professionals, such as agents, editors, reviewers, artists, publishers, and the like, may join as affiliate members. Institutional membership is open to organizations with a legitimate interest in science fiction and fantasy, such as schools, universities, studios, and so on, or to individuals associated with these groups.

Dues are collected annually for the July-June fiscal year, and all new members pay a one-time installation fee. First dues payment is prorated quarterly (as of the first day of October, January and April). Check with SFWA at the above address for any further details and current amount of dues.

Society of American Business Editors & Writers
c/o Janine Latus-Musick
University of Missouri-Columbia
School of Journalism
P.O. Box 838
Columbia, MO 65205
(314) 874-3889; Fax: (314) 756-5215

SABEW membership is restricted to persons whose principal occupation is reporting, writing or editing business, financial or economic news for newspapers, magazines, newsletters, press or syndicate services, or radio or television. Membership is also open to teachers of journalism or business subjects at recognized colleges, universities or other organizations deemed appropriate by the Board of Governors. Dues are $40 per year.

Society of Children's Book Writers & Illustrators
22736 Vanowen Street #106
West Hill, CA 91307
(818) 888-8760

No membership qualifications. Dues are $50 per year. Regular members have published for children, while Associate members have not.

Writers Guild of America (East)
555 W. 57th Street
New York, NY 10019
(212) 767-7800

Writers Guild of America (West)
8955 Beverly Boulevard
West Hollywood, CA 90048
(310) 550-1000

The Writers Guild has a system of 24 units of credit which must be accumulated to make one eligible for membership. Contact either office for brochure explaining details. Upon qualification, membership fee is $2,500.

The Television Market List, featuring contact submission information on current weekly prime time and television programs, is published monthly in the *WGAw Journal* and is available to nonmembers at $5 per issue or $40 for an annual subscription. Checks or money orders for the *Journal* should be sent to the WGAw address.

Chapter 8

❖❖❖❖❖❖❖❖❖❖❖❖❖❖❖❖

Plotting your career, with or without an agent

Getting your bearings

In selling articles, stories, even novels and nonfiction books, you can usually do fairly well without an agent. Joining a writing group always helps you find markets. You might even be able to build a successful, full-time writing career without the services of an agent, but I doubt it. That's why, before I get into chapters on areas of writing that require collaboration—particularly stage, film and theater—I wanted you to have diverse information not only on finding a good agent, but also on building a career.

Agents can be very helpful, even if getting a good one may seem an elusive quest. Where do you start? Well, before the advent of the technological age, the best agents for screenwriters were in Hollywood, while the best agents for authors were in New York. Now, with jet planes, picture phones, fax machines, e-mail and the Internet, a good agent can live practically anywhere on Earth and still do a good business.

If you're like me and write lots of different kinds of things, save yourself some trouble and quit looking for a "general" agent. If you only write one type of thing, all the better in finding an agent. Agents specialize; they don't generalize. Since they make only 10 to 15 percent of a writer's income, good agents have a number of clients. Accordingly, they don't have time to sell short stories, articles and such. Agents want writers who will provide them with a steady income, and 15 percent of $450 for an article isn't much. It might be worth a phone call, a letter and a stamp, but why bother when you can sell a screenplay for $50,000 or more and collect 15 percent of that with only a bit more effort?

Try to think like an agent and your chances of finding a truly good one will be multiplied. Here's a little exercise along that line: You're an agent, a really good agent with a fine income and the respect of your peers. What is the source of that income? Other than your own expertise, it's your writers. If a new writer comes your way, you want someone who has long-term financial rewards written all over them.

The best way to find truly fine agents is normally through truly fine writers. Hardly any writer who has had a book published, a screenplay sold or done any amount of work is without an agent, a manager, a lawyer or all of the above. Other writers are where you start looking for an agent. Rather than finding lists of agents that you know nothing about and sending them your manuscript(s) without contacting them first, try meeting some successful writers and getting referred to an agent. Granted, the writer(s) you meet will probably want to read your work before recommending you, but all the better. They might teach you something. Since you've read the chapter on the benefits of writers' organizations, you know how to go about meeting other writers and might have already begun to do so.

Negotiating the territory

Now, here's the big surprise. Even if you get referred by a successful writer and even if you get signed with an agent, chances are, your agent won't do a lot for you until you generate some sales on your own. Even then, you'll probably do a lot of the selling yourself. I once wrote successful science-fiction writer Poul Anderson to ask about his agent, H.N. "Swanee" Swanson. An agent at the Swanson Agency wanted to sign me, and I just happened to know that Anderson was represented by Swanson because of our mutual membership in the Science Fiction Writers of America (as it was known then). I admired Anderson's writing and had read about him in the SFWA Directory. Swanee Swanson was a legendary agent in Hollywood, having represented writers like Raymond Chandler (*The Big Sleep* and other Philip Marlowe novels). Normally, I would have gleefully accepted getting signed by an agent at Swanson, but since I knew about Anderson's relationship with Swanson, my curiosity was aroused. Anderson wrote back and said that he couldn't recall Swanson really selling anything for him—Anderson had done it all himself! But, he added, Swanson had negotiated some good contracts for him. In other words, Anderson had found the deal, but Swanson had made the deal a lot sweeter than it might have been.

I learned that this arrangement was more usual than unusual. Writers who get out and mingle make contacts, out of which come sales. This book, for example, was sold to its publisher after both my agent (David Andrew) and I pitched it to different people from Career Press at their booth at the American Booksellers Association convention in Los Angeles. We both generated interest; David closed the sale and handled the negotiations. When I sold my "You Solve It Mystery" novels to E.K. Gaylord II Productions, I made the initial contact. My agent Sasha Goodman (David's partner) negotiated the terms of the sale (increasing my money substantially), but I made the sale myself. When it came time to hash out the terms of the contract, Sasha did the initial work (with my input), and my lawyer, Bruce Grakal, added some important points and supervised the final contract.

The important point is that agents and lawyers know about contracts and the implications of certain contract items. Unless you have a legal background, you probably won't. That's why you need a representative.

Other than what I've mentioned, all the other sales I've made I negotiated on my own. My screenplays, videos, magazine articles, everything else, were all negotiated without the benefit of an agent or lawyer. There are a couple of exceptions. Larry Sternig, whom I described in an earlier chapter as the most successful short story agent of all time, put me in touch with two important magazine accounts: *Reader's Digest* and *Boys' Life*. Through Larry, my writing was introduced to Senior Editor Elena Serocki at *Reader's Digest*. I became the entertainment reporter at *Boys' Life* for over a year, thanks to Larry's relationship with the editor in chief, William McMorris. Granted, my writing had to measure up to Larry's recommendation, but without him those high-profile magazines would have been much tougher to break into.

Unfortunately, I paid dearly for flying solo. One how-to video I put together went gold, meaning it sold more than 100,000 copies. I trusted the producers I got involved with on a handshake deal. In the words of a popular country song, they got the gold mine and I got the shaft. I ended up getting bought out of the project for a small sum—and then only because I got a lawyer.

Good agents provide useful introductions, they negotiate terms, and sometimes they make sales that you have little to do with (other than the quality of your writing). Agents become the source, when they represent you well, of good "word of mouth" on your writing. And word of mouth is by far the most important means of convincing anyone of the worth of anything. Later in your career, when you are well-known, you might not need an agent, just a lawyer to handle the contracts that people offer you.

Agents develop relationships with publishers, production companies, films studios and producers. These writing consumers either find that the agent provides them with quality material on a regular basis, or they don't. Agents are the natural screening process of the entertainment business. They are part hype artists and part good friend. They may embellish the worth of something they sell, but they can't elaborate too much for too long and stay in business. They must supply quality product, time and time again.

Occasionally, writers refer other writers directly to producers, publishers, etc. Then writers get work without the "middleman." This "sans agent" practice used to be much more prevalent than it is today. Remember the story about F. Scott Fitzgerald referring Ernest Hemingway to his editor, Maxwell Perkins? Ah, the simple days of yore. Today, Fitzgerald would likely refer Hemingway to Michael Ovitz, the head of Creative Artists Agency (CAA) and the most influential agent in the entertainment business. Ovitz would have a subordinate read Hemingway's novel, synopsize and critique it. Then Ovitz would read (or have another subordinate read) the "coverage" on it and comment. If all was favorable, Ovitz would call up one of his friends who owns a publishing company and/or a studio and talk about his hot new "find," Ernest Hemingway. Hemingway's book would be sold to a publisher, with the film rights negotiated at the same time. Possibly, an auction would be held, with the publisher and film company making the highest bid getting the whole pie. Beyond that, a screenwriter from CAA would get attached to "the project," along with a CAA star client like Tom Cruise, a director signed with CAA, and other top clients of the agency. What started out as a novel manuscript would become a "package." CAA would make a percentage from each of their clients, then another percentage from the movie studio for "putting the package together." Roughly, that's what might happen if "Papa" Hemingway came around with a hot new novel these days.

Yes, you say, but I don't live in a major metropolitan area. I don't know Michael Ovitz. I don't know any successful writers, or even a writer who has an agent. Where does that leave me?

Well, there's a fine book called *Insider's Guide to Book Editors, Publishers, and Literary Agents* by Jeff Herman. If you can't find it in your local bookstore, it is available from Prima Publishing, 3875 Atherton Road, Rocklin, CA 95765, (916) 632-4400, (916) 632-4405 fax. Jeff, who has his own agency in New York, put the book together to give writers "fair access to the powers that be." With articles by himself and others, the book not only provides a directory of book publishers, editors and literary agents in the U.S. and Canada along with extensive and helpful descriptions, it also offers advice on contracts and other aspects of the writing business.

Unfortunately, it doesn't say much about the movie business, but that's just as well. To crack that nut, you're probably going to have to spend some time in a place where films are made. Meanwhile, you can also send $2 to the Writers Guild of America (see Chapter 7) for their agent list. If you display any talent at all, you'll probably find an agent who will pay attention. Believe me, though, if you join a writers' organization and mingle a little, the agent you need won't be far away.

Reaching your destination

The greatest thing a good agent does for a writer is listen. John Grisham told *Writer's Digest* that he comes up with 14 or so plots for books, then flies to New York to visit with his agents. They discuss the various ideas, and the one that the agents and Grisham agree is the best is the one Grisham writes.

As a writer, you need to pay attention to what the market is doing, what people are looking for, but you can't spend the majority of your time doing that. Otherwise, you'd never get any writing done. For an agent, knowing the market is a full-time job. That's one reason you need an agent. Another is to have someone to bounce ideas off of and who knows what will likely sell.

In the Joseph Campbell "myth structure," the hero of the story always finds a mentor early in his journey to guide him—Obi-wan Kenobi in *Star Wars*, for example. You may find a more experienced writer as a mentor for your writing. You will also, if you're smart, find a mentor in the marketing department. That's a good agent. If the relationship lasts, you'll become chums; it's like a marriage, with ups and downs, thrills and spills, and children of a literary sort.

Making your way

While you're seeking and finding the right agent, here are some other steps to take, to plot out a successful writing career:

Get your life out of the way while you're writing. Don't let anyone bother you; write the same time each day, with no distractions.

Find someone who will listen and respond intelligently. This could be a "significant other," an agent, an editor or all of these. You need someone to bounce things off of.

Until you're very successful, pick a genre and write in that genre. You'll succeed more quickly.

Don't be picky about where you get published or where you sell, within your own moral limits. Use any success you have to tout your next creation.

Work hard to develop lasting personal contacts and acquire industry information. Join writers' organizations. Take college classes from working writers. Read appropriate publications regularly.

Find common ground. Learn what the public is buying and why. Try to adjust your own writing to something the public wants.

Remember that other people have opinions, even if they're wrong. Editors might chop up your work. Movie people might tell you you'll never sell a thing. Take a hint from the rhinoceros, with regard to your career. Let it all bounce off your thick skin. Meanwhile, keep adjusting your writing when it makes sense to you. One day, people will stop trying to stick their two cents in. A greatly diminished number of people, anyway. At that point, you'll be "over the hump." You'll be an accomplished writer. But don't fail to stand up for yourself, if someone offers a critique that you don't understand. Get them to explain it. If they can't, or won't, what do they know?

Write your butt (or another part of your body) off. In the end, it will be your body of work that will be admired. The race in writing goes mostly to the prolific.

Promote, promote, promote! Great writers do not live in ivory towers, or seek to. Get whatever equipment, resources and knowledge necessary to allow you to write a lot more and send out a lot more. Many writers get the job over other writers simply because they are the most persistent, if not the most competent.

If it's working, don't fix it. If you're selling an article a week to your local paper, don't drop that to pursue the Hollywood dream or the American blockbuster novel. Let each success build on the previous one, as if you're building a stairway of easily negotiated steps.

If you make a big sale, don't get too "rich" overnight. A big paycheck may go a long way, but chances are you put a lot of days and a lot more sweat into creating the product that got you that check. If you get a million-dollar bill for your first screenplay, don't think you'll be getting a payday like that every other month. Your next script might not sell. It might be a decade before you sell another screenplay. Be extravagant and prolific with your writing, but be very conservative with your rewards. It's hard to write when all the money is gone.

Remember the people who got you there, or helped, which includes me. If my advice helps you, all I ask is that you pass it on to others. Tell them about this book, or what I advised you to do. There is an old Hollywood maxim that you see the same people on the way up as you do on the way down. If you reach the top, you'll discover how rarefied the air is up there. Don't forget "the little people," those lucky leprechauns of life who helped you when you needed it. Start helping other writers make it, once you've succeeded. Competition? I never worry about it. There's plenty to go around for everyone in the writing business. I've never heard a single person complain, "There's just too damn many great writers!"

If you follow the dozen hints above, by the time you do find an agent who is just right for you, he or she will probably think you are the greatest client they've ever had. Most agents are used to writers with egos the size of Mount Olympus. If you have your outlook on the writing life (and life in general) in order, you'll seem like a gift from heaven. It's also my opinion that if you are actively pursuing your career in a thoughtful, persistent and ethical manner, you will seemingly stumble across the right personnel to assist your career, as if the Angel of Serendipity is your personal guardian.

Speaking of guardian angels, I would have difficulty listing all the fortunate events that aided my literary career. Maybe that's why my first stage play was about a writer who screwed up, only to be rescued by his guardian angel, who was a frustrated apprentice. Viewing my top lucky breaks in retrospect, my being "in the right place at the right time" was mostly due to my dogged, relentless pursuit of my goals. I did not sit back and wait for someone to do it for me, unlike other writers I've known. The most successful writers I've met had a similar approach.

A career map

I get my students laughing every time I draw them a graph of what a successful career looks like:

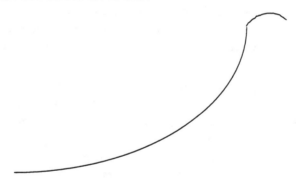

It looks like a side view of a wave, doesn't it? Plotting a career is like—okay, go ahead and laugh—surfing. You have to venture into deep water, way over your head, to ride that wave. It's tough, learning to keep your footing, to master your vehicle (your writing, your surfboard, whatever) and to catch that elusive wave of success. This might seem to be a ridiculous analogy, but allow me the luxury of explanation. When I started out, it seemed my career grew excruciatingly slowly—like the line with the long, slow rise I drew above. Then, when my career began to take off, it seemed to climb vertically until it reached a crest, a plateau of sorts at a whole new level. In my case, the beginning of the crest of the wave was where I went from just getting by selling magazine articles to where I began selling books. The crest of the wave was the sale of my "You Solve It Mystery" books for film and television.

Of course, there have been other waves of success in my career. I've ridden them all, with some "wipe-outs" and some enjoyable rides. My point to my students is that life comes in waves. Unless they create something that provides them the "endless wave" surfers travel the world trying to find, they'll simply have to start over every time they have a big success. How long each wave lasts depends on how well they ride the crest.

Note that my graphic has a curl at the top, like a real wave. There's a chance you might drop off the edge into the trough of the wave and, tumbling end over end, get caught in the undertow of ego or even "drowned" by a sudden big success. That's the "don't get too rich" type of thing I discussed earlier.

Some successful writers tend to ride only one wave for their entire career. J.D. Salinger had a tremendous success with *Catcher in the Rye* at such an early age that he seemed to never recover. He wrote *Franny & Zooey* and other works, but none like the international sensation that *Catcher* became. He retired to a New England town and was rarely heard from again. Harper Lee was of a similar mind after *To Kill a Mockingbird*. It's too bad. I feel great writers should write as much as possible and not let success get to them. Maybe they'll have a great ride next time; maybe they'll wipe out. That's just the ocean of life.

Seven steps to success

One of the early exercises I give my students—after I tell them all about the value of networking and how to go about it—is a one-year plan to achieve a goal. In a writing career, one year isn't a very long time. Here's what you do:

1. Define a goal for your writing that you feel can be achieved in one year. We've already talked about writing two pages a day and having a screenplay in two months. Figure out something you can reasonably achieve in a year.
2. Outline a seven-step plan to reach your goal. Why seven? Because it's a lucky number, or because most people feel comfortable with that number, which isn't as daunting as 10. Seven steps just seems to work, so that's what I use.

3. Write down a list of 10 people who might help further your writing career and your one-year goal, now that you have it clearly defined. Contact them, explain what you're doing and see what they can do to help. They'll probably be glad to be of assistance and refer you to other people who can do the same. Learn to "prospect at the close." If someone gives you some help but doesn't mention other contacts, or if they can't help you personally, ask for someone they know who might be able to help you. You'll be surprised who your friends know.

4. When you've completed step 3, take another look at your plan for the next year and reevaluate where necessary. For example, you may be hired as a writer through someone you know. If your seven-step goal was to get hired as a writer, you've already achieved it. Don't just pat yourself on the back, redo your one-year goal so that you keep moving up.

Here's another Hollywood story and an illustration of why you need to plot out your career. I heard Burt Reynolds tell a story once about how he and Clint Eastwood had their contracts terminated at Universal Studios the same day. Supposedly, it took both of them 15 years to reach the top. I've known scores of successful writers and other people in the entertainment business who took well over a decade to reach the success they envisioned. There may be "overnight successes," but most of them lived through a very long night to get where they were going. It took me roughly 15 years to "make it." I didn't always draw up a written plan for myself and actively pursue it. I feel I would have succeeded much faster if I had. When I was 30, someone told me I might not really make it until I was 40. That was a common age for writing success, I was told. I was aghast. I vowed I'd get there quicker, but that person was right. So if you're planning to make it big, get ready to put some years into getting there, and don't worry about it. The rewards will be worth the struggle!

Chapter 9

❖❖❖❖❖❖❖❖❖❖❖❖❖❖❖❖

The passionate stage

"The play's the thing!" Shakespeare exclaimed.

"Is the theater really dead?" Paul Simon wondered in a song.

How could I start a chapter about playwriting without quoting the Bard? And how could I deny the fact that Broadway may not be what it used to be? Personally, I don't think theater will ever die. People love intimate gatherings and shared experiences. Theater provides that. You might own a 50-inch TV, but do you want to watch the Super Bowl or the Academy Awards alone? Not likely. It's my belief that, as our electronic society and all-encompassing media grow larger and more available, people will feel an increasing need for real, human connection. The kind they get in a theater, for example.

Obviously, the basic writing form for theater is a stage play. Most anyone knows that, but do you know the proper format in which to present your play? I had plays professionally produced and had qualified to become an active member of the Dramatists Guild before I found out about and began using the accepted standard format for stage plays. I learned the proper format from a small booklet published by the Dramatists Guild. Since that time, I've come across numerous references that lay out play format, but the Dramatists Guild reference was the first I ever found.

That said, the next page shows how your title page should look. The title line should be 20 to 24 lines from the top, but no one will reject your manuscript if it isn't. It should simply look nice on the page. Most purists specify not using any special type style or font, but I disagree. Something that attracts attention might make your play stand out.

YOUR TITLE

BY

YOU

There are four lines between each of the lines on the title page, but it won't hurt if you use only two or if you don't capitalize all the letters in the "by" or your name:

YOUR TITLE

by

Your Name

At about the 50th line or so (again, as long as it looks good) you should put:

Your Name
Your Address
Your City, State, Zip
Your Phone

Your Agent's Name,
Address and
Phone (if you have one)

Copyright © (year) by Your Name
(Spell out the word "copyright," and use the symbol as well.)

Remember what I said about an agent pasting his or her label over your address? Most agents don't want anyone directly contacting the people they represent until a deal is made. Your name and information might not even be listed on this page. More on agents later.

The first page of a script is the most important, because it will often determine whether or not anyone reads further. Since many theaters have limited resources with regard to sets, available number of actors, etc., the first page often tells a dramaturge (the person who determines what plays to consider doing) whether your work is feasible to produce. If your setting is "The Follies Bergere, turn-of-the-century France," chances are you'll be out of luck. That's why you see so many plays set in motel rooms, dilapidated lobbies, living rooms, and so on. Sets that don't cost much money to put together are highly desirable for most small theater companies. Similarly, a cast list on the front page should not be too lengthy.

❖❖❖❖❖❖❖❖❖❖❖❖❖❖❖❖❖

SETTING: MOTEL ROOM IN ANY CITY IN THE MIDWEST.

UPSTAGE WALL, STAGE RIGHT, IS A WOODEN BED WITH A WORN CHENILLE BEDSPREAD. ON EACH SIDE OF THE BED ARE BEATEN-UP NIGHTSTANDS THAT DON'T MATCH.

ON THE NIGHTSTANDS ARE DILAPIDATED LAMPS WITH RAGGED LAMP SHADES HALF-HANGING OFF THEIR BRACKETS.

OVER THE BED IS A FADED POSTER OF MARILYN MONROE, STUCK TO THE PAINTED WALL WITH MISMATCHED PUSH PINS.

UPSTAGE WALL CENTER IS THE MOTEL ROOM DOOR, ABOVE WHICH A RUSTY HORSESHOE HAS BEEN TACKED IN PLACE.

UPSTAGE LEFT AGAINST THE WALL IS AN OLD TELEVISION ON AN OLD TV STAND. IT LOOKS LIKE IT PROBABLY DOESN'T WORK. THERE IS A CHAIR BY THE TELEVISION. THIS PLACE HAS SEEN BETTER DAYS, AND EVEN THOSE WEREN'T VERY GOOD.

CAST:

CASSIE MILLER....AGE 35, A RARE BEAUTY.
JAKE JACKSON.....SOMEWHERE IN HIS 30s AND NOT SURE WHY.
MADGE MILLER....CASSIE'S MOM, ON SOCIAL SECURITY.

BOB DOBSON, MOTEL CLERK, IN HIS 20s.
DEPUTY JACKSON, JAKE'S COUSIN, IN HIS 20s.

TIME:

THE PRESENT.

❖❖❖❖❖❖❖❖❖❖❖❖❖❖❖❖❖

"Upstage" is the rear part of the stage, away from the audience. "Downstage" is the front half of the stage, near the audience. Stage directions are written from the point of view of the actor, who normally enters the stage from the rear, or "back-stage." So if you mean for an actor to move toward what the audience would consider its left and front of the stage, you would write "downstage right."

So that is the first page, which should tell you clearly where this play takes place and who is involved. Note that Bob Dobson and Deputy Jackson are not listed in the same manner as the top three characters. That's because they are minor characters. The major characters are listed in their order of importance. The minor characters are listed in their order of appearance. You don't need to make any comments about the characters (like "a rare beauty") but I do. Again, it's just something to catch the attention of the readers and pique their interest. "In his 30s and not sure why" is a humorous commentary, and I've rarely seen humor hurt. You'll have to determine what you want to say. If unsure, leave out any commentary except age.

If the play takes place over different time periods, those times would be listed. For example: "MID-'60s," "LATE '80s," "PRESENT."

Note the single-spacing of the script. Play scripts, like film scripts (screenplays), are always written single-spaced. Here's how the body of the play should look:

❖❖❖❖❖❖❖❖❖❖❖❖❖❖❖❖❖

ACT I: LIGHTS UP. JAKE IS STAGE LEFT, LOOKING UP
                AT THE POSTER. MADGE ENTERS, FOLLOWED BY
                CASSIE, WHO QUIETLY SHUTS THE DOOR
                BEHIND HER. MADGE LIGHTS INTO JAKE
                IMMEDIATELY:

MADGE

There he is, daughter of mine! Your dream prince,
ensconced in his castle!

JAKE

(SITTING ON THE BED)

What was that old song?

(SINGING)

"The devil must have sent you here, mother-in-law, mother-
in-law..."

(IMPROVISING LYRICS)

I think I need a beer, mother-in-law, mother-in...

CASSIE

Jake, that's really enough! We came here to try and work
things out.

MADGE

Out. What a good word. What a useful word. What an
apropos term!

(MADGE GOES OUT THE DOOR, SLAMMING IT
BEHIND HER.)

JAKE

What a relief!

(PAUSE)

Cassie, Lassie. Look, I...uh...

DEPUTY JACKSON ENTERS, HAT IN HAND.

DEPUTY

Howdy, you lovebirds.

❖❖❖❖❖❖❖❖❖❖❖❖❖❖❖❖

A comment on the above: Some of the stage direction (THE PART
IN CAPS, LIKE THIS) was enclosed by parentheses. That was the
direction for the individual actors. When Jake is SINGING, it's from a
real song, which means as a playwright you might have to get an

okay from the song's publisher, if you have your character sing more than a certain number of bars. You'll have to investigate the copyright restrictions. When I have Jake IMPROVISING, he's making up lyrics, but he's still (we assume) singing the same tune. For this reason, if you want to make your life simpler I advise you to use songs that are in the public domain. That means no one owns the copyright on them. "Greensleeves," for example, or any other song you normally see denoted "traditional" when published.

Again, make sure you know the legalities of using any song you haven't personally written. The same goes for a poem or a quote from another author.

The stage direction not enclosed in parentheses bears reference to the stage as a whole, such as Deputy Jackson entering the room. Some playwrights, such as David Mamet, don't like to use stage direction. They feel that's the job of the director and/or the actors. I somewhat agree, but it's your call. Some direction is usually essential, particularly if you think your play might be a success, get published as a play and be sold for years to come. If Madge needs to leave the room, have her leave the room. Other directions, such as Jake sitting on the bed, could be left out. That's the kind of stage direction the director and actors will "play with," anyway. In the plays I've written, I used minimal stage direction—enough to tell a reader what the characters are doing, but not so much as to intrude upon the creative choices of the other people involved in putting on the play.

Unless it is one-act in structure (usually not much longer than an hour in running time), your play will be divided into two or three acts. The norm these days is a two-act play. At the end of each act, use the following format:

END OF ACT I

At the end of the play (let's say you have a two-act play), use the following format:

END OF ACT II

THE END

That's basically what you need to know about the proper format of a play. I suggest you contact the Dramatists Guild for their booklet on play format. It's a fun read, and you'll probably learn more.

The playwright's passion

Despite experience over a number of years, I don't claim to be an expert on the stage. That's why I've consulted some experts for this chapter. When you write an article, a story, a book or even a play, you're usually alone. When it comes to the stage and other entertainment mediums, however, if you want to succeed as a writer you'll have to learn about collaboration. That's why, before I got into stage, television, film and the other writing disciplines in this book, I told you first about writing groups. If you're serious about being a playwright, join the Dramatists Guild as an associate member. Start reading their publications. If you live in one of the major metropolitan areas where the Guild holds workshops and meetings (most often in Los Angeles, Chicago and New York), all the better.

So now that you know the proper format to use for your play, how about the proper content?

That's easy. There is no "proper" content. That's the wonder of the stage. Writing for the stage may not be my best contribution to the culture, but in many ways it is my favorite thing to write. Why? The people. To put words on paper, to feel and express strong emotions and deep philosophies, and then to see someone else feel and express them, using your words in perhaps an even more artful manner than you originally envisioned, is a thing of rare beauty. When you write any other form of script, it could be years before you see your work performed. If you do what it takes to get your play staged, though, you'll see your words come to life with a vigor and immediacy that will amaze and perhaps frighten you—the latter, when you see that it doesn't always sound the same in real life as it did in your mind.

We'll get into working with actors later. Right now, let's discuss how some successful modern playwrights go about their craft.

Great playwrights fall in love with the stage at an early age. For Peter Shaffer, winner of the 1992 William Inge Award for lifetime achievement in the theater, the moment came at age 8, when he "became an addict of the theater and the worshiper of William Shakespeare."

In a Liverpool classroom, Shaffer and 19 other students were transfixed as a teacher told them the details of a "ghost story" which Shaffer later learned was Shakespeare's *Hamlet*. The teacher broke off at 3 p.m. without finishing the story, and Shaffer was hooked. Years later, after authoring a successful play, he traveled to Morocco and watched raptly as a marketplace storyteller held a crowd transfixed. These incidents, Shaffer told an audience when he accepted the Inge award, convinced him that narrative is the bedrock of drama. The playwright is, to Shaffer, an enchanter.

In the same issue of the *Dramatists Guild Quarterly* where I read Shaffer's astute comments, Murray Schisgal said that playwriting is a "programmed outpouring of [one's] total self." I've found both men's comments to hold true. With a play, you allow an audience an intimate view of a unique world. You want them to be enchanted enough to at least sit through the performance. More likely, you want them to be charged with enthusiasm after seeing the play, so much so that they spread the word about your ideas like an unstoppable prairie fire.

To engender that type of emotion, wouldn't you need to be as honest as possible, to hold nothing back in your writing, to outpour your total self, as Schisgal suggests?

David Mamet reported in a *Playboy* magazine interview that audiences who first saw his play *Oleanna*, which is about sexual harassment, had very highly charged emotional responses. Some stood up and cursed; others applauded vigorously, but most left the theater talking about what they had just seen. This says one thing: When you write a play, it had better be about something that means a great deal to you. Even if it's a "light comedy," if you are compelled by what you are writing, the chances of an audience also being compelled are much greater. Just as you try to keep them turning the pages of a book, with a play you try to keep them in their seats, with their emotions and intellect constantly stimulated by the events on stage.

In the time of Shakespeare, the demands of the audience were high. The best seats were in the balconies of the Globe Theatre, not on the floor level. There was no front row, only a bare space where the "groundlings" watched the stage. These were the "cheap seats," except that there were no seats. The groundlings, who sat on the ground, were hard-working people who wanted rigorous entertainment, and the stout ale they drank loosened their emotional responses to the action. Thus, Shakespeare literally wrote to audiences on several "levels" with his plays. He offered sword fights and blood-letting, as well as tricks of language for the intellectuals.

The Bard of Avon obviously wrote from deep emotion and strong philosophical exploration. He was trying to entertain, certainly, but he was also urging people to examine life, to consider how life might be bettered. In addition, he was faced with a unique problem. He wanted to comment on the structure of society as a whole, starting at the top. In a day when beheadings were still common, it wasn't sensible to write too intimately about the English royalty. So, he did something very clever. He studied the history of royals and created characters based on them, with themes that had bearing on his own times. The groundlings were fascinated to see "how the royals lived," while the royals were fascinated by their own "history."

Of course, Shakespeare had many influences other than English kings, but you get the idea. His work aroused great commentary in his time, because it dealt with deeply felt (and argued) passions.

Today, work for the stage is divided, roughly at least, into three categories: 1) entertainment; 2) important work; and 3) experimental. Any given piece might be all three, like Tony Kushner's *Angels in America*. It's open to individual interpretation. Will Neil Simon's *Broadway Bound* one day be viewed with the same reverence as Shakespeare's *As You Like It*? It's possible, even if it seems unlikely from our current perspective. I would generally classify Simon's body of work as entertainment first and important second. It is certainly not experimental—a category in which you would find "performance art" and other such public offerings. But who cares? Simon's work is very funny and a fine comment on the human condition.

So what is "important work"? By that I mean any play that gets people thinking, and perhaps doing something about, an important public issue. Marsha Norman's award-winning *'night, Mother* was about suicide. Did the number of suicides decrease after the success of Norman's play? No, but it got people thinking about *why* anyone would commit suicide. Did Kushner's *Angels in America* inspire a cure for AIDS? Not as of this writing, but it painted a more sympathetic face on the plight of people dying from the deadly disease.

To me, the stage is a place where we can try to better understand community. That is, ourselves and our relations with each other. From the days of the Greeks who influenced Shakespeare, up to the present day, this has always been so. David Mamet, author of *Glengarry Glen Ross* and other noted works, disagrees somewhat. He says that the "purpose of literature is not to do good, but to delight us."

Like Peter Shaffer, Mamet became fascinated with the theater at an early age. He was a child actor, but it wasn't until he was 14, when he discovered the works of Samuel Beckett and Harold Pinter, that he got his "wake-up call" and became enamored with writing. By the time he was 27, his *American Buffalo* was on Broadway. Still, the gap between 14 and 27 is a long time, which might explain why Mamet feels that persistence is the only sure route to success.

The same holds true for Wendy Wasserstein, author of *The Sisters Rosenzweig* and other fine plays. Once she saw her first Broadway play at age 8, she, too, was hooked. Persistence must be her middle name, because she never gives up on a project. *The Heidi Chronicles* took eight years to finish, and she doesn't show her work to anyone until she's done "eight or nine drafts." Edward Albee, author of *Zoo Story* and numerous fine works, admits to a similar amount of drafts, but most of them are "in his head." He usually uses the first draft he commits to paper.

The actor's passion

So what goes in your drafts? Horton Foote says each character has to want something. David Mamet goes further, saying that no one ever speaks unless they want something. Actors call this "motivation." Actors and even directors will, in fact, drive you crazy at times trying to get you to explain character motivation. John Guare, author of *Six Degrees of Separation* and other famous plays, turns the table a bit. When auditioning a director for a new play, he asks the director to tell him the story of the play. The director who can do that with an understanding most like Guare's own gets the job.

The great thing about playwriting—and hopefully it will never change—is that in the theater the writer is given the ultimate power of decision. Playwrights are respected. If they say a line stays, it stays. The director is never—as opposed to film—seen as the "author" of a stage production. When the audience cries "Author!" it is the playwright who comes out and takes a bow. When you write a play and it gets to the point where it's being read aloud in your presence by real, live people, you maintain the ultimate authority. If it doesn't sound right, you can change it. Remember the rule Stephen King uses: If 10 people make the same comment, maybe it needs to be changed; if 10 people make dissimilar comments, leave it alone.

Similarly, your influences as a playwright may differ from other writers. You may enjoy Sam Shepard's *Buried Child*, while others will think it's the sickest thing they ever saw. Foote advises that you learn from all sources, then "find what best serves you in your material."

There is a term in the theater called "chewing the scenery." That refers to an actor given free rein to emote wildly, even out of control. Too often, acting, to many thespians, means loudly expressing anger or rage. That is not acting, but chewing the scenery. Even when Marlon Brando yelled "Stella!" in *A Streetcar Named Desire*, there was something held in reserve. Otherwise, he'd have yelled it all right then and there. Everything that was on Stanley Kowalski's mind would have come pouring out.

Which brings us to the legendary American playwright Tennessee Williams. I've already told you how I met Mr. Williams. Now let me share some comments he had on writing for the stage, as featured in my article for *Black Mountain Review*. Williams revealed that he thought any beginning writer should write about material that was "most organic, most emotional" to that individual. He said he wrote "just about what I am emotionally concerned with." He was also glad for his southern upbringing, because of the "rich and protean" background of life in the South.

"I have more sensibility than intellectual power," Williams said. "I don't like cerebrating over things, you know, thinking them out. I like to function from intuition and inspiration."

Williams once remarked that he tried very hard to "not only attract observers but participants" in the performance of his plays. To affect this, he had to be deeply emotionally involved in his characters and situations himself. How deep? When I asked him if his most famous character, Blanche Cutrere in *A Streetcar Named Desire,* was based on a girl he'd been fond of in his teen years, he laughed. No, he told me, the lady who utters the line about always depending on the kindness of strangers was actually "closest to a self-portrait."

So let your emotions run deep. It's worked since the time of the Greeks and will work on the stage into infinity. If you don't believe that, read *Oedipus Rex* by Sophocles, the tale about a boy separated from his family, who grows up to become a great warrior, kills his father and marries his mother, then blinds himself when he finds out what he's done. If comedy is your ticket, then study *Lysistrata* by Aristophanes, about a sex strike by the women of Greece to get their husbands to make peace, not war. Like I said, strong emotions have always been the stuff of the stage.

The group passion

Another similarity that you will find among many successful playwrights—other than their early passion for theater—is that, at some point in their careers, they become involved with a theater group on an ongoing basis. David Mamet began as an actor and director before turning to writing plays, and even then it was mainly because his company couldn't afford to pay the licensing fee to use plays from other authors. For Horton Foote, the formative group was the American Actors Theatre. John Guare's first big break came when he got the job as assistant to the manager of the National Theatre, a post that actor Warren Beatty had abandoned. Wendy Wasserstein holds readings of her plays with the Seattle Repertory Company. For Eugene O'Neill, the first American playwright to win the Nobel Prize for literature (1936), his early group was the Provincetown Players. French playwright Molière (real name Jean Baptiste Poquelin) worked with the Illustre Theatre in much the same way Shakespeare worked with the actors at the Globe in London.

If you can become involved with a group of actors on an ongoing basis, learning all the aspects of the theater and participating in the group effort, you'll stand a much better chance of having great success as a playwright. If there's no group near where you live, and you are passionate about playwriting success, either move to a major metropolitan center or start a group of your own. Regional theater has enjoyed a renaissance in recent decades, and New York's Broadway is not the ultimate goal it once was.

To further illustrate the importance of how a group can affect the theater, consider the Group Theater in New York. At one time, actors training under Lee Strasberg—people like Marilyn Monroe, Marlon Brando, Geraldine Page, Rip Torn, Paul Newman, Rod Steiger—could listen to Arthur Miller, Clifford Odets and Tennessee Williams discuss the play process on a weekly basis. My friend Manu Topou, whom I considered to be the finest acting coach in America, was trained by Strasberg, in fact, to pass on the knowledge the master had acquired. Knowing that Manu has often starred on Broadway (Black Elk in the original *Black Elk Speaks*, for example), I am always fascinated listening to him discuss the Group Theater days.

"There was always an irony to the work," Manu told me once, "and a built-in internal combustion taking place, a dramatic explosion from within. Everything, everyone there, was concerned with social issues, and the impact of our work. We talked about issues of repairing damage in society, the worth of labor based on sex. It was wonderful, all-around training for writers and actors, and we were consumed with the new drama of a changing world."

I hope you find such passion and such people, and emotions as deep as the people mentioned here have put into their work. Just don't forget that the word "drama" is derived from the Greek verb "dran," meaning "to act" or "to do." In writing your plays, keep in mind the need to make things *happen* onstage. A good play does not consist of people standing around merely talking. A great play is a true wonder, filled with happenings, and it's not easy to bring a great play about.

Composer Stephen Sondheim, who has had no small success on Broadway, thinks playwriting is the most difficult creative discipline. Sondheim, like most great geniuses of the stage, is inspired by the natural music that comes from the rhythm of the speech of the common people, in all languages. Whether you write for the groundlings or the people in the balcony (or, hopefully, them all), I implore you to listen to the music of life, and write passionately of the melodies, harmonies and even discord of your world.

Hope I see you—or your words—on a major stage.

Chapter 10

❖❖❖❖❖❖❖❖❖❖❖❖❖❖❖❖

Screenplay savoir faire

Savoir faire is a French term that literally means "knowing how to do." Hollywood is a place where anything is possible when it comes to writing, but not many people truly know what to do. Chances are that no 10 so-called script experts would be able to agree on what scripts should be made and what scripts should not be made. This isn't merely my opinion. In the 1970s, screenwriter William Goldman was viewed as the dean of all screenwriters, thanks to his script *Chinatown*, which many thought to be the perfect screenplay. In his book *Adventures in the Screen Trade*, Goldman offered one maxim for dealing with Hollywood. "Nobody knows anything," he said.

I began making money in the film industry shortly after my entry into it. The first story I wrote for film was "optioned," which is to say I received a small amount of money upfront, with the full price paid if the budget to make the film was raised by the people who "optioned" my story. The term "option" means someone buys, or talks you into giving them for free, an option to purchase a script within a given time period. In the film business, the usual option is 10 percent—that's when they're paying you. When they don't want to pay you, or claim they can't, they want the option for free. In most "free" cases, you should tell them to take a hike and hope they find money on the trail; if they do, they should come back to you and get serious. I never saw the rest of the riches I envisioned because the film budget never got raised.

In any event, I continued making money for film stories and scripts for more than a decade before receiving the full price for a screenplay. My first story sale still hasn't been made into a film or even a script. This isn't unusual. The screenwriting duo of Cash and Epps (*Top Gun* and other blockbusters) made a large living for a long time writing scripts for studios before one of their scripts finally got made. So why does this kind of thing happen so often in Hollywood? Because nobody knows anything.

No one has ever devised a sure-fire formula for gauging public taste in films. An added burden is the fact that most film studio executives do not come from creative backgrounds. They are lawyers, accountants and agents who worked their way up. Scripts that executives think are terrible one month might be the hottest thing in town the next month. These execs commune with each other, trying to guess what the other is doing. They "copycat" each other's moves. They jockey for the best table at Morton's on Monday night. Their underlings want their jobs and make a practice of saying yes to the bosses and no to creative types.

Hollywood is a corporate atmosphere that is, to a large degree, deadly to creativity. When you're an executive getting a nice six-figure salary, it's much safer to say no and not take a chance. Saying yes might mean you authorize spending $100 million to make a box-office flop. You might bankrupt your studio. Accordingly, film executives tend to hedge their bets and play it safe. They try to "package" films with scripts from writers who have written other hits, directors who have won awards and stars the public is likely to come see in any film. This makes agents at large agencies—who champion talents from all areas of filmmaking—some of the most powerful people in town.

To write to sell in this kind of atmosphere, you have to understand Hollywood. That's important if you have any desire whatsoever to succeed as a screenwriter. It took me a long time to figure this out, even though I lived in Hollywood for years. When I fell out of love with the image of the town and faced its reality, I finally began to get somewhere.

Books are where the real money is

I tell my writing students to forget about writing screenplays, unless they're eaten up with the desire to make films. But don't be screenwriters—make films. If a student has a good story, I advise him or her to write a book first, get it published, sell it to Hollywood and *then* get a job writing the screenplay. Why? Two reasons: 1) They'll make money three times with a book; and 2) Hollywood filmmakers, though they might vociferously disagree with me, still consider films to be a secondary medium after "serious" writing like books and plays. Let me give you an example:

In 1983, I wrote a screenplay with Michael Sean Conley called *Fair Game,* about modern piracy in the Caribbean. The first production team we showed it to immediately optioned the script. They didn't get it made on their first attempt, but they kept at it. When one option ran out (we gave them exclusive rights to the script for a year), they picked up another option. In all, Ron Hamady and George Braunstein had three options on *Fair Game.* Mike and I made the full price of the script, but still owned it. In 1994, we sold the script to another production company, who had the money in the bank to make the movie.

After that sale, we ended up making—considering all the options and the sale—twice as much as the Writers Guild basic screenplay price. Not bad, but not as good as a book. In contrast, my "You Solve It Mystery" novels brought me a small advance for each of the first three books, but a nice chunk of change nonetheless. When I later sold the books for film and television, I got money for the book rights, and was hired to write scripts. Which means I made money on those stories three times: a) book sale; b) book rights sale; c) scripts.

And let's say you have a story that is good for the "interactive" market, as I described earlier. You might make additional money for "interactive rights." You can also sell your book's electronic rights, which is an electronic text version sold online over the Internet. You can't do that with a mere screenplay.

On the other hand, if you write a great screenplay, you could be set financially for the rest of your life. You could enter a world of amazing money and amazing frustration to match. You might be able to direct the filming of your next screenplay. If you're one of those people convinced that writing scripts is the way to go, let's take a trip to Hollywood.

From script to screen

Let's say you get lucky. Let's say you write your first screenplay, find someone who will buy it and it's so brilliant someone puts up several million dollars to bring it to the silver screen. Here's what will most likely happen:

1. You sign a contract that, hopefully, gives you the chance to write any revisions that are made to the script.
2. Your first rewrite is not very much enjoyed.
3. Another writer comes on board.
4. The producer, director and studio executives decide they have a script that they can live with.
5. The director writes a "shooting script."
6. Actors are cast, locations are found, a detailed production and shooting schedule is drawn up—in short, "preproduction" is done.
7. The film is shot, hopefully on schedule.
8. The film is edited, special effects are added, sound is "mixed" and the score (music) is added.
9. A "rough cut" is shown to all who have an interest in making money from the film.
10. The film is exhibited in theaters, then on television, then goes out on video. It might go "straight to video."

A large number of people are involved in getting your story from script to screen. Film is the most heavily collaborative medium that exists. That's why selling a script is akin to creating the blueprint for a multimillion dollar skyscraper, which is also built within a corporate atmosphere.

Naturally, there are low-budget and very low-budget films that are made for what seems like little or no money by Hollywood standards. For example, 1994's *El Mariachi* was created for only $35,000. Exceptions like these are made by skilled filmmakers, however. Unless you are willing to make the commitment not only to write a script but to do whatever is necessary to get that script on film, forget those examples.

From story to synopsis

There is a basic difference between a screenplay and a novel. Almost all screenplays are written in the present tense, while most books are written in the past tense. Perhaps it comes from the natural transition of the stage directions for stage plays to plays written for the screen. The first screenwriters, by the way, were called "scenarists."

Some were playwrights, but most were not. They wrote action sequences, since films were silent and there was no dialogue to be heard.

Using the present tense makes sense because movies primarily deal with the immediate culture. Filmmakers strive to disseminate to the whole world the happenings of smaller portions of the world. A dance form might have been around for years in a region, but when it is popularized in a hit film it can become the hottest thing in the world for a time. Books can do the same thing, but not with the same sense of immediacy that belongs to film. I was first truly convinced of the world impact of films when an acquaintance, a filmmaker from Tunisia, told me a story. He was in the heart of Africa, in tribal country with only rudimentary structures for hundreds of miles around, when he stepped into a mud hut and saw the famous *Saturday Night Fever* movie poster of John Travolta in a disco pose. I can think of no better example of the enormous reach of films; it's no wonder that the annual Academy Awards ceremony is one of the most-watched (and longest) television events of the year.

You don't have to be able to read to watch a movie. You don't even have to speak the language used in the film to understand it. You usually watch a movie straight through. You don't set it aside to be continued later as you do with a book on a nightstand. A movie is immediate, a "witness this now" type of event. That's why it seems appropriate that scripts are written in the present tense. The most notable exception I ever saw to this rule was the script for *The Wind and the Lion* by John Milius, which remains my favorite screenplay. It was written in past tense, with the description reading like a novel. The subject of the film was a turn-of-the-century story, however, so past tense seemed right.

Before you try to get too clever with a script, I suggest you become competent. Milius is a very skilled screenwriter and was able to make the example I gave work. When you write your first script, unless you have a very good reason for doing something different, use the present tense in your description of the action.

Here's the next thing you need to remember about films: They are "moving pictures." Although you might remember and repeat great bits of film dialogue for years, films are primarily an action medium. As a playwright, it took me a long time to really get this point. I was in love with dialogue. As a result, my early screenplays were filled with pages of people talking to each other. "Talking heads," it's called in the business. The person who got me out of this was Edward Hunt, a writer/director who had done 10 films by the time we met. Ed and I collaborated on three feature film scripts, and by the time we finished the first one I was convinced of the need to keep things moving and cut down on the dialogue. All my writing improved as a result.

When Harry Cohn ran Columbia Studios during its heyday, he was famous for the "butt twitch" method of determining whether or not he liked a film. If he shifted in his seat too many times—if his butt twitched too much—he felt that audiences would do the same, and the film was boring, no good or needed more work. When you write a script, think of what it would look like if you were sitting in a theater watching it. As a good index of what I mean, you should know that most screenplay scenes are no longer than three pages long. Since one single-spaced screenplay page averages out to one minute of onscreen time, that means few film scenes are longer than three minutes. Some scenes are much shorter, and as more filmmakers graduate from the ranks of music video makers, very short scenes will become more common.

So try to keep your characters doing something, not just talking, and have them do it in three minutes or less whenever possible.

Wesley Strick, the writer of several hit films including *Arachnaphobia,* uses a simple method of constructing a film story line. He writes a short description of each scene on a Post-it™ note. The Post-it notes are then placed on a blank wall in sequence. If he wants to move the order of a scene, he merely pulls it off the wall and sticks it in another place, adjusting the other notes. Other writers use a similar method, shuffling index cards, but I like Strick's method. Forty Post-it notes at three minutes each equals 120 minutes of screen time. You can "see" the entire film in front of you, in sequence. Remember, 120 minutes is just an index. Some films are only 90 minutes long. The more action you have in a film, the shorter the script will likely be.

So let's say you have a story you want to turn into a script. You know you should keep your scenes down to three minutes or less, and you have a supply of 40 Post-it notes. Now what? The next step is figuring out the beginning, middle and end. Film scripts roughly follow a three-act structure. Syd Field, whose show business career began as a reader of scripts, was for many years the resident "authority" on scripts, thanks to his book *Screenplay*. Was Field an expert because of the hit scripts he'd written? No, he had simply read a lot of screenplays and noticed a pattern. He wrote that pattern down in book form. He proposed that the turning points of a 120-page script were at the 30-minute, 60-minute and 90-minute marks. The 30-minute mark was the end of the first act. The 90-minute mark was the end of the second act and the 60-minute mark was the crucial turning point of the story. He noted that Steven Spielberg, the most financially successful filmmaker of the last two decades, had an extended third act in his films.

Before Field penned his observations, Lajos Egri had been the "guru" for Hollywood writers. In Egri's *The Art of Dramatic Writing*, he stated that a play should deal with premise, character and conflict. He emphasized characters in constant change working out their own destinies. Then came the influence of the works of Joseph Campbell, who wrote *The Hero with a Thousand Faces*. John Truby, one of the main screenwriting teachers currently in vogue, breaks Campbell's findings down into nearly 30 steps that should go into a script.

I do not intend to break down the works of any of these men any further than I already have. There are many books available on screenwriting, and screenwriting teachers who tour all the major cities. There are correspondence courses available, and most likely, courses at your local college. None of this changes one fact: A good story is a good story. Syd Field studied successful scripts and noticed a pattern. Lajos Egri studied great writing and wrote down his observations. Joseph Campbell studied the great stories, myths and religions and noticed a pattern. Scores of people have studied Campbell and made a nice living out of passing on their findings. None of the people mentioned, however, ever made a living writing screenplays. That should tell you something. If you can write a great story, you can learn to write a great screenplay of that story.

Your screen story begins with an event or an action that impels the main character or characters toward a great change. The middle of the story is the sequence of events that puts the main character in some sort of peril or conflict that must be resolved. The end is the emotionally stirring resolution of the conflict. It's basically that simple. Why do you go to the movies? To be entertained, primarily. One Hollywood studio boss was reported to observe, "If you want to send a message, use Western Union." Whether it's a horror film that scares you to death, a love story that makes you cry, a comedy that makes you laugh or an action film that leaves you breathless, most people go to the movies with the primary purpose of having their emotions roused.

So, when crafting your movie story, ask this question: "Will anyone really care about this but me?"

If the answer is "probably not," maybe you'd better pick another story. On the other hand, if you are so compelled by the story that you will do anything to put that story on film whether anyone else cares, you probably should pursue it. You might find there are a lot more people out there than you think who will care about your story. Given all the hurdles necessary to write a script, sell it and get it filmed, only those passionate about a script ever get it made. I advise you to be completely passionate about any screenplay you write. Director Richard Donner (the *Lethal Weapon* films and a score of other hits) told me that the main determining factor of whether he wants to make a movie is if he reads a script and wants to see the film. With a story you're passionate about, it shouldn't be too difficult figuring out a beginning, middle and end. In figuring out the beginning of the story, remember what I told you earlier about Steve Allen's comment on "where does this story really begin." The middle is where the great transformation takes place—hence Syd Field's observation that it is twice as long as the other turning points, and the fact that the middle portion has its own midway turning point.

With the primary portions of your story determined, get your supply of 30 to 40 Post-it notes (or index cards) and figure out the sequences. Remember, each scene should lead to another. There should be no sudden jumps that go unexplained. Think of what it would look like to you, sitting in a theater. Write down a paragraph describing what happens in each scene. Once that is done, you'll have what is called a "step outline," which can then become a polished story.

Producer Joel Silver, known for his ability to turn out action hits, believes there should be a big explosion and/or breathtaking action sequence every 10 minutes of a film. It's also a commonly held belief in Hollywood that at least five times during the film there should be some major piece of action. Naturally, they should be spaced evenly through the script. If you want to write action, study action films.

Once you've figured out your story you may want to go on to a treatment. Don't get this term confused with a synopsis. A synopsis can be one, three or five pages. A step outline shows, scene by scene, the entire action sequence of a film story. A true film treatment is a step outline expanded. It could be upwards of half the length of a script, with bits of important dialogue added in various places to flesh out the scenes for the reader. A synopsis describes a film. A step outline provides the sequences, while a treatment allows the reader to see the film mentally, minus most of the dialogue.

In trying to get someone to read your script, you might be asked to explain the "high concept." That means, "What's it about, in 25 words or less?" Currently in vogue is combining two hit films to describe your story. For example, you might describe a script about a frontier widower coming to a city to meet a mail-order bride who turns out to be a Native American as "*Sleepless in Seattle* meets *Dances with Wolves.*"

From step outline to script

You'll probably need to do a good deal of study to learn to write a great screenplay. With some scripts selling for $1 million or more, the stakes are high and the competition is voluminous if not fierce. Given that admonishment, here's your next rule: Make your script as perfect as possible and you'll greatly increase your chances of success. When I first met producer Ron Hamady, he told me of a successful writer who spent a year and a half perfecting the first script he ever wrote, before he showed it to anyone. Ron told me that although the script never actually made it to film, the script got him one writing job after another. It was one of the finest "spec" scripts he had ever read.

You'll hear that term a lot in Hollywood. A "spec" script is one written speculatively. You write it without commission or pay, hoping someone will buy it, or merely to show what you can do as a screenwriter. Your first screenplay, unless you're very lucky or your Uncle Joe plans to finance the making of your movie, will most likely be a spec script.

The same elements of any good story go into a script. Read the screenwriting books I mentioned earlier. Meanwhile, here's the basic screenplay format:

❖❖❖❖❖❖❖❖❖❖❖❖❖❖❖❖❖

FADE IN:

EXT. YOUR HOUSE—NIGHT

We see a small house in suburbia, distinguished only by a light in a corner window. We hear the sounds of a late-night talk show.

> TALK SHOW HOST (O.S.)
> And that's my opinion whether you like it or not!

CUT TO:

INT. SMALL HOME OFFICE—NIGHT

It's your office. Sitting at a desk cluttered with papers and bills is *you*, red-faced, on the phone, talking to the radio man. A computer sits in front of you. Near it is the radio, the volume turned down.

> YOU
> You opinionated jerk! You can't treat me this way!

> TALK SHOW HOST (O.S.)
> Oh, yeah!? Watch me!

We hear a PHONE HANG-UP. The talk show isn't off the air, but you are. You SLAM the phone down in disgust and turn up the radio. The host DRONES ON, congratulating himself on the air.

> YOU
> I could do better than that. I really could.

❖❖❖❖❖❖❖❖❖❖❖❖❖❖❖❖❖

(Note: This is a feature film script format, not a script for any form of television show. It is also a "master scene" script, which is to say it only describes the scene and dialogue, and not things like camera angles and special effects.)

Let's examine the various components. "FADE IN:" means you gradually focus in on the scene. Not every script has FADE IN at the beginning, but in recent years it has become the generally accepted form to use. "EXT" means "exterior." The first shot in a screenplay is the "establishing shot," but you don't need to say that. Just know the first shot should orient the reader and give an idea of where we are. Once we've done that, we "CUT TO" another scene. This means we switch from one scene to another quickly, as if the film has been cut with scissors. Some writers don't use CUT TO at all, but simply begin the next scene. Speaking of which, the next scene in our sample begins with an "INT," which means "interior." It could be EXT if it was another outdoor scene, but I chose an indoor one, which moved in closer on the location of my first shot. After we know whether we're outdoors or indoors, we tell the reader IN CAPS where the action is taking place: "YOUR HOUSE" and "SMALL HOME OFFICE." Then we say whether it's "DAY" or "NIGHT." The first time we see a character on-screen, his or her name is CAPITALIZED. After that, it's not capitalized. "BOB" becomes "Bob" (as long as he's the only Bob) thereafter.

When we hear someone talking but don't see them onscreen, that is noted to the side of their name. I use "(O.S.)," which means "off-screen." "V.O." for "voice-over" would also be okay. If you have some direction for the actor, such as "whispering," that would be given this way:

YOU
(whispering)
You jerk, I'm losing my voice arguing with you!

The "(whispering)" line is called the "slug line." In screenplays, less is more. Unless it is imperative for the scene, leave off directions for actors. Similarly, don't get fuzzy and cute by adding "WIDE SHOT" or similar camera directions in your script. That is the director's job, and many of them take offense if you attempt to tell them where the camera should be. Unless it's absolutely imperative that you do so to illustrate a point, leave out camera directions.

Back to FADE IN. Let's say the director might not want to fade in. He might want the action to begin immediately. Bam! There's the scene. Similarly, at the last scene of a script many writers add the following: FADE OUT.

Should you? Might as well, since it's generally accepted. If you're ever in doubt about what to put in or leave out of a script, remember the K.I.S.S. rule: "Keep It Simple, Stupid." You'll be better off.

Lastly, when you describe a sound or special effect in a script, you put it in CAPS, such as "PHONE HANG-UP." There are people who will comb through a script and find this type of thing when figuring out a budget for shooting the film. Special sounds and special film effects cost money. It's not absolutely necessary that you put such directions in CAPS, but you'll make the budget-maker's job much easier by capitalizing. Why not help them out a little?

And that's it. Everything else about a script is extra. Instead of CUT TO: can you say "DISSOLVE TO:" or "FADE THROUGH TO:"? Okay, go ahead, even though it's a director type of decision. Unless it truly emphasizes a point though, a simple "CUT TO:" (don't leave out the colon, please) will be sufficient.

I hope you noticed that there is no space between the character name and the dialogue. Dialogue is roughly two tabs in, with a similar margin on the right. One-inch margins should be used on all four sides. What if someone's dialogue gets cut off at the end of the page? Here you go:

YOU
(hoarse)

You jerk, I'm losing my voice arguing with you! And furthermore, if you don't let me tell you why I called and what I have to say, and by golly I mean absolutely everything I have to say, buster boy, I'm...

(MORE)

On the next page:

YOU (cont'd)
(yelling)

...going to come down to that radio station and cut your little power line!

There's an easy shortcut to getting the format for a screenplay right. If you have a computer and a commonly used word processing program like WordPerfect, Microsoft Word, WordStar or MacWrite Pro, you can get a software program like "Writing Screenplays" or "Scriptor," which work "on top of" those programs.

As you know, this is a "basics" book. There are dozens of books and hundreds of classes on screenwriting. I suggest you read the books I've mentioned previously and do your own further study. Do a lot of studying before you write your script, but start your story right away. With the idea that a two-hour script should be 90 to 120 pages long, with scenes usually no longer than three minutes each, you know the basics. As I mentioned, the more action description there is on a page, the more likely the page will have more than one minute screen-time. That's why some action scripts are no longer than 90 pages. Comedies are generally shorter, too. But that is all "extra." Start with the basics, then learn the variables and exceptions.

Here's another piece of Hollywood wisdom. Alfred Hitchcock, who made amazing films like *Vertigo* and *Psycho,* said that suspenseful movie plots should revolve around something called "the MacGuffin." Other people call it "the cookie." It's a real object, such as the maltese falcon or the treasure of the Sierra Madre or the ark of the covenant in the first *Indiana Jones* film. In action and suspense movies, the MacGuffin is most always something tangible. In other films, the MacGuffin is a person, a place or a status. In the case of Scarlett O'Hara in *Gone with the Wind,* the MacGuffin she wants is to never go hungry again. The MacGuffin in *The Wizard of Oz* is the ruby slippers, as far as the Wicked Witch of the West is concerned. Judy Garland's Dorothy has the slippers, but that's not what she wants. She wants to go home to Kansas. In *It's a Wonderful Life,* George Bailey's MacGuffin, at first, is to leave home and travel the world. Later, after a visit from Clarence, the angel, George does a drastic rethinking of his MacGuffin. Life, he realizes, has to do with friends and family and loved ones, not so much with the glamour and adventure of world travel.

When you're plotting out that first script, ask yourself: "What is the MacGuffin? What is the main thing in this story that everyone wants?" Answering that can greatly help you clarify your story, if you don't have it focused already.

The last element of a good script is the "tag." In fancy French terms, it's the *denouement.* This is the wrap-up of any loose ends of the story, often—but not always—with a laugh or a cheery note. Think of Rick being confronted by the authorities at the end of *Casablanca* and what happens. Simba and Nala showing off the new lion prince at the end of *The Lion King.* The bell tinkling at the end of *It's a Wonderful Life,* showing that Clarence got his wings. Or the feather floating away in the wind at the end of *Forrest Gump.* Audiences love tags.

From script to sale

So let's say you get your script finished. Now what? How do you sell your script?

Your best bet in selling a script is to write a wonderful script with an original story that gets Hollywood types salivating at the commercial potential. What sort of script is that? First of all, it's a great story. It's a story that will appeal to audiences forever. A classic. To learn what that is, you should study scripts. Get your hands on the scripts for films that won Academy Awards for writing and for best picture, like *Forrest Gump.* Study the works of highly successful screenwriters—read *It's a Wonderful Life* by Albert Hackett and his wife Frances Goodrich, *Chinatown* by William Goldman, or anything by Ernest Lehman (*North by Northwest, The Sound of Music,* and others).

Tony Bill, who produced *Hearts of the West,* once told me that a great script was so hard to find that it was worth its weight in platinum. That is darn near literally true, given the prices some scripts sell for these days.

A great script gets a lot of attention. A friend of mine was working with Mel Gibson once on a rush basis to complete the video about the making of Gibson's *Hamlet.* Gibson and his producer dropped everything to read a hot script in the parking lot, one that top people all over town were supposed to bid on that day. This is the kind of attention a great script will get. Everyone in Hollywood will drop everything they are doing to read the script by bidding time.

So let's say you've written your script, rewritten your script, perfected your script, and now it's time to try and sell it. What next? You could contact the Writers Guild and ask for its list of agents who will look at scripts from unknown writers. You might get lucky, but by and large the top agents in Hollywood aren't on that list. I suggest you do what I advised earlier: network. That's how most projects (and writers) get discovered in Hollywood. Someone knows someone, or knows someone who knows someone. A script comes to their attention, someone falls in love with it and it eventually gets bought. Dale Launier sold producer David Permut on *Blind Date* by telling him a true story at a party. Permut was floored by the story and brought Launier to the studio to "pitch" it for a film.

Which brings up a very important point: *Someone must fall in love with your story/script for it to ever be made.* *Forrest Gump* (which came from a book by Winston Groom) received six Academy Awards at the 1995 Oscar ceremony. As one of the producers, Wendy Finerman accepted her Oscar for best picture, explaining that it had taken a decade to get *Gump* from book to screen. This sort of thing is not unusual. It took Sir Richard Attenborough decades to get his epic film *Gandhi* to the screen, even though Mahatma Gandhi was one of the major political figures of the twentieth century. If Attenborough had not been in love with the project, it would never have been made and would never have won the accolades it did.

Even if you write a truly great script, you'll have to find someone who not only realizes its greatness but falls in love with it. Even though people all over Hollywood drop what they are doing to bid on your script, someone will still need to fall in love with it to outbid the others and turn it into a film. It's merely the nature of the business.

If you ever compare the number of books submitted to publishers with those accepted for publication, and then compare the number of scripts submitted to movie studios and production companies with those actually made into films, you'll be aghast at the odds of selling an original script. You have a much better chance of selling a book. That's another reason I advise writing a book if you have a great story. It's harder work, but the rewards and percentages are better. If you're a determined aspiring screenwriter, however, here's how to get it sold:

1. **Study everything you can get your hands on about screenplays.**
2. **Write a great script.**
3. **Move to Los Angeles.** It's possible you can sell your script without ever coming to Southern California, but your chances are greatly diminished. New York City, or the film studios in Florida, North Carolina or even Vancouver, British Columbia, are also possibilities. But L.A. is still "the

place" for the movie industry and should remain so for the foreseeable future.

4. **Make sure you have a means of support.** This could be a job, an inheritance or a significant other who supports you while you try to make it, as Sylvester Stallone's first wife did until he sold *Rocky*.

5. **Subscribe to publications of the Writers Guild of America West.**

6. **Study the catalog of the UCLA Extension Writers Program and find a screenwriting course (or several) that appeals to you.** Sign up and go to class. You might also check out the American Film Institute.

7. **Find out where directors and producers hang out.** For example, Morton's restaurant on Monday nights is currently "the place." That's where the big post-Oscar party takes place. But this will cost you some serious money. Other writers are nice to meet and can introduce you to their agents, but only directors and producers will get your script made into a film. These folks hang out at certain places, such as: Mr. Chow's, Drai's, Eclipse, Matteo's, Spago and, that old standby, Trader Vic's. Of course, by the time this book is published, the current "in spots" could very well have changed.

8. **If you haven't met an agent you like by this time, start looking for one.** Have your storyline ("high concept") ready to pitch.

9. **Read the industry trade papers daily and pay close attention to their thicker issues.** For example, when the American Film Market (a gathering of independent filmmakers trying to sell to overseas film distributors) is held each year, the *Hollywood Reporter* and *Daily Variety* do special issues. All the films being shown at the market are described, along with the principal owners of the production companies, their addresses and phone numbers. It's a simple matter to send a letter to each person in that issue telling them about your script. Better yet, you can attend the Market (and other such gatherings) and meet people who might buy your script. Study the trades on a daily basis, developing more contacts

and learning what's going on in the business. There's nothing worse than being industry-ignorant if you are at a party or watering hole where movies are being discussed.

10. **Keep a log of everyone who reads your script.** Who, where, when and the result. You'll not only learn from this but have a written record, should you ever need it for legal purposes.

11. **When you find an agent who will work with you not only on your first script but on developing an overall career plan, sign with that agent and get your script sold.** If the agent doesn't seem to have time for you at any point, find out why or find another agent.

12. **Write some more scripts.** Your career will depend upon your body of work, not a single screenplay. Your writing will improve the more you write, so keep on writing, keep perfecting and keep learning.

The view from the top

Would you like to know what the most financially successful filmmaker of all time has to say about screenwriting? I just happen to have interviewed Steven Spielberg. What many people don't know is that Spielberg's first success was as a writer, and the frustration he had with the studio who bought his script is one of the big reasons he decided to direct. The 1973 script was *Ace Eli and Rodger of the Skies*, co-written with a friend. Spielberg sold it to 20th Century Fox while still in college, and after all was said and done they received credit for the story alone. Given that the director is generally seen as the author of a film, Spielberg advised me that in the film business one should aspire to be a filmmaker, not merely a writer.

"You have to be a self-starter these days," he said. "Get interested the way I did. Make a movie, and then make two, and then make five, and then make 10. By the time I got to college, I had made over 18 amateur short films in 8- and 16-millimeter. So I was ready when the studio came to me, finally, and said, 'We want to offer you a contract to be a TV director.' I had had years of teenage and preteenage experience making movies."

What inspires his films and the stories he chooses? Much of it has to do with childhood memories. It's no wonder that his films appeal not only to children, but to the child in all of us. *E.T., the Extra-Terrestrial* was based on an alien from space that Spielberg imagined lived in a tree behind his home in Arizona. His interest in U.F.O.s came from a description of an encounter by some fellow Boy Scouts.

"For the first time," he told me, "I was listening to eyewitnesses describe how they saw this great bright light in the midnight sky taking some screwy turns and disappearing behind a mountain. Hearing it from friends made it that much more realistic. My whole interest in U.F.O.s was the reason I made *Close Encounters of the Third Kind.*"

The last time I checked, Spielberg's films alone had made around $5 billion. That's a five, followed by a dozen zeros.

The last scene

So learn about writing great scripts, then work at it until you get a great one. Do what Spielberg advises, and write scripts that really inspire you. The kind you'd just love to see as a movie, like Richard Donner says. After you've studied the books I've mentioned, found others on your own, taken classes, broken down scripts to see their structure, written a few scripts and perfected that sample script of yours, it's all marketing, and with the stakes so high, you'll need intense marketing. If you can't or won't move to Los Angeles, you can probably still sell your script—if it's a great one. I'm sure you can find an agent who will work on selling it for you. Excellent scripts tend to rise to the top. If, however, you ever want to stand on the podium and say, "I'd like to thank the members of the Academy...", I suggest you work on getting to know some of the members of the Academy by immersing yourself in the community where most of them live.

Somewhere up the road, I hope it's your special screenwriting touch that thrills me in a darkened theater. I'd love to see your name 20 feet high on the silver screen, and I'll bet you would, too.

Chapter 11

❖❖❖❖❖❖❖❖❖❖❖❖❖❖❖

Television is terrific

It began on Broadway

Early television, broadcast out of New York, was heavily influenced by events on the Broadway stage. Early hits like *Peter Pan* with Mary Martin, and the variety program *Your Show of Shows* starring Sid Caesar were the kind of entertainment that theater patrons of "The Great White Way" knew well. There was a clear division, however, between TV and film people. Generally, film stars wouldn't be caught dead on television, and film studios saw television networks as potentially putting filmmakers out of business. That "opposite poles" sentiment lasted a long time, but the eventual studio involvement in television is obvious. What you may also have noticed is that only in the last decade have film stars done original television shows without being seen in the entertainment business as fallen stars, no longer popular with the film-going public.

I cite this example merely to point out how television has grown in popularity over the last four decades. As an aspiring writer, you should realize that television may offer you the most lucrative potential of all mediums, particularly if you also learn to produce programs. In television, writer/producers like Steven Bochco of *Hill Street Blues* and *NYPD Blue* rule the roost. The richest man in Hollywood, in fact, may well be Aaron Spelling, the producer of *Beverly Hills 90210* and dozens of other hit shows. Spelling was as an award-winning playwright before coming to Hollywood from his native Texas. Although television shows produced by Spelling and other TV mainstays regularly get trashed by intellectuals and cultural critics, the medium remains the most influential cultural force in the world.

Newton Minnow, the former head of the Federal Communications Commission, called television "a vast wasteland." Marshall McLuhan predicted that after three generations of television watchers, we would have a society of savages. Maybe they were right or maybe they were way off base, but the fact remains that television eats up writing and spits it out on a regular, daily basis. Writing for television may be hard to break into, but it also offers writers great rewards, often far beyond their wildest dreams. Just ask Aaron Spelling, in his castle overlooking Beverly Hills.

It ended up "Due South"

Back to film versus television. I started out in Hollywood at the same time as Paul Haggis, a friend who went on to write and produce a number of hit TV shows, including *Due South* on CBS. I was determined to remain "true" to film, while Paul actively pursued TV, hoping to break into films later. His first break came when a strawberry grower from Canada, who wanted to get into the film business, came to a meeting of a writers' group Paul and I put together. The man invested $10,000 in Paul's fledgling career, which gave him the freedom to write some sample scripts for animated shows and Saturday morning cartoons. Once Paul started working in animation, he wrote "spec" sitcom scripts, which eventually led to sales to a number of situation comedy shows. That in turn led to writing and producing *Facts of Life*, which led to writing and producing for the popular drama *thirtysomething*. Paul won an Emmy for a script he co-wrote on that show, which established him firmly as a writer who could do it all.

His next venture was co-writing and directing a feature film. But fickle fate fingered the feature, and Paul ended up in a legal battle with the producers, although he finished the film and did a fine job.

Back to television he went, ending up creating *Due South* for CBS and having a hit show that was all his own. How long did all this take? About 15 years. Of course, there's every reason to believe that Paul will return to his main dream, which is writing and directing feature films. Meanwhile, he has the respect of his peers, and the public loves his work. He might have done as well if he had stuck to writing films, but I venture to guess he would not have been as consistently successful or had the training of being a staff writer, had he not gone into television from the start. If you do some research, you'll find that a number of top writers and filmmakers got their start in television.

All over the compass

Like Paul Haggis, Emmy award-winning writer David Axelrod also started out writing for a young audience. David's Emmy came for 1979's *Hot Hero Sandwich,* a show for adolescents on NBC. He also wrote for two other Emmy-winning shows, Dick Cavett's late-night variety show on ABC, and *Irving Berlin Celebrates His 90th Birthday* on NBC. David got started in TV in 1962, writing for *Captain Kangaroo.* Television was much less structured in those days. He discovered that even though the medium was more than a decade old at that time, there was no established format for scripts.

"Each show did it a bit differently," he told me. "If I came into an existing show, I just looked at copies of older scripts to see how they did it. If it was a show we were starting, we just made up our own logical construction for the script format, based on whatever scripts we were familiar with, and how they were structured. There was no 'right' or 'wrong' way to do it." Now, he says, "I struggle with WGA-approved formats. I keep hearing horror stories about how someone's script was rejected because even though it was good, it was in the improper format."

If he were starting out now with the knowledge he accumulated over the years, David says he would write more and "learn how to pitch better. It's so different now from when I started, I don't know as I would have started!" he exclaims. "There were no schools for TV writing, or sitcom courses or anything much to learn from. TV was still newish (and black and white) in those days."

Directions you need

My, how things have changed. To keep you from becoming one of those horror stories David has heard about, I offer you some basic TV script formats to help get your scripts taken seriously. Remember, if you think the stakes are high in film, think of what they are in television. The chances of your creating a new TV show and selling it, and then remaining on board for its production, are about as remote as an astronaut landing on Mars in this century—but that's not to say it couldn't happen. It worked for Susan Harris when she created *Soap,* but that was a fluke. Try to approach breaking into television realistically, and you won't have your hopes easily crushed.

A TV movie script, called a teleplay, is normally shorter than a feature film script (screenplay). Some sources say 105 pages is correct, others say scripts can run 120 or so. The length of the script and the act breakdown relates directly to commercial breaks, in case you didn't guess. You'll be safer with the shorter length—if a network has to choose between cutting minutes out of your script and selling advertising time, guess which will win? Contrary to the three-act structure of feature film scripts, a teleplay is usually seven acts. Naturally, this varies with different TV movies, but you can get a good index of where the breaks are by watching a few movies and timing the breaks. Since tastes change at networks, rather than advise you on exactly where to put the act breaks I simply advise you to time them yourself. That way, you'll get a better idea of currently accepted structure.

Basic guidelines, however, are as follows: Act 1—first 20 minutes; Act 2—shorter, about 15 minutes; Act 3—longer, about 25 minutes. Note that the first three acts comprise an hour. Acts 4, 5, 6 and 7 are all about 15 minutes long.

Act the end of each act, insert the following: <u>END OF ACT [NUMBER OF ACT]</u>. For example:

<u>END OF ACT ONE</u>

Other than that, teleplay scripts look the same on the page as the format I gave you for screenplays. Note that I said "about" a few times above. The actually running time will be less, since there will have to be room for commercials to air. Also, each act should end on something that arouses your attention. A cliffhanger, a dramatic revelation or a turning point in the story, perhaps. The house catches on fire, for example. Just as long as it's something that impels the viewer to hurry back from the fridge with that sandwich!

Michael McGreevey, a highly successful TV writer who has also produced hit shows (*Fame*, among others), has another bit of advice for the aspiring TV writer—visit an editing room.

"That's where you see the little nuances that advance the story," says McGreevey. "You get to see all the different shots that were filmed, which ones go in and which ones stay out. It enhances your ability to tell a story to watch this process."

It also gives you an idea of writing within financial boundaries, McGreevey adds. The average "license" (price to broadcast it a specific number of times) is currently an average of $2.9 million. A film for the USA Network is less, about $2.4 million. A film McGreevey wrote, *Bonanza: The Return,* was a little more, done for NBC for $3.2 million.

"You need to know that kind of thing," McGreevey adds. "Otherwise you could write something beautiful that will never be filmed. In TV, you also need to know network tastes. ABC and NBC mostly buy TV movies that are oriented toward women. CBS is a bit more eclectic, while Fox does shows that appeal to a younger audience. If you want to write about politics or religion in a TV movie, forget it. It's broadcasting, remember. No matter how well you treat a political or religious subject, someone will object."

What do TV development execs look for? McGreevey laughs. "Something unique, but derivative," he says, shaking his head.

Another tip this experienced TV veteran offers is that you must know how to "pitch" to make it in television. That is, once you've done something to prove you can write, such as impressing someone with a spec script, then you have to go in and explain your show to a development executive. That's where some fine writers fall short, because they are not adept at speaking, or at telling a verbal story.

"You're dealing with a generation that grew up on TV, in these executives," McGreevey confides. "They're smart, and many of them have Harvard MBAs, but they are verbal and visual, not literary. If you have visual aids to add to the story you tell, all the better. I've had writers get completely tongue-tied when pitching to me as a story editor and producer. In one case, I told the man to go home, write it up and mail it in to me. I knew he was a fine writer who just couldn't pitch to save his life. We bought a script from him, but usually you don't get that chance."

Some writers these days, McGreevey adds, take acting lessons to get over the fear of pitching. There is even one acting coach in Hollywood who makes most of her living coaching writers to pitch.

There's another reason you should live in Southern California, if you have any aspirations of making it in television. It's one of the few places where you can find acting (and pitching) coaches in the yellow pages.

Your map to success

The next thing you need to know about writing for television, particularly writing TV movies, is that there are lists of "approved writers" at networks. That is, people who have proven themselves to be competent at writing for TV; things they wrote received high ratings and/or awards. Also, if you are not a member of the Writers Guild of America your chances of selling a TV movie are greatly diminished. The Guild gets quite upset when non-Guild members write for television. Since producers for major networks are all "signatory" with the Guild, meaning they agree to abide by Guild rules when hiring writers, almost everything you see on network television (other than feature films that are being shown on TV) is written by members of the Writers Guild. The Guild also supposedly gets upset about lists of approved writers, which are not legally supposed to exist, but it's a well-known truth that they are used. Similarly, there are lists at networks of actors who have "TV Q." This is a public popularity index—a quotient—which is also not legally supposed to exist, but does.

Many proven TV stars (if they are smart) start their own production company and acquire "pay or play" deals from networks. This means that the networks want these stars to be in TV movies and thereby, hopefully, draw high ratings. So they pay them to do a certain number of TV movies. If no movies are made (because of inadequate material, or whatever), the star still gets to cash the checks. If you think you have a great TV movie possibility going, you should contact a TV star who could be in your story and solicit his or her interest. Find out if he or she has a production company and who the director of development is at that company. Forget calling or writing the network. It's very simple to contact any star. Just called the Screen Actors Guild at its Agency Department, which fields calls about who represents who. All TV stars are members of the Guild—they have to be, because of collective bargaining agreements. The Agency line is (213) 549-6737. The main line of the Screen Actors Guild is (213) 954-1600 if you have any problems. Its address is 7065 Hollywood Boulevard, Hollywood, CA 90028.

What if the SAG Agency Department doesn't have a representative listed for a star? Try reaching them through the network. Get the network's main phone number from your local affiliate. But before you do that, watch the star's TV show (if he or she has one currently running) and find out what production company produces the show. You can then call the network and ask for the phone number of the production company and the address. Chances are the production company is "on the lot" of the network, meaning it is housed at the network studio where the show is filmed. Other times, it may be located at a major studio such as Paramount Studios in Hollywood (the only major studio actually in Hollywood).

If you don't have success in calling the network (although you shouldn't have a problem), call Los Angeles information. This might require some work, because there are a number of area codes in Southern California, and the production company could be at an 818, 213, 310, 619 or other area code. Still, it's going to require a lot of work to break into writing TV movies, so making dozens of phone calls is a good way of getting used to what you're up against. Once you locate the production company's phone number and reach someone there who will take your call, explain what you have to sell them.

Once you know who to send your script to, call an agent. If there aren't any agents where you are located, call a lawyer. In a later chapter, I'll go into where to find a representative. Once you've found someone you think might do a good job as your legal representative, tell him or her "So and So at [a Star]'s production company wants to see my script. Will you represent me and send it to them?"

If you're speaking with a reputable person, he or she will probably say "Sure!" or at least, "Let me read it." This is how you get around the "Catch-22" in Hollywood of "Can't get my script read unless I have an agent, can't get an agent unless someone wants my script." The worst an agent (or lawyer) could say is, "Sorry, I'm too busy." With someone at a production company "asking" to see your script, the agent or lawyer probably won't turn you down.

Could you send a script you intended for a feature film to a TV star with hopes it could be a TV movie? Sure you could, but movies for major networks usually have to do with family horrors, like stolen children or "disease of the week." If you watch many TV movies, I'm sure you know what I mean. Also popular are true stories, but if the story has received any national publicity at all, chances are very good that a TV producer has already contacted the personnel involved in that true story long before you have. If you can secure the rights to someone's true story, however, or if you have a personal story that you feel would make a good TV movie, then you're in the driver's seat. A good agent or lawyer can advise you on the steps to take in "tying up the rights." That's the question a production company person will ask if you're trying to sell a true story: "Do you have the rights?" *Never* lie about this, hoping you'll tie up the rights later. It will get entirely too complicated.

TV movies also take on different characteristics among the cable networks. The Lifetime cable network advertises itself as "the women's network." All their films have strong women characters who are usually in jeopardy. The Turner Network (TNT) owned by CNN magnate Ted Turner, loves political and historical themes. A movie made for HBO or Showtime is little different than a feature film. Do your homework, and figure out which network is best for your story. Then try to determine if the star you have in mind would appear on that network. You'd probably see Meredith Baxter on a CBS, NBC or ABC movie, for example, rather than something on Lifetime, but nothing is written in stone unless the star has an existing deal—which is to say a signed contract—with a network. You *might* be able to find this out by calling the star's production company. There are hundreds of people who keep up with who has network deals and who doesn't. If you call and are ignorant of such contracts it could make you look like an amateur. A good agent should be "up" on all this sort of information.

How much can you earn for a TV movie script? Call the Writers Guild and you can find out. They have a standard "Writers Guild minimum" for every conceivable form of script written for features or television. That is what all Hollywood script prices are based on, when a production company is a signatory of the Writers Guild. See what I mean about the corporate nature of Hollywood?

Where the jokes are

There are Hollywood writers who spend an entire career writing only situation comedy scripts. Let's define what that is: a 30-minute TV program in which the comedy springs from an ongoing situation. Roseanne's sarcastic but oddly normal family, for example, or the fact that affable and amorous bachelor John Ritter was a roommate with two beautiful women in *Three's Company.*

Each particular episode is unique and comprises part of the ongoing situation. Lucy going to work in the pie factory in *I Love Lucy* is one example. So is the *Brady Bunch* kids sneaking around their parents to enter a talent contest and getting the prize money to buy something for Mom and Dad.

Beyond that, the structure of a "sitcom" is pretty easy. It's a running string of dialogue jokes as the plot moves along. The jokes are like this: 1) setup, followed by 2) payoff. Let's use one of the oldest jokes in show business as the example:

"Who was that lady I saw you with last night?"
"That was no lady, that was my wife!"

My all-time favorite is when Jack Benny was approached by a robber. "Your money or your life!" the criminal demands. Benny, whose onscreen persona was that of the biggest tightwad in show business, hesitates and doesn't answer. "Your money or your life!" repeats the thief, waving his gun. "I'm thinking about it!" Benny barks.

If you can't write jokes, forget about writing sitcoms. One writer told me of selling his first sitcom script (for *Barney Miller*), then sitting with the story editor, going over the script page by page. The TV veteran would mark a "J" at various points on the script without comment. When my friend finally asked what he was doing, the wizened old writer smiled wryly and said, "Jokes. You need two jokes a page. That's the rule." Since sitcom scripts are double-spaced, meaning two pages make up a minute, two jokes a page equals one every 15 seconds.

Sitcoms began to change with the advent of a program called *All In the Family*. Prior to the appearance on TV of the household dominated by Carroll O'Connor's wonderful bigot "Archie Bunker," little political or social commentary took place in sitcoms. Currently, sitcoms are often a proving ground for testing societal issues. Roseanne being kissed on the mouth by Mariel Hemingway's lesbian character caused an uproar for more than a week before the episode aired.

When you are starting out, social and political "cutting-edge" commentary is best left to the successful writer/producers. You might be the exception to this advice, so don't let me stop you from writing your heart. Just know that the chances are not good of your writing an episode of a sitcom and selling it to that sitcom. This kind of "over the transom sale" is very rare in television, although one new writer sold three spec scripts to *Cheers* in one season, years before that hit series ended. He subsequently became a staff writer for the show. (A "transom," by the way, is that small window above office doors in older buildings, made so it could be propped open in hot weather. Writers encountering locked doors in old Hollywood would hurl their scripts over the transom in an attempt to get them into the office and read. Actors would do the same with their pictures and resumes.)

If you are serious about writing sitcoms, you must get your hands on some sample scripts. Again, you'll simply have to do research. Check your local bookstores. If they don't have scripts available, call the Los Angeles yellow pages and ask the operator what they have under scripts. You can also contact the Academy of Television Arts & Sciences for information on where to purchase sample scripts.

You should understand that the common practice in breaking into writing sitcoms is that you write a spec script good enough to get you an agent who deals mostly with TV writers. Pick a long-running TV series *that is still on the air* for which to write your spec script. Since people in Hollywood know hit series well, which is to say they know what the characters are like and how they would normally behave and speak, your "take" on the characters and the situation(s) you put them in will tell the person reviewing your script if you: 1) have done your homework; 2) can write authentically; and 3) can write exceptionally well.

I mentioned earlier that, when you are breaking in as a writer in Hollywood or in mainstream adult New York publishing, your first works need to be spectacular to get attention. I emphasize that even further in breaking into writing for television, particularly for sitcoms. With thousands of proven writers available in Hollywood at any given time (the Writers Guild could give you some idea of the numbers), the competition necessitates that you do something that gets you noticed. Think of that spec script of yours as a first job interview where first impressions not only count, but may be your only chance.

So what if you just can't wait to get started? It's a mistake to write a sitcom without reading at least one script from an established show as a reference, but here's what a sitcom script is all about.

On the title page, the show goes first, spaced down at the same place the script title would go on a feature. This is followed by the name of the episode, the by-line, the scene and page indicators, and your representation. Scene and page indicators aid the reader in finding various scenes. Scripts that are filmed or videotaped often go through scads of rewrites, with the different rewrites designated by pages of different-colored paper. Don't worry about that for now—if you sell a script, they'll explain it. Meanwhile, here's what your script should look like.

❖❖❖❖❖❖❖❖❖❖❖❖❖❖❖

CHEERS

"The Last Shot"

Written by

Your Name

SCENE—PAGE NO.

A—1

B—10

C—19

Representation:

The Great Agency (Your Agent)
Address
Phone

❖❖❖❖❖❖❖❖❖❖❖❖❖❖❖

To explain the scene numbers, a sitcom runs about 24 minutes onscreen. The rest of the 30 minutes is taken up by commercials. The page numbers given are where the acts in "The Last Shot" begin.

In the actual script, many things are different than a feature film screenplay or TV movie. The dialogue is double-spaced, for example, and the stage directions (most sitcoms are shot on a studio set, so it's like a stage) are IN CAPS and single-spaced. The beginning of a new act has only about half a page of typing. Don't ask me why—this simply developed over time. The double-spaced dialogue has to do with the fact that TV actors and directors like to tinker with things. With dialogue double-spaced they can more easily jot in their changes.

I hope you're getting an idea now of why I advise you to get copies of scripts to study. You might also invest in an excellent book called *The Writer's Digest Guide to Manuscript Formats* by Dian Dincin Buchman and Seli Groves. I don't always agree with them on all the formats, but it's a well-done guide that will save you time and headaches. Formats and preferences can still, believe it or not, vary slightly from show to show, like they did in the "good old days" mentioned earlier by David Axelrod.

You can also get a scriptwriting software program, as I've suggested, and save yourself the worry. But if you're anxious to get going, here's a rough guide.

❖❖❖❖❖❖❖❖❖❖❖❖❖❖❖❖❖

ACT ONE

FADE IN: (you can put this in or leave it out)

EXT.   SAM'S BAR   HAPPY HOUR (the time)

SAM AND WOODY ARE BEHIND THE BAR, LOOKING GLUM. THE PLACE IS COMPLETELY EMPTY. SAM SADLY POLISHES THE BAR WITH A TOWEL, WHILE WOODY SPITS AND POLISHES A SPOTTY GLASS.

REBECCA COMES THROUGH THE DOOR AND LOOKS AROUND, UTTERLY AMAZED.

REBECCA

What happened, did everybody in Boston die or
something?

WOODY

(AMAZED) How did you know that, Miss Howe?

REBECCA

Sam, am I dreaming or can you explain this empty
bar to me?

SAM

If I explain will you sleep with me?

REBECCA

Oh, I get it. I'm not dreaming, you are!
(PEEVED) Woody, what is going on!?

WOODY

(DREAMILY) It's a long story that began when I
was just a lad, Miss Howe...

FADE TO

Obviously, we're venturing into some sort of dream or flashback
story here, and you can see the setup/payoff joke structure. Actually,
Cheers almost always began with a big joke scene of some kind that
preceded the opening of the show and the theme song. Still, you get
the idea of how a show begins and the format. When you start another act or any new scene, you use the same structure of the blank
top half of the page. An act ends like this:

<u>END OF ACT ONE</u>

One last note on sitcoms. Since there are 24 minutes of onscreen time available for a sitcom, and since the dialogue (which makes up the majority of the script) is double-spaced, most sitcom scripts are in the 48-page range. Don't take my word for it; get some sitcom scripts and study them thoroughly. I can't emphasize that enough.

Where it will seem no one has ever gone before

I could give you examples of other types of TV shows (like soap operas), but I'd be wasting my time and yours. Those one-hour shows like *MacGyver* are written by highly paid, experienced TV writers who mostly all live in the Los Angeles area, or at least in the area where the show is filmed. The format is roughly the same as that for a screenplay or teleplay. Obviously, in a one-hour show you would not have the seven-act structure of the TV movie. If you are interested in writing one-hour TV episodes, you should get your hands on some scripts, write your spec script and shop it around.

To give you an idea of how tough it is selling one-hour scripts or selling yourself as a "green" writer for one-hour shows, here's a personal story. The only spec TV script I ever wrote in my life was for *Star Trek: The Next Generation*. I wrote a controversial script about a civilization that had outlawed sex because of nuclear contamination and mutation. To literally keep life pure, sperm and eggs were combined scientifically; it was a post-nuclear "test tube baby" society that had devolved into one where few knew how the science worked. Science had become religion; if they followed established procedures they could have children. If not, the race ended. The catch was that the daughter of the leader wanted to mate (that is, have a baby normally) with someone from the *Star Trek* crew. The penalty was death, and this caused some problems.

Actually, I never wrote the Star Trek script to sell it to the show; I just wanted to get an invitation to come in and pitch show ideas. I knew someone who worked on the show, who gave the script to the executive producer directly. The script was good enough that it was considered for a long time before it was finally turned down. And it came in handy as an example of my TV writing abilities when it came time to sell my "You Solve It Mystery" novels and get myself attached as a writer and producer when we tried to turn the books into a TV series. So I didn't waste my time. The point of the story is to give you an example of how tough it is to break into writing "one-hour episodic" shows for TV, even when you have an inside track and a fine track record.

The way to Toontown

The animation field is similarly dominated by established writers, but it's one of the places where it is much easier to make your first sale. Since the prices for animated series scripts are half, or less, than those for "prime time" sitcom or other TV scripts, the competition is not as fierce. That's a big reason your chances of breaking into the medium are slightly better. Several of the successful TV writers I know (remember the Paul Haggis story?) got their first break in writing Saturday morning cartoons for companies like Hanna-Barbera, which produced *The Flintstones* and other cartoon hits.

Cartoons are created by far fewer people than films or TV shows are. Likewise, the scripts are somewhat different. In some cases, every single detail must be written out, so that the artist knows what you want drawn. An animation script is akin to a novel, where everything is fully described. Unlike a novel, you normally wouldn't attempt to depict a thought in an animation script, because the only way to show it effectively is by a character looking upward into a "cartoon balloon."

Michael Maurer is one of the prime animation writers in Hollywood. He has the added distinction of being the grandson of legendary funny man Moe Howard, the leader of *The Three Stooges*. About 90 percent of everything Michael writes gets produced, which ain't bad. He was the story editor for the animated versions of *Karate Kid* and *Police Academy,* and for the long-running hit *Scooby Doo*. He has sold more than 200 animated scripts, writing for top animated shows like *Darkwing Duck, Captain Planet* and *Gummi Bears*, and he wrote the series "bible" and pilot for a number of shows. (A TV show "bible" is a full description of the characters, world and basic plot lines of a show.)

Michael has helped a number of writers get successfully started in animation. First, he advises them to study the different genres of animation. Some, such as *X-Men,* are akin to live action shows. Others, such as *The Simpsons,* are basically sitcoms. Warner Brothers cartoon shows use a lot of visual gags, while shows like *Bobby's World* are along the lines of the traditional animated show. Michael got started in the family business by writing some scripts for a cartoon version of the Stooges called *Robotic Stooges,* which his father Norman was producing for Hanna-Barbera. If you think he made it only via family connections, think again. Michael's brother Jeff Scott (who changed his last name because he got tired of spelling it) is also one of the top animation writers, with numerous awards to his credit. Talent runs in this family.

Michael learned to break scripts down, and that's what he advises other writers to do. First, he isolates the genre. If it's "like a live action" show, then the script can be roughly like a feature film script, although the sound effects should be written in. For these, Michael uses the following description: <ROAR OF ENGINES> (or whatever the sound may be). If it's more a cartoon-like show, that means the visual gags must be described fully. You can't simply say "Bobby rides his tricycle through the big house." It would be more like:

❖❖❖❖❖❖❖❖❖❖❖❖❖❖❖❖

EXT. BIG HOUSE—DAY
<WHIRRING OF WHEELS> as BOBBY speeds along the sidewalk away from CAMERA toward the front door of the house. The door opens wide as Bobby BOUNCES across the front step and pedals inside.

INT. BIG HOUSE—DAY
JEEVES the butler stands behind the door, trembling, as Bobby whirs by him. WIDEN to reveal a house full of newly constructed wooden tracks, which resemble a makeshift roller coaster, throughout the expansive rooms of the mansion.

> BOBBY (VO)
> Wow, is this the life or what!?

ON JEEVES, looking petrified by this display of childish danger.

> JEEVES
> Bob-by! Young man, your uncle won't like this!

WIDER TO INCLUDE BOBBY as he catapults off a track through the air.

❖❖❖❖❖❖❖❖❖❖❖❖❖❖❖❖❖❖

Note the spacing (with the beginning action line jammed up against the location line), and how the character line and dialogue are closer to the left margin than in a screenplay. Also, you're writing in camera angles and the like because you are in essence the director of the script—you're providing the "what to draw" direction to the animators, at least. (There are directors of animated shows who oversee the animators and voice-over talent, in case you wondered.) Once again, you need to get your hands on an animation script (or several) and do some study.

The current boom in animation began in 1985, when Disney came out with the first season of *The Gummi Bears*. The quality of that show inspired all animators, and the popularity helped boost a surge of animation activity that shows no signs of decreasing. Despite all the attention, animation is still an area of Hollywood where, Michael says, you can still call a story editor and get in to pitch a show. With scripts going for $2,000 (for 11-minute shows, such as one-half of a *Doug* on Nickelodeon) to $6,000 for a full half-hour, the money isn't bad. How long do the scripts run? About half a minute per page. Michael's "Bad Luck Duck" for the *Darkwing Duck* series, for example, is 49 pages, or roughly 25 minutes. Don't forget, you have to leave room for the commercials.

Michael is a member of a group you can contact to get tips on getting started in animation writing. This wasn't always the case. The group is the Animation Caucus at the Writers Guild of America, West (see the chapter on groups for the address and phone number). Caucus members will tell you which agencies represent animation writers, and offer personal advice to beginning writers. In addition, he offers the following tips to those who want to write for animation:

1. You have to really want to do this kind of writing; it's lots of hard work.
2. Duplication is the key word. You should tape shows you admire, then outline them scene to scene. Read scripts and get to know the show before you try to write for it.
3. You need a great sample script, one that stands out.
4. Find a mentor in the business. Pay attention to the notes you get, and be prepared to do a lot of rewriting.
5. Persist. Be willing to throw away everything you've done on a script if it just isn't going right.

Perhaps not surprisingly, one of the reasons Michael says he's willing to help others get started is that he often needs someone to help him when he has more work than he can handle.

Are you an aspiring animator as well as writer? Contact the Cartoonists Guild, located in Los Angeles. A combination writer/animator (or vice versa) is a very rare breed, however. There hasn't been one who's really made it big since Walt Disney or the team of Hanna-Barbera (*Tom & Jerry, The Flintstones, The Jetsons, Yogi Bear* and a dozen others).

See you in Toontown!

Where the news is

On television you'll see a lot of other kinds of programs as well. How-to videos, "infomercials" and commercials fall under a different heading, as far as I'm concerned. They are made for business and/or advertising purposes, and usually follow the audio-visual script two-column format. Educational films may or may not be written in that format—that will probably depend on what the producer prefers or has grown used to. I'll discuss all these in a later chapter.

The last big area of writing for television is news, which ranges from your local news report to tabloid shows like *Hard Copy* to prime-time hits like *60 Minutes*. They are also commonly referred to as "reality-based programming." To keep things simple, let's discuss how you might be able to break in, which is most likely at your local news station. That's what Steven Weakley did at WSMV-TV in Nashville, Tennessee. Based on the strength of a short story he wrote, he got a job as a writer and eventually became producer for a program that won the Edward R. Murrow Award in 1984 as the best newscast in the United States and Canada. Steven went on to become producer for the KTLA-TV *Morning News,* then senior producer for *Good Day L.A.* on Fox Television's KTTV in Los Angeles. *Good Day L.A.* won an Emmy Award in 1993 as "Best Morning News Program." Staying on the cutting edge, Steven moved on to software giant Microsoft and the world of multimedia.

Formats for writing television news, Steven says, are fairly standardized in structure. "As in all journalism," he related to me, you need to "tell the audience the four W's: When, What, Where and Why.

The key is to write simple but descriptive declarative sentences. Write simply but clearly as if you were describing the story to a friend. The more your words sound like speech instead of prose, the more natural they will seem on the air. Active verbs are preferable to passive ones. The lead should summarize what's new or exciting about the story and intrigue the viewer to listen to the rest of it.

Since video is crucial to television, the aspiring newswriter needs to learn to write to pictures. This is a delicate art; one needs to learn to time the pictures and write to the action so that the words and pictures augment each other onscreen.

Video directions for the show director and tape editor are generally typed in all capital letters on the left side of the script page. While each producer and station have their own idiosyncratic lexicon for these instructions, their basic function is to tell the director when to roll the tape for a voice-over (newscaster reading over pictures), a package (reporter voiced piece prerecorded on tape) or a voice-over with a sound bite (a prerecorded piece of sound on tape, like a witness description of a murder). The most common abbreviations are, in order, TAKE VO (voice-over) and TAKE SOT (for reporter voiced piece or sound bite)."

Steven also offers advice on news computer programs:

"While there are a variety of oddball computer programs and even primitive typewriters still in use in some markets," he said, "the dominant programs that are designed for TV news production are BASYS, NEWSTAR and NEWSMAKER. These are basically all simple DOS-based word processor and timing programs."

Should you buy one of these programs? Not according to Steven. He says the news industry is moving to Windows-based word processors "as they creep like reluctant dinosaurs to the latest in technology." But he does advise that you learn one of the above programs, if you want to be a news writer. "Training on any of these systems will be a real advantage to the new job seeker and is available at many universities, or training manuals may be acquired from the companies who designed the programs. One of the best recommendations that you can give to a news manager is that you already know how to operate the computer system in use at their particular station. And one of the most arduous tasks for your prospective employer is teaching you how to use their system. Usually, there are no formal training programs or trainers and one is thrown into the frying pan after an hour or so of instruction on the program. Excellent books on news writing for television are available at most bookstores and libraries."

If you think the competition is fierce, you might not be correct. "Surprisingly," Steven said, "many news writers, even in large markets, are poor writers." After sharing his thoughts about the news business with me, Steven also showed me "an abbreviated but illustrative" sample anchor voice-over script, which follows.

❖❖❖❖❖❖❖❖❖❖❖❖❖❖❖❖

SIMPSON ESCAPE (This is the slugline assigned to story by producer)
04/04/95

(ANCHOR'S NAME)

	O.J. SIMPSON FLED FROM A FRIEND'S HOUSE TODAY AND LED POLICE ON A WILD FREEWAY CHASE ACROSS SOUTHERN CALIFORNIA.
TAKE VO	(ANCHOR VOICE OVER)

SIMPSON JUMPED INTO A BRONCO WITH HIS EX-TEAMMATE AL COWLINGS AND ESCAPED SHORTLY BEFORE HE WAS SUPPOSED TO SURRENDER HIMSELF TO POLICE ON MURDER CHARGES.

THE DAY-LONG CHASE RIVETED THE NATION ON TELEVISION AND PARALYZED L.A. FREEWAYS. COMMUTERS CHEERED FROM OVERPASSES AND MILLIONS OF OFFICE WORKERS STOPPED THEIR WORK TO WATCH.

SIMPSON REPORTEDLY POINTED A GUN AT HIS HEAD AND THREATENED TO KILL HIMSELF, WHILE PURSUING COPS PAVED A CLEAR PATH FOR THE LOW-SPEED CHASE THAT ENDED AT O.J.'S HOME.

SIMPSON FINALLY GAVE HIMSELF UP TO POLICE OUTSIDE HIS ROCKINGHAM HOME IN BRENTWOOD AFTER HOURS OF TENSE NEGOTIATION WITH SWAT TEAMS.

THE FORMER HEISMAN TROPHY WINNER FINALLY GAVE UP PEACEFULLY AFTER BEING ALLOWED TO SPEAK BRIEFLY WITH HIS FAMILY.

THE MAN MILLIONS ONCE WATCHED FROM
THE SIDELINES AS A RUNNING BACK AND A
SPORTSCASTER WAS LED AWAY IN HANDCUFFS.
HE IS ACCUSED OF KILLING HIS EX-WIFE
NICOLE BROWN SIMPSON AND HER FRIEND RON
GOLDMAN AT HER BRENTWOOD CONDO THREE
DAYS AGO.

TRT:30

❖❖❖❖❖❖❖❖❖❖❖❖❖❖❖❖❖

("TRT" stands for total running time of the tape.)

The script as you see it is exactly as Steve presented it to me. Again, be warned that script formats might vary from station to station, but if you write a sample script with the above guidelines and know one of the word processing programs mentioned, your chances of getting a shot as a news writer are greatly enhanced.

I also asked Steven where writing for the news could lead, and this is what he told me:

"Breaking into television news writing is most easily done in smaller television markets where the standards and the pay are lower. Take journalism courses in college extension programs or major in mass communications if you are a student. Many television stations offer paid or unpaid internships and this is the golden path to employment. Hang around as long as you can as an intern, do the dirty work no one else wants to do, be ambitious but not overly pushy, and when you have made yourself indispensable ask for a job.

"Other courses of action involve more *chutzpah* and chicanery. Write some sample scripts and send a resume to the news director of the television station in your town. Emphasize your experience, enthusiasm and experiences as a writer. Beg, crawl and cajole until he or she agrees to grant you an interview. You can then graduate from writing to actually producing the show, and even become an executive producer, news director or reporter yourself, given your talents and the size and upward mobility of the market. Salaries in small markets typically pay as little as $15,000 a year, while a news writer in Los Angeles or New York can earn as much as $50,000 to $75,000 annually."

Which isn't bad, if you have a nose for the news and a desire to offer "breaking stories" to the public.

Across the "vast wasteland"

So, is television awful, terrible and mind-numbing? Surely it can be, but so can anything, taken to excess. I prefer to think that although I grew up with a "TV baby sitter" for a number of hours after school each day, I still managed to come out all right. So did my younger brothers, and I don't feel that my young children's minds have been unalterably ruined by hours of watching Disney videos over and over again (their choice). It seems to me that, for all the bad effects of television, people have enough of a self-correcting mechanism to know when to turn it off.

It used to be you had to take what you were given—namely, "free" network TV. Now, with the explosion of satellite, cable and computer technology, people have so many choices it's hard to know where to begin, even if it often seems like Robin Williams was right when he said, "What do you know? Fifty-two channels and nothing on!"

In the last few years, coffee houses have proliferated across the United States. People get together, go out, watch live performances, drink coffee and talk. Even characters on popular sitcoms like *Seinfeld* do this. Why? I think it's because no one can be coerced into watching a "boob tube" (television) all their waking hours. When so many people look at a computer screen all day long, the last thing they want to do after work is sit in front of another small screen. It's my prediction that the more people there are using computers, the less people will watch the old standard network television formats. There are only so many computer games you can play and only for so long, before you go into mental meltdown. People nowadays watch only what specifically appeals to them. This is "narrowcasting" as opposed to the old "broadcasting."

Maybe I'm wrong about this, but you'd better hope I'm not. The more choices there are, the more writers will be needed to write that programming. Which makes me think that, all things considered, television is indeed terrific. Used correctly, it connects societies, informs and entertains, in a way the world has never seen before. If you write for any form of television, I just ask that you try to keep the welfare of the world in mind. As you've no doubt seen on television, ours is an increasingly smaller world.

Chapter 12

❖❖❖❖❖❖❖❖❖❖❖❖❖❖❖❖

Right on radio

Theater of the mind

"The main difference between radio and television," Susan Steinberg told me, "is that with television the picture can augment the words. In radio, all you have is words. With radio you're painting a picture on the canvas of the mind."

As simple and obvious as that might seem, no truer words could describe what you need to know when writing for radio, and Sue should know. A radio veteran now working in television, as music director for KMET in Los Angeles she created the "Breakfast with the Beatles" show that ran every Sunday morning for years and made its host, Deirdre O'Donahue, famous. Radio is special, Sue told me. No matter how far you get away from it, there is an affinity to working in radio that remains. "Radio people" can spot each other across a crowded room, she claims. "There's just something about it."

Why? The immediacy of radio, and the intimacy. Sue cited an example. When musician John Lennon was killed, TV news crews scrambled to find file footage of Lennon and snippets of music. With radio, all anyone at a station had to do was reach up on a shelf and pull down a Lennon or Beatles record. A few bars of music and the awful, fateful news of Lennon's assassination, and the point was made. Bloody pictures and wailing fans weren't necessary.

"Think about it," Sue said, "when there's an emergency what's the first thing you do? You turn on the radio."

A good place to get started

The first script I ever sold was a radio script, to a nationally syndicated science-fiction drama series called *Alien Worlds*. It was my mother's generation that grew up huddled around the radio listening to dramas like *The Shadow* and comedies like *Fibber McGee and Molly,* but I knew enough of the shows to feel fondly toward them.

I came to Los Angeles to pursue an entertainment dream. What I didn't know was that I could have started right where I came from, in North Texas, had I started in radio. I learned that from Susan Steinberg. Let me explain by capsulizing her story. It's as good an example of successfully climbing the show business ladder as any I've ever come across.

Sue was a student at San Francisco State, majoring in broadcasting. The station she'd grown up listening to was KSAN, a major outlet owned by Metromedia Broadcasting. It occurred to her that the station might have an internship program, so she inquired, telling them she was willing to work for nothing, just to learn. They didn't have an intern program, but she persisted, telling them she could get college credit if they'd let her come aboard. So they considered it.

Meanwhile, she went back to the college and told them that KSAN might take her on as an intern. Could she get credit for the work?

The college wasn't sure. It had never been done. So they turned her down, good academics that they were. But KSAN took her on after getting an okay from the national office in New Jersey, and Sue was in heaven. She worked for nothing, but the "perks" were tremendous. Like the time she helped rocker Tom Petty pick out music to play on a show, or "all the vinyl [free record albums] you could eat."

She wrote a thesis about her experience, and got extra college credit after all. And the next year, interning at KSAN became a course at San Francisco State. Ten years later, after working at KMEL in San Francisco and the RKO Radio Network, Sue moved on to KMET in Los Angeles, a station which was also owned by Metromedia. She had to laugh when KMET asked her to do something special—start an intern program. Could she do it? Maybe, she told them. After all, she'd been the very first intern Metromedia had ever hired.

Her secret was simple. "No job was too small," she confided to me. "And there was plenty to do, because radio stations were relatively cheap. You could buy them cheap, sell them cheap, and staffs were not as large as they are these days."

Will it play in Cleveland?

Sue first began to look for other horizons when the program director at KMET wouldn't let her, as music director, program David Lee Roth's version of "California Girls."

"It didn't test well in Cleveland," she was told.

"Cleveland!" she exclaimed. "This is L.A., this is local boy David Lee Roth, formerly of that small local band Van Halen. Maybe you've heard of them? Who cares about Cleveland?"

Spoken by someone who "grew up" working for radio stations in the large cities of San Francisco and Los Angeles. In the majority of the United States, staffs at stations are still small, and the opportunities for someone who wants to break in like Sue still exist. The "I'll do anything" (within reason and the limits of the law) attitude is still applicable, as I learned from disc jockey Dave "Sandman" Barravechia, who holds forth at station WZLE in—can you guess?—Cleveland.

In these days of talk radio domination of the airwaves, there isn't much room for anyone who doesn't aspire to be an "on-air personality," but that doesn't mean programs aren't scripted. You can use your writing talents to get started in radio, possibly writing Public Service Announcements, or "PSAs." You might also try writing commercials for your local station.

"At WZLE we have scripts for PSAs, scripts used in commercial production, as well as promos," Dave informed me. "At our station, our production director is in charge of everything that has to do with our commercials. Sometimes our salespeople write scripts for commercials because they know better what their clients want to say. As far as PSAs and promos, our program director picks out which events to promote."

What's the secret of a good radio script? Dave had the answer for that as well.

"When a script is written to be spoken over the air, the more succinct the better," he said. "They are as short as they can be while getting the point across. It takes a lot of practice and training to be able to use a few words and get a big message across. If someone wanted to get into this area of radio, I would suggest that the best training they could get would be from any radio journalism classes they could enroll in." He offers a word of caution, though. "It's hard to make a living in radio," Dave says. "You have to develop several skills in order to be successful. Only a small percentage make it to the big-time in radio."

There is no set format for radio scripts; they vary from station to station. If you wanted to write a sample script to show the program director or production director, just remember to make it a large type-face and at least double-spaced, so it's very readable.

If you write a sample script and want someone to see it, you should already have some idea of where to take it, just from what Dave Barravechia mentioned. If you don't, just drive down to your local station, go to the reception desk (if they have one) and ask. Radio stations are still, by and large, relaxed operations, even in larger markets. In the radio shows I do on a continuing basis promoting my books, I have yet to encounter anything but a friendly atmosphere.

If you want to write for radio in a larger market, there is also hope for you. Do you think Howard Stern makes up all those loony things you hear on his show?

Even Rush Limbaugh isn't clever enough to do it all himself.

"Howard Stern even talks about his writers," Sue Steinberg says. "All those wonderful bits that seem like they're so spontaneous and ad-libbed are well-rehearsed. If someone is trying to break into writing for radio, they should write bits, and it's usually topical bits. What's going on in the news, what's happening politically. If you're in Cleveland and you know the Rock 'n' Roll Hall of Fame is there, write about it, because that personalizes it. It's knowing your market, which goes back to being in touch with the listener, that intimacy thing."

Back to those golden days of yesteryear

Is radio drama dead forever? Maybe not. At the Gene Autry Museum in Los Angeles, original radio Westerns have been broadcast in the last couple of years. With the parts read by well-known actors like Bruce Boxleitner and Melissa Gilbert, the shows have live audiences, a studio band, and are broadcast live. There's a wonder and—what else can I say but—"intimacy" to it that's like nothing else. Watching *The Tonight Show* live isn't as good, and I've done both. The actor's expressions, the timing of the band and the sound effects created by the "Foley artist" all make for a tremendous evening of entertainment unlike anything else.

In major markets like Los Angeles and New York, radio dramas are a regular item. It might not be the same in your locality, but who's to say you couldn't put something together? A piano player, someone doing the sound effects, some actors who can deliver lines well and a microphone are all you need.

Except for a script, of course, which is your job. Looking for a format to use? The format I gave you for a stage play will work just fine, with one big difference—SOUND EFFECTS. There are no stage directions in radio scripts, only sound directions. Put them in CAPS so they won't be missed when the Foley artist starts figuring out what tools of the trade to use to make the right sound at the appropriate moment.

Who knows where you can go with a good radio script? Why, you might even come up with a title like *A Prairie Home Companion,* talk about a fictional place named Lake Wobegon, have yodelers and banjo players on the same show, and get someone interested in listening. Call up a guy named Garrison Keillor at National Public Radio and see if he thinks it'll work.

In radio, the theater of the mind, anything is possible.

The last word

If you aspire to do more than just write radio scripts, or write and produce radio shows, such as becoming an on-air radio personality, you could also start just about anywhere. While you're working on the proper intonations of voice and delivery, do yourself a favor and get a subscription to *Talkers* magazine. It is a trade publication covering the explosive area of broadcasting that seems to be at every other stopping point on the radio dial these days. You can't find *Talkers* on your local newsstand—it's subscription only—but you can reach them at: P.O. Box 60781, Longmeadow, MA 01116, phone (413) 567-3189.

Just how far can you go, starting in radio? All the way to the top, and not just in radio. Consider bestselling author Mary Higgins Clark. She had been fascinated by radio dramas as a child; after losing her husband she turned to writing for radio to support her family. The four-minute programs she created were broadcast five times a week on 500 stations, hosted by major celebrities. If you don't think there's room for such a program these days, you haven't heard Paul Harvey lately.

If you're looking for a place to get your writing career started in a big way, try your local radio station. I'll be interested to hear how you do.

Chapter 13

❖❖❖❖❖❖❖❖❖❖❖❖❖❖❖❖

Business bucks, bucks, bucks

Why should a chapter on business writing follow one on radio? Because they go hand in hand. Radio depends on its sponsors more heavily than any medium except "free" television, and vice versa.

If you have ever worked in a corporate atmosphere, it probably shouldn't surprise you that business writing is where the most money is spent on writers. The amount of copy written for advertising overwhelms us all on a daily basis. If you don't want to be a copywriter, how about penning a business plan, a year-end report, a newsletter, a technical manual, an audio-visual script or even a corporate speech? If you can write well, you can make a five-figure or even six-figure income. That is, if you know how and where to market your valuable services.

The key to the kingdom

Stev and Mary Donev are a good example of a successful business writing team. They've done everything from year-end reports (both written and video) to scripts for shows at theme parks. In comparing notes about writing for businesses, I found we share a similar approach. Their secret is they don't approach a job as writers.

"We're problem-solvers," Stev told me.

"And business people first," Mary added. "Then we're writers."

The basic problem each business has, Stev explained to me, was that no one there can do the job, so they hire freelancers. He and Mary told me about one instance when they were contacted by a tractor manufacturer.

"So what do you folks know about tractors?" the CEO asked them in the first meeting.

"Nothing," Stev replied quickly. "That's your job."

"We're writers," Mary told the executive. "You're the expert on tractors. You tell us what your problem is and we'll figure out how to put it in writing the way you want."

No, they didn't offend the man. They got the job. Remember what I told you earlier about writing taking the reader or viewer some place that he or she cannot go, has not gone or hasn't seen from your unique perspective? That principle still applies in writing for business. You might not smile when you think of Alka-Seltzer, but the phrase "Plop, plop, fizz, fizz, oh what a relief it is" will put a smile on your face. I'd be willing to bet that the copywriter who came up with that had the problem of "How do we sell Alka-Seltzer in a new and fresh way?"

In interviewing Stev and Mary about their decades of experience writing for businesses, I found that no matter what the business was, no matter what kind of personalities they encountered, there were some things that kept coming up, time after time. Combining their tips with my own experience, I sketched out an approach that has worked for them and for me:

Don't expect to get the job overnight, but be prepared to do it overnight, once called. Lasting relationships are cultivated over time. It was five years between a couple of jobs I did for one company; it just worked out that way because of my schedule and their need for my services. Stev and Mary Donev told me of a job they got writing scripts for a major theme park attraction that came after a year of Mary calling the company and offering their services once a month. They never got so much as a returned phone call. Then one day a call came and they were asked "Could you be here at 2?" They wrote the script in a week and it was performed as soon as it was finished. That's not an uncommon occurrence in the world of big business.

Know your audience. If you are meeting with the head of an organization, do your research. If possible, find out what publications the organization puts out, what kinds of ads it places in newspapers and magazines (if any), and how the business is doing. Any new client appreciates someone who is prepared and ready. The story about the Donevs and the theme park is a good example.

Isolate the problem. After you get down to business, find out what it is your client is trying to accomplish. It may be obvious, or it may not be. Sometimes, the client won't know exactly what it is he or she wants. You might even encounter someone who will say, "So what is it that you can do for me?" right away. Others will know specifically what it is they need, but don't know how or don't have the time to accomplish it.

Be flexible. If you come up with some ideas, don't marry them. Be willing to throw it all away. If you are billing by the hour, it won't matter, anyway. Don't let your pride get hurt if one of your precious ideas gets discarded. On the other hand, be willing to stand up for something that you think will work. Maybe the client simply isn't seeing what you see, and can be convinced. Still, it's their business that is on the line. Truth be known, your business is, too. Word-of-mouth is a large part of Stev and Mary's business, which has grown steadily over the years because of pleased clients who tell other businesses about the fine job the Donevs have done. People who are flexible and friendly are a lot more fun, and people remember them.

Look for the hidden agenda. A client may be embarrassed by the job done by an in-house employee who blew it. Stev and Mary told me about one client who wanted to present a new product on video. An employee who thought he was the next Spielberg hired a couple of actors and shot a video, which was shown to the Donevs without the employee present. It was an awful, boring 15 minutes worth of "talking heads." One actor explained the new product to another, with the "student" looking on wide-eyed and asking obvious, leading questions. Doing a new, effective video was the obvious problem. The hidden agenda was doing it without embarrassing the company's employee. So they used the basic story of the video and presented it in a more engaging fashion. Thus everyone won and the Donevs did not make any enemies.

Don't talk money until you've worked out the job. Some clients may ask you that immediately. Usually, this means they have limited funds to work with. Most companies budget out their year in January, which makes that a good time to promote for new clients. If you're being asked to do a job in November and you're asked how much you charge up front, it could mean that the funds to pay you are limited. On the other hand, it could mean that the person dealing with you needs to get some figures in order to report back to a higher-up what the job is going to cost, at least roughly. Don't hesitate to quote your price once you've gone over the job and established a rapport, however. If you seem uncertain when talking money, that can easily be seen as personal uncertainty about your abilities to perform.

What should you charge? Naturally, it will vary from region to region. The Donevs have clients all over the nation, but most of their jobs are for people in Southern California, where they live. The non-L.A. clients, they told me, pay only about half of what clients in Los Angeles will pay, but they're usually much more relaxed and easy to work with, which provides its own compensation.

Here's a good shortcut to determine your rates. Get the latest edition of *Writer's Market* and look for the chapter on rates. It's usually called "How Much Should I Charge?" or something like that. After you read that and have an index, look in the yellow pages. See if you can find anyone listed under advertising, copywriting, public relations or any other listing applicable to what you want to write. Call them, pretending to be a potential client, and ask what they charge. If they say, "Well, that depends on the job" (and they probably will), be ready to tell them about a specific job you have in mind. A 48-page full-color catalog, for example. Again, this will depend on what you want to write, so you'll have to figure this out. If you can find several people in the phone book who might answer your question, call them all and compare notes. Then compare that to the suggested rates in *Writer's Market,* and you'll have a good idea of what to charge.

If you can't find anyone in the phone book, that's to your advantage. That means your client can't find anyone, either, so he or she probably doesn't know what the "going rate" is, until you reveal it.

If you can't figure out what rate to ask for, see if you can find something listed in *Writer's Market* that is *like* the job you want to do. It's unlikely you can find your area of writing listed, however.

The requirements of business

In the headlong rush to get products to market and ace out the competition, corporate executives usually don't have the time to think through the minute details of what they present to the public. That's why advertising agencies make so much money. Some executives are generally nervous as well, which is why they rarely entrust their entire company communications to a single person or to a team of persons. This often works to their detriment and leads to financial depletion, which gets passed on to the consumer. Let me give you some examples:

I was once hired by a major Los Angeles bank to write a manual to be used by their executives to schedule employee work hours during the 1984 Summer Olympic Games. The air in Los Angeles was relatively free from smog, and traffic on the freeways was manageable, even during rush hour. Why? Because all major businesses staggered their hours. Some banks would open at 6 in the morning and close at 2 p.m., for example, while others would open at 11 a.m. and stay open until 7 p.m. My job was to tell the execs of the bank how to figure this out. I was given a computer study that had taken a year to compile. I had to learn the bank's in-house word processing program to write the manual. In all, I spent three months on the bank payroll and came up with a decent manual. After the bank execs got through tearing apart what I'd done, they ended up using only two pages of what I'd written, and they were happy with my work!

Another time, I worked a full quarter for a major health food company, running a marketing department. Supervising three other writers and a large art department, I got out a monthly magazine, a monthly newsletter, several brochures, a new company business plan and several translations of the new corporate video. In addition, I wrote all the collateral materials for the yearly convention of 2,000-plus people, hired the event coordinator, picked the major talent (Marie Osmond), wrote the program for the convention, supervised the events and wrote and produced the multimedia slide show presentation. Money was no object when it came to putting on the yearly convention, and there's the rub.

The new corporate video, already finished by an expensive outside advertising agency at the time I came on board, cost $350,000 for a 20-minute program. Since the company was operating in 10 foreign countries, it had to be translated into versions usable in those countries, including an "Australian English" version that wouldn't offend the distributors "down under." I hired a trusted associate to direct that work (under my supervision). Meanwhile, among all my other duties, I wrote the slide show that was the opening presentation of the convention. The distributors from around the world wanted it, instead of the new video, to use in selling the company's products! It cost less than $40,000. The last time I inquired, more than 100,000 copies of the slide show, converted into video, had been sold to distributors.

Does this give you an idea of how businesses throw money around? It should. Any freelance writer should know that most businesses have a good deal of money to spend, particularly at the first of the year when their budgets are approved, and just before major company events like stockholder meetings and yearly conventions. With that in mind, let's delve into some of the products you might produce for a business.

The corporate speech

When you think of speeches made by former President George Bush, is there any phrase that comes to mind? Chances are good it's "a thousand points of light." When you think of President John Kennedy, do you hear "Ask not what your country can do for you, but what you can do for your country"? These phrases added to their speakers' fame, but they were both written by well-paid speech writers. Similarly, few corporate heads write their own speeches. Instead, they find the best writers possible to put words in their mouths. As an example, Emmy award-winning David Axelrod has written speeches for executives at companies like Dow Jones and Gallo Wineries.

The first freelance writing money I ever made, other than for articles, was $75 for a speech I wrote for a corporate "roast." There is no set format for a speech, and each person you write a speech for can vary considerably, but I can give you a few tips:

1. Double- or triple-space the text, and print it in large type. (If you have a computer with scaleable fonts, the last part is easy.) The extra spacing gives the exec room to make notes. Large type makes the speech easy to read. If the company is sophisticated enough to use a TelePrompTer during the speech, they'll still probably want a printed version of the text.

2. Spend a lot of time determining who the executive's audience is, including details about specific individuals. For example, for the "roast" speech, I dug up "inside information" about the person being roasted from his friends in the company.

3. Once you know the audience, get to know the speaker. Ask him or her about speeches given in the past, what worked and what didn't. The speaker might volunteer this information without your asking, but probably won't. Do your best to get him or her relaxed and in your confidence, and you'll get to the heart of the matter. You'll cut past the superficiality and find out what truly motivates this person to do a good job. If you can get to the core of the speaker's passion and then translate that into a speech, chances are you'll have a lasting client.

4. Be prepared to rewrite endlessly, but don't give up your integrity. If you've worked and worked a speech but the executive still isn't satisfied, even though you think it's a fine speech, it might be time for you to hold your ground and state the reasons why you think the speech is fine. You're hired to do a job, but you shouldn't be required to be a doormat for anyone's ego (or anxiety).

5. Draw from the masters. It's no accident that good speeches contain quotes from leading figures of history. If you've never heard of *Bartlett's Quotations* or similar books, you'd better spend some time at the library before you attempt to write a speech. Knowing that author Kurt Vonnegut called New York City "Skyscraper National Park" (in his 1976 novel *Slapstick*) can not only bring a laugh but make the speaker appear to be well-read and humorous, thereby putting his audience into better rapport as he launches into the important parts of his talk.

How much should you charge for a speech? Again, it will vary by the market in which you live, but you can always refer to *Writer's Market*.

The company newsletter

As the use and affordability of desktop publishing increases, there is little excuse for any company, no matter how small, not to offer a newsletter to clients and prospective clients. The opportunity this offers freelancers is that the majority of people who run companies don't have a clue when it comes to laying out or writing a newsletter, computer or otherwise. If you're looking to simply write a company newsletter and not to also create it via desktop publishing, you'll probably be left in the dust. There are too many people out there who do it all.

So get over the "I'm just a writer" syndrome quickly, if you want to do newsletters. If you own a computer and can learn a program as common as WordPerfect or Microsoft Word, you can put together a professional newsletter, using ready-made newsletter templates that come with the programs. If you're a little more adventurous and learn programs like PageMaker and Corel Draw, you'll be able to create a publication rivaling those of Fortune 500 companies. Other than that, the written content of a company newsletter varies little from what you would write in an article. The important point is that you maintain a cheery, "good news" type of attitude, usually in a conservative tone.

To build a good business of doing newsletters for companies, I'd advise you to have the following:

- A computer with plenty of memory and a good desktop publishing program.
- A good laser printer.
- A color printer.
- A scanner (for incorporating photos and artwork into the newsletter).
- A good fax machine.
- A decent 35mm camera and the ability to take good pictures.

Just remember that your job is to make people feel good about the company. My best example of this is my family's *Press Gang* newsletter, which we send out on a regular basis. It's not hard for people to think about hiring me as a writer, because I continually keep them abreast of what I'm doing. Inevitably, when someone calls me about a job, it begins with "I read in your newsletter...."

Newsletters are their own separate art. You'll find lots of advice on them in your local library, and they are often a good way to develop stable business for yourself as a freelancer. If you've never done one, use your computer to develop one, then send that out to prospective clients as an example of what you can do. You'll get some business.

The company brochure

Just as the most common word processing programs offer newsletter templates, many have brochure templates as well. That aside, you should view a brochure as a continuing revelation. The cover should intrigue the reader, either with a statement or a posed question. "Why are Krazy Kornflakes the best on the market?" for example. "Because Chucky Jackson says they are!" exclaims the copy inside the next fold, which is under a picture of a grinning 8-year-old happily eating his corn flakes. "And Chucky isn't alone," leads off the paragraph at the top of the next fold, which launches into a description of a bar graph comparison of kids across the country who sampled all the leading brands of corn flakes. The last fold of this imaginary brochure might describe, in confident detail, the solid history of the Krazy Kornflakes company, a family-owned business dedicated to happy, healthy youngsters everywhere since it was founded 50 years ago by Korny K. Krazy. You get the idea.

The good thing about writing brochures is that they're done a lot more often than newsletters. You don't have to be able to create them via desktop publishing, but why not? Don't limit yourself to being a mere copywriter and your bank account will also be less limited.

The year-end report

It used to be that a year-end report was done only by high-paid advertising agencies or in-house communications departments. That changed with desktop publishing. These reports are created for the benefit of stockholders, both existing and prospective. These days, they come in two forms: in print and on video. Like newsletters, they are an art in themselves; they present the full corporate image to the public. Therefore, they are scrutinized to the minutest detail. Since they vary from company to company, and since you'll be competing with big advertising companies who want the business, I won't attempt to give you any kind of standard format here.

Instead, I'll offer some common sense. If you want to do a year-end report, contact a company you have your eye on and ask for a copy of its latest report. Study it and see if you can find ways to improve upon it. If you can, write out those improvements, be it better copy or better ideas or both. If possible, lay out a sample page with your desktop publishing equipment.

If it's a video year-end report, you'll need to know video format, which we'll get into later.

I don't know anyone who makes a living doing company year-ends, but I'm sure there are people out there who do. I would advise you to learn about them as merely one more piece of the business writing pie.

The business plan

You can buy software that walks you through creating a business plan. Barring that, if you're writing one for a company and have never done one, head for the library. If the company doesn't have one and doesn't offer you a sample of the kind of business plan they want, they are as clueless as you are. A good source of information is the Small Business Administration, 1441 L Street NW, Washington, DC 20416, phone (202) 653-6832. You can also call its answer desk at (800) 368-5855, or check the phone book for an SBA office near you. Since complete books have been written on writing business plans, I won't attempt that here.

The business guide

Businesses that depend on independent distributors, such as Amway, for their marketing have business guides that lay out the ground rules for each individual representative of the company. These are policies that have been developed over time and include "boiler plate" legal language that protects the company in case a distributor goofs. The company can always claim, "Well, it was right there in the business guide and the distributor signed a statement agreeing to uphold same." To give you some idea of the content of such a guide, here's a sample of the chapter headlines of one I worked on:

   I. Basic Principles
  II. Eligibility to Become a [Company Name] Distributor
 III. Rights Granted
 IV. Independent Business Relationship

V. Compliance by [Company Name] Distributors with All Applicable Income Tax, and Other Sales Laws

VI. Authorized Sales Region/International Business

VII. Pricing

VIII. Representations Made by [Company Name] Distributors

IX. Labeling and Packaging

X. Advertising and Use of Name

XI. Cancellation, Resignation, Termination, Death or Incapacity

XII. Excuse for Nonperformance [This was basically a disclaimer saying neither the company nor any distributor was responsible for delays and failures in performance caused by circumstances beyond their control, such as strikes, labor difficulties, riot, war, fire, death, curtailment of supplies or government decrees.]

XIII. Assignment and Delegation [This section explained how no distributor could assign or delegate his or her rights as a distributor without the prior written consent of the company.]

XIV. Limited Warranty [Covered what the company would exchange or refund and what it would not.]

XV. Infringement [A statement that the company had not infringed on any patents, trademarks, trade names or copyrights.]

XVI. Copyrighted Materials [A statement that all company literature and programs were copyrighted and could not be duplicated without written consent of the company.]

XVII. Exclusive Rules [A statement that the Business Guide, Distributor Application and Agreement, "and the instruments and documents referred to herein constitute the entire understanding of the parties with respect to the subject matter." Also, that the Business Guide and Distributor Agreement could be amended at any time by any instrument in writing signed by an officer of the company.]

XVIII. Waiver [It follows, in full.]
The failure of [the company] to exercise any rights stated in the Business Guide, Distributor Application Agreement or to insist upon strict compliance by a

distributor with any obligation or provision thereunder shall not constitute a waiver of [the company's] right to demand exact compliance therewith. Waiver by [the company] can only be effected in writing by an authorized officer of [the company].

I hope this gives you an idea of why business guides are written under legal supervision. While I worked for the company, I got constant complaints from distributors that this guide was impossible to comprehend. That's the way the in-house company lawyer wanted it. In trying to make the guide more readable and understandable, however, I encountered something that opened my eyes to corporate politics. Despite everything else I had to do during my three-month stay to get the company through its annual convention, I was also asked to supervise the revision of the business guide. Then I hit a brick wall named Cynthia, the in-house lawyer. It seemed that it took forever to get her legal stamp of approval on anything, much less a lengthy document like the business guide.

I'd advise you to stay away from things like business guides. It won't be worth the headache. A business plan is completely different. Leave the legal writing to the lawyers.

The personnel manual

Any company with more than a dozen employees should have a personnel manual. Don't count on the director of personnel to write it. Personnel manuals handle two basic areas for a company: 1) a description of company regulations and practices for the benefit of employees; 2) something in writing to fall back on, should a supervisor need to discipline an employee.

Will most employees read a personnel manual? Probably not, but that won't stop companies from having them written. There is no established standard for personnel manuals, but all of the following should be covered in detail:

- Basic company policies, such as physical exams or drug tests required for employment.
- Work hours, overtime, holidays, vacations, sick days, personal days, jury duty and leaves of absence.

- Salaries and benefits, performance reviews, merit increases, educational assistance and severance pay.
- Profit-sharing and pension plans.
- An equal opportunity statement.
- Safety regulations and advice.
- A confidentiality clause regarding company events.
- Causes for discipline, discipline guidelines and grievance relief.
- Any other information relevant to that particular company.

Again, much of this is the domain of lawyers. The list is to give you some idea of what a personnel manual contains. How much should you charge? I advise you to stay away from a flat fee. Because you'll very likely be dealing with lawyers to get a final approved version, do what they do and charge by the hour.

The technical manual

I'm sure you've had some experience with a technical manual. That book that attempts to tell you how WordPerfect works, perhaps, or the booklet that came with your VCR. Well, someone has to write those things, and that's where freelancers come in. I've done a few of them, including the first one for Miracle Ear, an almost invisible hearing aid. No, I didn't write a manual on how to use the hearing aid. I wrote a manual for the Franchise Consulting Group in Los Angeles, which had contracted with Miracle Ear to develop a manual explaining to new franchise owners how to set up and promote their hearing aid business. I did not write the "boiler plate" legal language of the manual, just the step-by-step "now you do this" type of thing, which came from my interviewing people in the company.

How do you format a technical manual? There's no standard. Just try to make it as simple as possible, and write in a language that is suitable for someone with a fifth-grade U.S. education. This is no slam against owners of hearing aid franchises—writing for the fifth-grade is the accepted standard "language" for most business writing. For any of the business manuals I've written, I've tried to approach the problem as if I were the recipient.

Don't assume readers know, or can logically figure out, anything. Take it step by step in the logical progression of use of the item or operation of the business.

Sometimes, this approach can drive you crazy. When I wrote a manual about the operation of an indoor amusement park for kids, I never saw the park. I had lots of audio tapes from the various personnel at the park, who operated different parts of the operation on a daily basis. I organized their advice into a manual, which was then looked over by the owner, who corrected what I'd written, and I continued to massage the writing until everyone was satisfied. The manual became the "bible" for all other franchises of the park around the country, although I never set foot in a single one!

One drawback you'll run into if you try to get into the technical manual business, is the problem of degrees. If you see an ad for "Technical Writer" in your local newspaper, most likely they'll ask for someone with years of experience. You might be able to convince them you can write anything and get the job, but in some cases, if you don't have specific technical know-how, you'll be up a creek. For example, if you have to write a manual on the operation of a new piece of high-tech equipment, but cannot read an electronic schematic, you're wasting everyone's time.

If, on the other hand, you have a degree in electrical engineering and can also put words on paper in a way that explains complex things in a simple, straightforward manner, you may be able to make a very good living as a highly paid technical writer.

And sometimes you don't even need a degree. A case in point is Andy Shafran, whom I ran across on CompuServe. Andy interviewed me one night for a book he was doing about (can you guess?) CompuServe. What struck me about Andy was that he was being paid to write the book while he was still in college! How did he get such a job? I'll let him explain it:

"About a year ago I saw a public job posting on CompuServe for a new author to write an entry-level *Lotus Notes* book. I called, faxed my resume and was generally annoying to the acquisitions editors at Que [the publisher] until they finally said, 'Enough already, take the damn contract and write the book.' It wasn't exactly like that, but I was persistent. I was very careful to meet all of my deadlines. A month after the project was complete, I called them up and reminded my editor I was interested in writing more. They shuffled me some smaller contracts, which became progressively bigger and bigger.

"Three months ago, someone at Alpha Books (they work in the same building as Que) called me up and said he had heard about me. He wanted to know if I would write *The Complete Idiot's Guide to CompuServe*. It was a book that paid royalties (my first one), so I jumped on it. I now have too many writing offers to handle. Since I am a full-time college student, I can only do one project at a time. It's too bad; otherwise I'd have written several more by now."

Andy told me he thought it was "pretty uncommon to be offered an entire book on your first time out," and right he was, in most cases. The exception is in technical writing, where it doesn't make any difference about your experience, *if you know the technical area well and can write about it so people can understand it*. Obviously, Andy has that ability in spades. A senior at Ohio State when we met, Andy got college credit for the *Lotus Notes* book. If he had any secrets, it was to "Be flexible in writing styles. Humorous, dry, casual—all have different places and are all important." Of course, it didn't hurt that Andy's father owns a computer store, and that he "grew up on Kaypros, Apple IIs, and CP/Ms," bought his own PC 10 years before and has been continually upgrading it. Then of course there's the fact that he's a computer science engineering major. He also has to read tons of trade magazines to keep up, like *PC World* and *Dr. Dobbs*.

The business script

You don't need a technical background like Andy's to write business scripts. You just need a good visual sense, a desire to make films and the ability to duplicate the vision of your client on paper. The business script is described in many different ways—the audio-visual script, the educational video script, the presentation script—but it's still a script written with one thing in mind: the education of its audience. Since one of the primary hurdles any business faces is getting the public to understand its product and what it can do for them, and since a visual presentation does that better than anything other than hands-on experience, I've saved my favorite and most lucrative form of business writing for last.

The first "how-to" video I attempted was a golf video for women, which ended up as *Jan Stephenson's How to Golf*. You won't find my name on this certified gold video, because I sold out my interest and walked away from the project after a disagreement with the producers, but I put the project together, wrote the first draft of the script and was paid handsomely for my efforts. I already mentioned the multimedia slide show I wrote that became a corporate video.

Before I actually tried to write one, I didn't know the first thing about writing this type of program. Whatever it is you do for a business client—a TV commercial, a slide show, a video year-end report or a how-to video—you'll use the same script format. It's considerably different from any other filmed or videotaped program format. At the same time, it's a very simple format:

❖❖❖❖❖❖❖❖❖❖❖❖❖❖❖❖

Work-Related Accidents: Something to Avoid

VIDEO	AUDIO
1. Jack walks toward the Ajax Building, eating a banana. He tosses the banana peel over his shoulder, paying little attention to the people following a short distance behind.	1. Announcer (O.C.): It's a normal workday for Jack, your happy working stiff, but it's about to turn unhappy for Sally, thanks to Jack's carelessness.
2. Sally laughs with her friend Ethel, not watching where she's stepping.	
3. Close on Sally's foot, as she slips on the banana peel.	2. Sally: Agghhhh!!!
4. Slow motion as Sally's feet go out from under her and she falls.	3. Announcer (O.C.):
5. Close on Jack's concerned face. Camera pulls back to reveal an ambulance, lights flashing, as it pulls away carrying Sally.	All it would have taken was one step to the trash can. Right, Jack?

00:18

Breaking down that opening sequence, you notice that the video column on the left is written single-spaced, just like a screenplay. The audio portion is written double-spaced, like the dialogue in a sitcom. At the bottom on the right you saw "00:18." That's the timing of the scene in seconds. Each page of an audio-visual script is timed in this fashion. Additionally, with each successive page, you "add up" the elapsed time and indicate it in this fashion:

00:30

01:00

The bottom number would be the total for two pages, or one minute. If the script was a 30-minute script, the bottom of the last page might read:

00:30

30:00

Some sources suggest a straight line across the top of the script:

VIDEO	AUDIO

Personally, I think that's a matter of style. You won't lose a job over it. Similarly, I've seen books advising you to put a line of technical information across the top of each page, but you needn't worry about that. This is sufficient:

Page 1 (etc.)

The only thing that really matters is the two-column format, the way your dialogue matches the action depicted and the timing of the scenes (which is based on the way the dialogue reads, so you can put yourself on a stopwatch and time it). Also, you must underline each successive person who speaks. The "O.C." stands for "Off-Camera," meaning that we don't see the announcer. "O.S.," meaning "Off-Screen," would also be acceptable, as would "V.O." for "Voice-Over." Remember what I said earlier about leaving out camera angles in a screenplay, since that was the director's job? This doesn't apply nearly as much in an audio-visual script. You as the writer are more in control with an audio-visual script. If you need to say "High angle, looking out over the valley," go ahead and do so, if it emphasizes your point. Remember my advice about keeping film scenes to three minutes or under? With audio-visual scripts, 15 seconds is a good limit. Don't fall into the "talking heads" trap. Generally, no one wants to sit and watch two people just talking about the merits of a product. Action, action, action, whenever you can and within your budget.

Don't worry about putting something in a script that you think might require too much expense. There's a thing called "stock footage." If you want a plane taking off from a major airport, an affordable film clip can probably be purchased and incorporated into your video from a company that specializes in supplying generic footage. If you're not sure about this, ask the people you're working with.

Remember to tell a story, even in the smallest film. Another good rule when it comes to something for a business is the "three times to be sure they'll get it" maxim. You've probably heard it before: Tell 'em what you're going to tell 'em, tell it to 'em, then tell 'em what you've told 'em. There's something about repeating three times that manages to get through to people. But you won't do it with "talking heads" sitting there repeating it, over and over.

Should you attempt to be a filmmaker or just write scripts? That's up to you. If you're trying to get brochure and newsletter business, I'd advise you to become a full-fledged desktop publishing operation. If you're at all technically inclined, it is now possible to shoot perfectly acceptable business videos on a "High-8" video camera and edit them on your computer, adding the voice-overs, sound and special effects yourself. That requires a good deal of dedication and expense, however, so unless it's something you have a great desire and ability to do, you might be better off sticking to writing.

I hope you have a great time writing for business. It's a continually challenging environment. Just remember the Stev and Mary Donev approach and go at it as a problem-solver first and a writer second. Solve some problems, write some things that increase business for your clients, and you'll never be out of work.

Chapter 14

❖❖❖❖❖❖❖❖❖❖❖❖❖❖❖❖❖

Telling the world about it: newspapers, advertising and public relations

If you ever publish a book and try to promote it, you will learn some big lessons fast. The first one is that your publisher will most likely not roll out a broad national campaign on your book. You won't get flown across the country, stay in the finest hotels, appear on *Regis & Cathy Lee* and meet with the President in the Oval Office to discuss the social merit of your tome. Of course, all that could happen, but don't count on it. Prospective authors I meet always seem a bit saddened by this revelation. That's when I tell them about the motivational author who put a trunk load of books in his car and traveled the country talking about it, eventually pushing the book to number-one bestseller status. I relate the story of poet Rod McKuen, who approached Random House founder Bennett Cerf at a talk the publisher gave in the San Francisco area. Would Cerf be interested in publishing a book of poetry, McKuen asked? Cerf politely declined—there wasn't much money to be made in poetry, he said.

"Strange," replied McKuen. "I wonder how I managed to sell 35,000 copies of my book."

"Let me see it!" Cerf exclaimed.

I wasn't there, but it went something like that.

As you become more established as a writer, you will begin to see how intricately connected the worlds of advertising, newspapers and public relations are. Originally, I intended to write separate chapters for each of these areas of writing. Then I realized that advertising is

193

the stuff of college degrees, even though it is based on one thing when it comes to writers—copywriting. The same goes for public relations.

In this chapter, I'll discuss good copy and good public relations, but mostly I'll clue you in on how a newspaper works. Despite our "Information Age," when computers and television seem all-pervasive, the majority of people in the world read their local newspaper each day. They most certainly depend upon it for information on where to shop, what's available to buy and where to go for good meals, entertainment, etc. It's my feeling that if you understand how newspapers work, you'll have a basic grounding in writing good copy and know how to promote anything you choose to tell the world about, including your latest creation.

Knocking around the newspaper

Craig Howson learned about the newspaper business in Prescott, Arizona. He held a number of jobs at the *Prescott Courier* at one time or another, beginning as a reporter. He was news editor, editor of the Sunday paper, business editor, feature editor and city editor. A part-time job at a Prescott radio station led to a job as news editor at the station. After getting to know the local newspaper reporters, he landed a job at the paper.

In the first five years, Craig covered just about every job on the paper, eventually supervising three other writers. "I did just as much writing as all the other people did," he adds. "I did all the layout for the pages, edited copy, that sort of thing. That was really fun. Basically, anything I wanted to do was a story. We redesigned the paper."

After a change in editor and publisher, Craig became city editor. Staff got cut to the bone, and experienced reporters were replaced to cut costs. Craig saw changes he didn't like. For example, he said, "Every real estate agent in town had his own column."

Not willing to push journalistic integrity aside, he moved on to the magazine *RCR* (Radio Communications Report), which covered the emerging mobile phone industry. From there he became editor of the *Aspen Daily News* in Colorado. Now Craig is freelancing, but he feels that if you learn to write for a newspaper, you can write anything. Plus, the sense of intimate involvement in the ongoing events of the world is immense.

Craig says, "The thing I miss about working on a paper is that when you see something on television, like the O.J. trial, you kind of miss being in the middle of it all, because you get to see things nobody else gets to see. There is a lot more material that comes in than is ever printed, because you just don't have room for it all, but you see it."

A downside of the job was the heavy personal involvement.

"When I went out to dinner, everyone knew who I was," Craig confided. "I did a series on teen suicides, and I knew a couple of the families. You're a lot closer to your readers, a lot closer to your community. You could walk right into our newsroom any time you wanted. You're just closer to people. You feel what they feel. It's the part of the job I really liked and the part that made me get out of it. It got to the point that if an accident report came in I was terrified that I'd send a reporter out there and find out the victim was somebody I knew."

Another drawback was the hours. "I basically worked 24 hours a day, seven days a week," Craig recalled. "My camera was always in my car. I didn't have a private life to speak of. I remember going home from dinner one night with a girl and a fire engine goes rolling by. There's a house on fire. I had to cover it and shoot pictures."

Also, the money was "terrible," according to Craig. Which was another reason he moved on to other things. Nevertheless, he wouldn't trade his newspaper experience for anything.

"Knowing where to dig up information, knowing there's more than one angle to something, knowing that everybody's got an ax to grind, learning to be creative and think on your feet—all these things have stood me in really good stead. I'm a journalist and I always will be. A part of me will always be a newspaper guy."

If you wanted to work on your local paper, you could try Craig's approach, but newsman Gene Koprowski offers a sure bet, no matter how big the paper.

"I can guarantee you a freelance job at any big city daily," he told me, "if you do the following. Call the high school sports editor. This is a beat that is understaffed, underpaid and underappreciated, but their output is probably the reason most suburbanites buy the big city daily in the first place. Best of all, there's not much competition for the

---

positions. Everyone is trying to break into the news or features department, but the editors there are jaded and rude.

"Call the high school sports editor and tell him you would like to cover one game—say basketball or football—a week. The pay is lousy and so are the hours, but if you need professional clips from a major daily, this is the fastest way to break into the profession. Take your clips from your college paper, local paper or whatever, and use them as a marketing tool to approach the prep editor. Tell him you know the coach at your old high school. Create your own story. In a month, you will have four clips from a major daily. And once that happens, you open up opportunities at other papers, magazines and newsletters for higher paying, higher profile jobs. I did this myself. I covered prep sports—about which I know very little—for just a few weeks before the editor asked me to write an opinion piece for the paper. The opinion piece caught the attention of the local CBS affiliate, and they called me for an interview. This kind of stuff is great for your career."

Seasoned reporter John D. Reger offers similar advice for breaking into newspaper writing. A journalism major at Long Beach City College, his first news job was covering high school sports and "some colleges and pros." Something that opened his eyes was the relationship between advertising and newspaper, and how integrity could be compromised.

"It's a business," John said of newspapers. "You can't ever forget that. The papers are not like *Lou Grant* [the TV show starring Ed Asner]. They are run by bean counters. If you are lucky, you will get to practice a slight variation of the journalism they taught you in college. I once wanted to write a column about a car dealer who was planning to buy a minor league hockey team. He only threw his name in to get the free publicity and had no intention of buying the team. The team ended up disbanding because any really interested parties left when they thought the car dealer was going to buy it. Well, I wanted to blast the car dealer, but was told by my editor that he [the car dealer] was a personal friend of the publisher and bought four full-page ads a day. He was off limits."

If this story seems cynical to you, be advised that reporters from urban papers around the world have similar stories. Craig Howson was right—you do see things as a journalist that most of the public rarely sees. I first learned how intimately connected advertising and the print media were when writing for *Palm Springs Life* magazine. The thick glossy Southern California monthly had a regular Beverly Hills section, which made sense because many of its readers' primary residences were in Beverly Hills, with second homes in Palm Springs.

"I want you to write some advertorials," editor Walter Bowart told me. "Four of them this issue."

"No problem," I replied. "What's an advertorial?"

It didn't take long to find out. Merchants would buy full-page ads and have complimentary articles written about them. Since I was adept at finding the good side to anyone, I was perfect to write advertorials, which come from combining the words "advertising" and "editorial." In fact, I wrote them for a Century City newspaper and several other Southern California publications.

Is this a compromise of journalistic integrity?

I never saw it that way. I never lied about anyone or painted a false picture. If I was writing about a rare coin dealer on Rodeo Drive, I talked about the fact that he could read the Coptic language an ancient document was written in. In journalistic terms, this type of article is often called a "puff" piece, which was fine with me. I didn't mind saying something nice about someone when it was paying my rent and allowing me to pursue loftier aspirations.

The previous stories should give you some ideas of how to break into newspaper writing. If you haven't studied journalism and don't know where to start in writing for a paper, just remember the basics I talked about in Chapter 3: who, what, when, where, why and possibly how. If you cover those bases in your article, you'll do all right. Also refer to that chapter if you want to know the proper formats to use.

Rather than waste your time with other ideas, let me refer you to the book that reporters around the United States use regularly. It's the *Associated Press Stylebook and Libel Manual*, available at your local bookstore and library. It's also available directly from The Associated Press, 50 Rockefeller Plaza, New York, New York 10020. Some big city papers, like the *Los Angeles Times*, have their own stylebook. The *Chicago Manual of Style* is also popular, but the AP book is more broadly used than any other.

Making money twice

Once you've published some articles in the local paper, it might occur to you to get them reprinted in other markets. One writer I knew who worked for a small newspaper in West Virginia was thrilled the first time one of his stories got "picked up" by the Associated Press and reprinted around the country. When that began happening on a regular basis, he found out that his editor was selling the stories to the AP but keeping the money for himself. Needless to say, the fur flew.

Whether you are on the staff of a paper or not, you can resell your stories via syndication. When you see "AP," "UPI" or a similar designation by a story, it means it's come from somewhere other than the newspaper in which you're reading the piece. *Writer's Market,* in fact, has an entire section devoted to newspaper syndicates, with pages of advice on who buys what from whom. There is also a good book on the subject, *How to Make Money in Newspaper Syndication* by Susan Lane, available from Newspaper Syndication Specialists, Suite 326, P.O. Box 19654, Irvine, CA 92720. If you sell an article locally that you feel may have national or even international appeal, don't simply mail it off to *Reader's Digest* and hope for the best. Investigate the world of syndication and see if you can expand your horizons.

One last thing about newspaper writing. Why not try writing an "op ed" piece? That stands for "opinion editorial." Contact your local paper, ask how long an op ed piece should be, then write it. Whether you want to have your say about the injustices meted out by the local dogcatcher or how you think a toxic landfill anywhere is a bad idea, you just might get published. If your piece is about a subject that is also "hot" in other parts of the country, chances are that you can sell the article again and again. Unfortunately, you'll probably have to do the marketing yourself. Syndicates might get interested in marketing your work, but they make money off volume, not "one-shot Charlies."

Advertising: awful or amazing?

There is a way to succeed in advertising without really crying. You don't always have to have a degree to get hired by an advertising agency, but in most instances it's required. Also, don't expect to make much money starting out, and be willing to work anywhere you're placed, such as the mail room or reception area. Ad agencies are by nature neurotic beasts.

When I first attempted to make a living as a freelance writer, I did word processing. One of my temporary assignments landed me in the office of the head man at Foote, Cone & Belding, one of the larger ad agencies in the country at the time. After completing one of the letters I was dictated and handing it to my employer to sign, I told him of my writing aspirations and asked him how I could break into advertising.

"Write something," he told me. "And let me see it."

So I did. I wrote several fictional TV commercials and some magazine ad copy and brought it back to him, weeks after my assignment at the agency had ended. To my surprise, I was ushered into his office.

"You came back," he told me. "You did what I asked. Most people never make it to that step."

I'd like to report that I went on to make a huge six-figure income coming up with catchy phrases, but it didn't happen that way. After my creations got dissected by this seasoned ad veteran, I didn't continue to follow up.

No one has ever been able to draw a distinct relation between advertising and public consumption, although millions are spent daily in all forms of the media to achieve exactly that. Advertising people measure their effectiveness in things like "impressions."

Here's an example of an impression. Let's say a radio station manages to come up with some figures that say it reaches an average of 3 million people each hour. Or a magazine with a circulation of 300,000 figures that each copy of the magazine passes through five people's hands before being discarded, resulting in 1.5 million actual public contacts. The radio station and the magazine would deliver 3 million and 1.5 million "impressions," respectively.

What's a good ad? One that someone remembers. After all, you might only get one chance to sell someone on your product, or one impression. Will they remember it, and thereby seek it out in the market? That's what you want them to do.

One ad exec I knew built a huge business in Dallas. He was the number-one man at the largest agency in town, with major clients like the Dallas Cowboys football team and the Dr. Pepper soft-drink company. One of his main tricks was something he'd learned from an old ad veteran. When he created a new TV ad, he didn't hire an expensive composer to come up with new, memorable music. Instead, he used songs everyone knew that were in the public domain, meaning he didn't have to pay anyone a royalty.

You knew the tune and remembered the commercial. That's why celebrities get so much mileage out of advertising. Michael Jordan, the greatest basketball player of all time, not only promotes McDonald's, he gets his own burger named after him. Will it help a kid to play better hoops? No, but it will make them feel like it will. That's what advertising is all about—emotions and feelings first, and facts second. The next time you listen to a car commercial, see if you can't recognize the voice. Isn't that movie star Michael Douglas touting that luxury car? You don't see his face, but you're familiar with (and therefore, advertising logic says, you feel comfortable with), the voice.

As I said, I won't attempt to delve very far into the world of advertising in this book. There's too much to cover. If you want to make money writing advertising copy, find a local agency and offer your services, like Gene Koprowski did in approaching the sports editor of a newspaper. Advertising, even for someone with a college degree, is an area where the "I'll do any job while learning" approach still works. If you lean toward Madison Avenue with your writing aspirations, be prepared to make a full-time pursuit of it.

It's a PR world

Did you know that many of the shorter stories in the newspaper weren't written by reporters? Often, particularly in smaller papers, the stories are merely reprinted from a press release, sent to the paper by a public relations specialist. When I say it's a PR world, I mean a public relations world. In Hollywood, it's not uncommon for a movie or TV star to pay a PR firm $3,500 a month or more to get favorable press. When someone holds a press conference, he or she doesn't just sit in front of a microphone and make an announcement. How do the reporters know to get there? Did they all get a phone call? Probably not. They probably responded to a press release.

A press release, like a newspaper article, should answer who, what, when, where and why. It can come from the person who is seeking the publicity, but that's generally not a good idea. It's a strange thing with the press, but they like to learn about something from someone other than the true source. That's why press agents stay in business. Most people I know who can't afford to hire a PR firm get around it by typing their own press release and sending it out as though it came from someone else. It needs to be printed on some form of stationery that connotes a business, not a person. If you are promoting a book, it could be your publisher's stationery. At the top, in large, bold type, the type of news you are providing should be prominent. Also at the top on the left side should be the phrase FOR IMMEDIATE RELEASE. At the right, indicate the date, so the reporter knows when you sent it out. If possible, keep the press release to one page. It's good to double-space, for readability. At the bottom, after you've said what you have to say, give a name of a person to contact and a phone number, so the reporter can pick up the phone and call with any pertinent questions.

On page 204 is an abbreviated example of a press release on a book of mine. It was printed on the stationery of the publisher, B & B Publishing. To keep it on one page, it was single-spaced. The press release also gave my phone number, if anyone wanted to call me to schedule an interview. Since B&B is in Walworth, Wisconsin, and I'm in Southern California, and since Katy O'Shea at B&B would have to relay phone calls to me, anyway, I let them list my phone number on the press release, to save time for everyone.

If your press release is about an event rather than a specific product, write it so that any reporter reading it can use your paragraphs intact, with the most important information in up front. (See example on next page.)

At the bottom of this fictional release would be the name of someone who is serving as George's campaign manager, along with the address of his campaign headquarters and the phone number. A fax number should also be listed, if there is one. Basically, answer all the questions you can in the press release, but say only enough to intrigue the recipient and get him or her to call the person listed. After all, that's the point.

A press release can be a potent tool for anyone wanting media coverage, but a press kit is the full package. For one how-to video I did, I not only wrote the script, co-produced the production and played one of the roles, I also got the job of putting together the press kit, even though we had hired a PR firm at $3,500 a month.

ANYTOWN ELECTION NEWS!

<u>FOR IMMEDIATE RELEASE</u>   <u>Today, 1995</u>

George Gump will announce his entry into the mayoral race to-day with a press conference scheduled for 9:00 a.m. Gump states a simple reason for running for mayor.

"I'm sick of being sick of the sickos in city government," says Gump, a local veterinarian since 1949. "If you're not part of the cure, you're part of the disease, and I'm just the man to clean up the epidemic of stupidity we've had to endure in Anytown for the last couple of years."

Gump brings a convincing bag of political knowledge and common sense into the race. He won the first race he ever entered, Anytown's first Soapbox Derby, in 1939. The winning attitude has always...

A press kit consists of the following:

- A press release describing the main event, such as the release of the video, book or whatever.
- A bio of the principal people involved.
- A synopsis of the production, movie, book or whatever.
- A photo or photos of the principal people involved.
- Photocopies of any other pertinent and notable press that has been received, such as a good review.

A bio is a short biography about a person or a production. It shouldn't be any longer than three pages, double-spaced. If you can keep it to one page, all the better. I usually take the approach of current event (the show or event), followed by the past (what the person has done of note), then more information on the current event, wrapping up with future plans. It's a past, present, future structure that seems to work pretty well.

The synopsis is merely the beginning, middle and end, making it sound as compelling as possible. It's more of an advertising piece than a scholarly dissertation or critical review.

If you include photos, get them taken by a professional photographer, and use black and white. Remember, they go mostly to newspapers, which will usually run the photo you send rather than send out their own photographer and incur extra expense.

A word of caution in photocopying articles—clear it with the people who printed them. This is rarely done, even by top PR agencies, but they break copyright laws when they photocopy and broadly distribute hundreds or thousands of reviews, articles or whatever without obtaining permission first.

You might have been wondering—could you make a living writing for public relations firms? I doubt it, unless you were on staff. You could pick up some extra cash writing bios, however. When I was doing it, $50 for a short bio was the norm. Check your *Writer's Market* for currently acceptable rates.

I wouldn't advise anyone to try to make a living in public relations if they have higher writing aspirations. Why? Because you'll be asked to put on a front, bend the truth a little, puff up people who may not deserve it. One PR person I know started out as a serious journalist. He did good interviews with top musicians, and made a living as a freelancer. Now he concentrates on "lines and inches" all day. Lines about his clients and column inches of print about them in publications. Still, many newspaper articles appear only because of materials received from PR people. If the subject of the press release is a big advertiser in the paper, it'll get plenty of attention.

Now you have some idea of how the newspaper/advertising/public relations machine works. Many fine writers started at a newspaper. You can make a lot more money in advertising, but you might feel a bit hollow at the end of the day. Public relations? I barely consider it writing, but it is essential that you know how that game works when you're out promoting something worthwhile that you've written. After all, one day you might plan to tell the world about something you've done, maybe even something that makes the world a better place.

BOOK NEWS from B&B

<u>FOR IMMEDIATE RELEASE</u>   <u>DECEMBER 1994</u>

AWESOME ALMANAC: California

B&B Publishing, Inc. is proud to announce the publication of a new title in the AWESOME ALMANAC series of state trivia books—AWESOME ALMANAC: California! This book closely follows AWESOME ALMANAC: Florida, which was published in November. All the "awesome books"—Indiana, Illinois, Michigan, Minnesota and Wisconsin—have been well received. B&B will add to the series with Ohio, New York and Texas, scheduled for Spring 1995 release.

Award-winning writer Skip Press, a California resident, is author of the California book. He brings a unique and entertaining tone to this fun and fact-filled book.

Each AWESOME ALMANAC contains comprehensive coverage of the best, the worst, the most, the least, the good, the bad, the famous, the in-famous, and much more. They are loaded with essential as well as fun information. New features include a subject index, bibliography and de-tailed state map.

Here are some comments we have received on earlier books in the series:

(quotes follow)

AWESOME ALMANAC: California
by Skip Press
$14.95 list
Trade paperback—7 3/8" x 10 1/4" 206 pages
ISBN 1-880190-21-4
Publication date: December 1, 1994

The AWESOME ALMANAC series is published by B&B Publishing, Inc. Distributed by Login Publishers Consortium.

For further information contact Katy O'Shea (414) 275-9474.

Chapter 15

❖❖❖❖❖❖❖❖❖❖❖❖❖❖❖❖

It's a funny life

As you might have surmised, I'm a person who is interested in just about everything. I've always had the attitude that if it was something that could be written, I could write it. As I was finishing up this book, for example, I sold a comic book.

This is a chapter for "everything else." If you want to write and sell calendars, greeting cards, jokes, recipes or novelty books, this chapter is for you. I can't see making a living at any of the above, but who knows? You might be one of the ones who does.

Bob Lovka was the perfect person to speak to about "everything else" because the company he works for publishes it. Bob is the senior editor of adult trade, humor and creative development for Price Stern Sloan Incorporated, a Los Angeles publishing house that is a division of the Putnam Berkeley Group, Inc. Like me, Bob came to town not knowing anyone. Also like me, he got a job by answering an ad. He was hired by a gift company to write things like posters and bumper stickers. He got the job first, then figured out how to do it. Could he do a few "on spec"? Sure! He wrote a few, they hired him and he was a working writer.

From there, Bob branched out to comedy skits, writing for a humorous game show called *Bedtime Stories*.

In Bob's office at Price Stern Sloan were dozens of books his company had published, some board games and calendars galore. He told me he was looking for a good calendar, in case I had any ideas. If there was one unifying element of all the various items, it was humor. In the world of "specialty" publishing, humor is king. If you have a good sense of humor and can write, you can do well. If you can also draw, like Gary Larson of "The Far Side" fame or Charles Schulz of "Peanuts," you might become a millionaire seemingly overnight.

Seeing all the funny things around the office prompted me to ask Bob the question, "So what's funny?"

"It's just a feeling inside that something is going to work," Bob said. "It just makes you laugh."

Bob told me that, despite all the talk of market research that one continually hears about, the decisions of what the company publishes have mostly to do with gut instinct.

This surprised me, because Price Stern Sloan is perhaps the most recognized publisher on the West Coast. I asked him to give me an example of a book they had published on instinct—just because they thought it was funny. He offered me *Sheldon & Mrs. Levine*, a satirical takeoff on the bestselling Griffin & Sabine books. *Sheldon* was written by the writing team of Sam Bobrick and Julie Stein. When I saw Sam's name, I wasn't surprised Price Stern Sloan had published the book. Sam is a funny and highly accomplished playwright who made a fortune when he created a long-running teenage sitcom that became an industry all its own called *Saved by the Bell*.

Why did they publish Sam's and Julie's book? Because it was funny, Bob told me, and indeed it was. It chronicled a Jewish mother who won't leave her son alone. Even if they hadn't known who Sam was, Bob said, someone at the company would have read the book. If it could make it up the chain of command with everyone thinking it was funny, they'd publish it.

The only exclusion in Price Stern Sloan's submissions policy was drama. "We don't do dramatic novels," Bob said. "Don't send 'em."

Okay, so maybe I haven't told you what's funny, but I've given you some idea of the inner workings of comedic publishing. Mark Twain said that all comedy was based on sorrow, which has some truth. Having written a book on Twain, I know that he suffered a good deal of personal pain, yet managed to turn it into humor.

If you want to sell your comedic writing, you'll go a lot further with humor than you will with what's currently called comedy. What's the difference? Humor is socially acceptable. A chuckle, maybe even a guffaw, results from humor. You wouldn't be surprised if a comedian was banned from the radio, as George Carlin was when his famous "seven words you can never say on television" (all profanities) bit came out on a comedy album. You would be surprised, though, if you heard that a humorist had been banned from air play, wouldn't you?

Humor is rarely mean-spirited, while comedy often is. Also, comedy can vary widely by culture, while humor is universal. An example: A popular Japanese TV show is based on a group of people surprising someone who is sleeping by screaming as loud as they can, shocking the person awake. That's comedy. One of the most popular Japanese TV commercials of all time, on the other hand, featured two small children taking a bath together. A large bubble appears on the surface of the water and bursts, causing one child to look at the other, wide-eyed. When Johnny Carson played the commercial on the *Tonight Show*, it got one of the biggest laughs and was the most popular of all the foreign commercials he showed that night. That's humor. Humor touches on the universality of the human condition everywhere, and is not limited to time or culture.

Just joking around

When I wrote a book on Joan Rivers and her daughter Melissa, I was amazed at how Joan had struggled to make it as one of the first female stand-up comedians. Starting out writing for the old *Candid Camera* TV show, she got her break and first appearance on the *Tonight Show* by getting the producer to book her as a comedy writer, not a comedian. Joan was determined and never gave up, no matter what the setbacks were. Her story is common in the world of stand-up comedy.

I once contemplated doing stand-up because it was the obvious route to getting one's own TV show. I haunted the Comedy Store on Sunset Boulevard in Los Angeles on Monday nights for years, watching Robin Williams, Martin Short, Jim Stahl and others in the Comedy Store Players make people laugh with improvisational comedy.

What kept me from pursuing stand-up was the amount of time it took: years on the road getting good enough to become a regular at the Comedy Store or the Improvisation. I watched too many comedians struggling and didn't laugh when Taylor Negron joked onstage, "Comedy isn't pretty."

Do you want to write and sell jokes? You won't make much money. Try $25 for a joke, if you're really good. How many of those can you write in a day? Can you do it every day?

If you want to be a comedy writer, but don't do your own stand-up, you're probably not going to make a living. There are simply too many jokes out there. If you're really good, though, you might land a job as a staff writer for Jay Leno or David Letterman. Guess what the odds of that are? But if you're serious about it, move to New York or (preferably) Los Angeles and start making the rounds. Hang out at the comedy clubs, offer some sample jokes to comedians and see what you can do. It's that simple and that difficult. I suggest Los Angeles over New York for two reasons: 1) that's where the TV shows are filmed; and 2) it's easier to stay alive while starving in a warm-weather climate.

Format? Whatever you can type on a 3- by 5-inch card. Milton Berle, the comedy pack rat of all time, has file cabinets full of them.

Comic books: where the real money is

Let's say you have a wacky mind but you don't plan on becoming a stand-up comedian. How about writing comic books? That's actually a misnomer now, because most of them aren't comic. Many stars who began as comedians, however, are making box-office history starring in films that started out as comic books. Jim Carrey in *The Mask,* for example. Michael Keaton in *Batman,* for another. The latter got serious attention at Warner Brothers as a possibility for a live-action movie only after the astounding success of a "graphic novel" called *The Dark Knight Returns.* When I was a kid, we would have called a graphic novel "a big comic book."

As I said in the chapter opening, I sold my first comic book as I was finishing this book. It was basically a fluke, because of my friendship with Dave Simons, a well-known comic book artist and illustrator with whom I collaborated. Still, I hope our *Tribe 13* does well.

Another writer who is now a big success in writing comics also fell into the profession by chance. Peter J. Quinones had friends who were trying to break into the field as artists. A friend named Glenn Johnson read a fantasy novel Peter was writing and created four "beautiful pages of artwork" to accompany it, Peter told me.

"At that moment," Peter remembered, "I decided I really wanted to see my words illustrated. I'd grown up reading comics and had always made up stories. And being a member of the TV generation, I was used to thinking visually."

Peter and Glenn took the four illustrated pages to ComicCon, a yearly convention in San Diego for the comic book trade. They found a publisher who liked the artwork and asked if Peter could tell the story in 32 pages.

The book was published in 3-D, and was a hit. Small, independent publishers gave Peter more work, and he learned his craft, little by little. To him, those early books were his resumes. One of them was noticed by an artist who went on to become one of the top illustrators for Marvel, which then published a project they created together. There was no set format and no one to teach Peter—he merely learned by doing, which he says has not changed to this day.

"You have to work for a lot of independents to learn your craft," he advises. "It helps if you're in New York. You don't have to live in a major metro area, but just make sure you go to the conventions. The only person who can buy your work is an editor. If you don't go to their office (and odds are, they wouldn't see you even if you did), you can go to conventions. However, what you want to give them is a published work. My experience has been that they don't really read your proposals. They can't really tell if you can pace a book, do dialogue, etc. It's like in Hollywood. You have to have the right format, and the best format is a published comic book."

Most of Peter's stories—which he presents these days in one-page synopsis form—have been connected with an artist like Glenn Johnson, Kelley Jones or Ron Lim. So he recommends hooking up with an artist right from the start. What if you don't know one? Go to a comic convention and meet some.

"Usually you are also helping the artist," Peter said. "You give him a story to draw, so that he's not just submitting pinups."

Selling comic books, like selling jokes, is that simple. You go where the people are and give them a sample of what you can do. If you don't live in Southern California or New York, spend your vacation this year where a major comic book convention is taking place and start making the rounds. It is probably the only way you'll ever get started in that business.

Greetings and gewgaws

Do you want to write greeting cards? Do you want to be the next Hallmark? You don't have to move next door to a greeting card factory, but you would be better off if you were affiliated with an artist.

Like writing for comedians, you probably won't make a living writing greeting cards. One successful greeting card writer I knew had a full-time job as a secretary at a firm where my wife worked. Her advice to me about selling greeting card slogans was, "Write something that makes people laugh." But don't get too encouraged. Carole King, an "idea person" at Hallmark, told me that it was a fluke if they published something other than a card created by a staff writer. I've known people who made a success of greeting cards, but only because they self-published them.

A "gewgaw," in case you didn't know, is a trifle or bauble. A desk calendar, for example—the kind of thing Bob Lovka publishes when he finds one funny.

If you want to be a success with the more obscure areas of writing, I'd advise you to come up with a character or characters. This means you should either be an artist *and* a writer, or hook up with an artist.

Bizarre as Gary Larson's humor may be, the people in his cartoons seem to be from the same unique world. They're like strange children who he manages to love, and gets us to love, who remind us of ourselves in a way that makes us laugh. Because of that, we buy T-shirts, calendars, coffee mugs and books about "The Far Side." We buy the humor.

It's a funny life. I hope these stories and advice on "other" areas of writing have helped you and that, if you're interested, you pursue them vigorously. We could use a few more laughs in this world!

Chapter 16

❖❖❖❖❖❖❖❖❖❖❖❖❖❖❖❖❖

Doin' it your own dang self

If you decide to publish your own book, you won't be in bad company. Maybe you read a book recently entitled *The Celestine Prophecy*. It was originally self-published. I'm sure the story about poet Rod McKuen publishing his own book of poetry and selling 30,000 or so copies before being picked up by Random House got your attention. Perhaps you've heard of that fellow Mark Twain, or that playwright Shakespeare? How about Benjamin Franklin?

Self-publishers all.

I've known a number of people who self-publish books, some with fine success and some...let's just say they could have spent their money more wisely.

One of the better aspects of the Information Age and all the electronic marvels we have is that people can more easily exchange notes, keep in touch with each other and make their books look like everybody's else's books, at least as far as layout, art, and so on.

Can you spot a self-published book when you see one? If you can, you know something I don't. In this day of "trade paperbacks" and perfect binding (paperback books held together with glue as opposed to stitching), the only way someone will know you self-published your book is if it's stapled together and has handwritten photocopied pages instead of nice type. Even then, if you have worthwhile information or entertainment within those pages, you can probably sell what you've written.

The biggest problem you'll run up against is bookstores. I'm not talking about unique stores that are a mainstay of the community, like The Midnight Special in Santa Monica, California. I'm talking about the Crown Superstore down at the mall, or even the book section at Kmart. For mass market booksellers, public profile is the key.

If the author's name is Jackie Collins and the title is *Hollywood Wives,* that doesn't take much advertising to move. The public recognition of that book is instantaneous.

If you've written *Bed & Breakfasts of Montana,* however, don't count on the Crown in Boca Raton to order mass quantities. You're going to have to advertise that in magazines and sell it through travel agents and the like. A major publisher doesn't have the time, so chances are you'll have to self-publish the book.

So what if you either want to self-publish or can't find anyone to publish your book? Should you go to a "vanity press," a publisher who takes your money, prints copies of your book and says, "Thank you very much, you're a fine person"? I advise you against doing so. Unless you have money to burn and/or just don't want to put in the work of marketing the book you slaved to write, stay away from vanity presses. They'll tell you about people who have self-published and gone on to great success, but they won't show you many books that *they* published for authors that went on to great success.

Before I go any further, what constitutes a successful book? For a hardcover book 5,000 copies sold is respectable. Double that for soft cover. If you can turn out books that generate that kind of sales, your publisher will continue to work with you. You won't be on any bestseller lists, but you'll get another contract, or several. Even if you find someone to publish your book, however, you'll still have to do the bulk of the promotional work to get that book to sell. Unless, of course, you come up with a book that gets you a chunky six-figure advance. Then the publisher will buy the big ads, spring for the PR firm to get you booked on the talk shows, and pay for your air and hotel bills. But how often does that happen, realistically, for a first-time author?

Self-sufficient Sutton

One of the best examples of a successful self-publisher is artist/writer Scott Sutton. Over the last eight years, Scott and his wife, Sue, have sold more than 50,000 copies of Scott's *The Land of Ree* children's books. They are whimsical, full-color books written in rhyme, and loved by kids, parents and teachers around the country. Scott's more recent creations, *The Kukumber Kids* and *The Adventures of Dinosaur Dog are enjoying similar success. Not only has Scott sold a lot of books, but he and Sue have made all their sales without the assistance of a single book distributor and without much reliance on store sales. Their secret is sales via schools. Scott appears regularly at schools and tells kids about his books, using dolls of his characters that were sewn by Sue. He doesn't charge the students for the visit, although he'll accept whatever honorarium the school can pay. In exchange for Scott's performance (and it *is* a performance), the school passes out *Land of Ree* flyers. Scott doesn't just show up and act out stories from his books, however. He teaches the kids to draw. Not only does he entertain them, he tries to spark creativity in the youngsters. In all, Scott estimates he speaks to more than 11,000 kids a year, which is a lot of inspiration (and perspiration).

Scott and Sue also sell their books through art galleries and at art shows. When the world-famous Laguna Beach Art Festival opens in the summer, Scott is there with a booth. When the harvest festivals are held in the fall, he's there pushing the books. During the winter and spring, he does his school tours. At last count, the Suttons had more than 15,000 people on their mailing lists, with approximately 45 percent of their business coming from repeat customers. They continually try to improve the products by surveying parents, teachers and kids to find out what works and what doesn't. The *Ree* books, which have commonsense values and educational basics woven into their stories, have received widespread acclaim and are now being packaged as a possible television series and/or feature films.

"If someone wants to self-publish," Scott confided, "there's a couple of things they'd better know. First of all, they'd better have money in the bank. If you run out of books, yet have orders you need to fill and no money in the bank to reprint, you're in trouble. Also, you need to be free from debt. Have all your debts paid before you try to get into the business of self-publishing. Otherwise, you'll just never make it."

Before he self-published his first *Ree* book, Scott worked for a dozen years in publications in Southern California, doing everything from printing promotional materials to binding books to drawing illustrations. He knew something about all the mechanical aspects of publishing before he turned out that first book.

Even with all that know-how, he didn't intend to publish the book himself. With 400 advance orders and other people asking when his book was going to come out, Scott fell into the awful predicament of having his scheduled publisher go out of business.

Scrambling fast to get the book out himself, he met the orders and never looked back.

"I never really looked for another publisher," he told me. "I'd heard stories about how even Dr. Seuss had had a hard time getting published at first, getting turned down by publisher after publisher. I didn't want to go through that. I knew how to publish books, so that's what I did."

If you want to find out about Scott Sutton's *Land of Ree*, write to Sutton Publications, 14252 Culver #A 709, Irvine, CA 92714.

Some Poynters to ponder

If you haven't worked in publications and you're thinking of publishing your own book, what do you do? There are a number of self-publishing experts around the country who can help you. One of them is Dan Poynter of Santa Barbara, California. His *Publishing Poynters: Book/information marketing news & ideas from Dan Poynter* will appear in your mailbox on a regular basis if you write Dan at Para Publishing, P.O. Box 2206, Santa Barbara, CA 93118-2206. You can call him at (805) 968-7277 or fax him at (805) 968-1379, or e-mail him at 75031.3534 @ CompuServe.Com.

Dan travels the country giving lectures, like "How to Write and Publish Books," and touring with other information professionals who advise you on all aspects of book marketing, promotion and distribution. In a recent packet from Dan, I learned of a 50-page report about college publishing, an Internet book-listing service, how paper prices rose 48 percent recently, the number for the Publishers Marketing Association (310-372-2782), publications that were advertising for books to review, and an affordable book promotion service. Dan offers "fax on demand" reports, which "provide you with the latest condensed answers to your book promotion questions." For example, a four-page report on "Selling Books Through the Gift Trade" (gift shows, magazines, mailing lists, reports and consultants) is available for $2.95. The five-page "Raising Money to Publish Books" is $5.95, as is "Cooperative Book Promotion" (a nine-pager), which comes with an action plan and addresses of more than 100 cooperative publishing programs.

If you're really serious about self-publishing, you should also consider joining the National Small Press Publishing Institute, or at least attending one of their conferences. Contact them at 6893 Sullivan Road, Grawn, MI 49637, or call at (800) 345-0096.

Setting your price

I'll leave it to you to figure out the details of your book if you decide to go the self-publishing route, but I'll try to offer you a bit of help in figuring out how much to charge. One hint: Dan Poynter has a report on it. Based on my own research, however, here are some things you need to know. Publishers call the costs of production of a book "PP&B," meaning "paper, printing and binding." Of course, they also factor author advances and royalties, promotional costs and staff salaries into this figure. Bookstores usually get the books for at least 40 percent off the list price.

One book I did recently was sold to the distributor for a third of the list price of the book, or about $5 per unit. (The list price was $14.95.) I know this because my publisher asked to renegotiate my royalty contract. Landing the big distributor allowed a lot more books to be sold, but at the old royalty rate I had negotiated for myself, it made it tight for the publisher. Willing to bet on long-range, high volume sales, I struck a new deal and the publisher gave me the exact details on everything (which publishers don't normally do). Since the book was in its second printing after only a couple of months on the market, it was a good educated guess.

You know how many hours it took you to write your book. You know the costs that went into producing the manuscript. (If you don't, your business sense is lacking and I hope you have money in the bank and no bills, as Scott Sutton advises.) You can then figure out how much it costs for PP&B. Remember to factor in promotional costs, which include mailings, phone expenses and travel. If you have a normal size book, you can mail it in a $3 two-day overnight post office "priority mail" hard envelope, so also take that into account. To get someone to talk about your book in the newspaper, or to put you on their radio or TV show, you're going to have to send a copy of the book. Count on licking a lot of stamps, by the way.

Add all these things up and divide the total cost by the amount of books you plan to print in your first run. After someone revives you with smelling salts, you can add the profit margin you think you can get away with to the average cost per book, and that will be your cover price. Why do you need to know this? Because most likely you'll print a "trade paperback" and you'll print the suggested retail price right on the cover. You have to print it on the cover so the bookstore can slap their less-than-that price label on it, and their customers will think they're getting a big bargain. That's the way it works.

Where this leaves you

The good news about self-publishing is this: No one has to know you self-published, and they won't know unless you tell them. I'm assuming you won't make the mistake of calling your publishing outfit "John Doe Publishers" if your name happens to be John Doe. Don't call it "My Own Dang Self Publishing Company," either. If you can't come up with a decent enough name, ask a friend or relative to help.

A word of caution: Be sure you incorporate your publishing company. Why? Because if you make a claim in your book or offer advice that someone later decides to use as the grounds for a lawsuit, your company will get sued, not you personally. This might not seem important to you until you are served legal papers at your front door.

Once you have a book in hand, whether someone else published it or you did it yourself, you'll need to know how to let people know about it. You'll be facing that cold, cruel PR world. If you did what I suggested and got some journalism experience under your belt and if you joined writing groups, you'll have developed some media contacts and will have an idea of where to go to get your work noticed.

If you were sleeping in class, though, I can still help you. Call Bookzone at (800) 536-6162 and ask them how they can help you get promoted on the Internet. Get in touch with Publicity Blitz and ask about their database of more than 15,000 reporters, editors and producers (both radio and TV). They're at (800) 989-1400.

You could also get yourself listed in a magazine called *Radio-TV Interview Report,* put out by the Bradley Communications Group, 135 East Plumstead Avenue, P.O. Box 1206, Lansdowne, PA 19050-8206. You can call them at (610) 259-1070. Ever wonder how that psychic belly dancer got an appearance on the *Jerry Springer Show*? She probably wrote them a letter. That author of a book on the Social Security system, however, probably got on the *Oprah Winfrey Show* because she was mentioned in the *Radio-TV Interview Report,* which is read by producers across the country. The emphasis of the magazine is on nonfiction subjects. They're easier to sell, both through traditional publishers and on your own.

Possibly the best source is *Talkers* magazine. Editor Michael Harrison says that if an author wants to stay up-to-date on talk radio and on what radio people want to see from authors needing promotion, this is the magazine that really counts. I tend to agree with him.

The closest thing to self-publishing is the small press, a publisher who will offer you little in the way of a monetary advance and probably little help in the promotional department. No matter how you get a book in print, though, you'll still have to do a lot of promotion. But remember, if you go to all the trouble of writing a book, self-publishing it and promoting it, make sure your product is in place, so that the public can find it when your publicity machine is in high gear.

Dean Blehert has been self-publishing and distributing his work successfully for years. Dean publishes his own poetry newsletter, called *Deanotations*. Rather than poetry news, however, it consists of new poetry written by Dean and illustrated by his wife Pam. He has only recently made a living at it, after years of publishing books of his work. The last time I asked, *Deanotations* went out to more than 10,000 people. For a long time, the price of the newsletter was left up to reader donations. In the last year, Dean set a fixed price. Maybe he finally figured out his PP&B.

You can do very well at self-publishing if you choose that route, but it might take some time to be able to make a living at it. If you're a poet, you'd better be prepared to self-publish. It worked for Rod McKuen. And it's been working for a long time. There was a famous Chinese poet, Lao Tzu, whose lines were so clever that someone decided he was a philosopher. He tried out his poems on the little old lady selling flowers down at the corner. If she understood his *Book of Changes,* he decided, then shouldn't anyone be able to?

Poetry is probably where writing began, and it's not a bad place to end. I'm not a philosopher, but I hope I've given you some instructional, inspirational and beneficial advice.

Now go out and do the same, and we'll have a better world.

Index